THE W✵RLD
DREAM
BOOK

THE W❖RLD
DREAM
BOOK

Use the Wisdom of World Cultures
to Uncover Your Dream Power

Sarvananda Bluestone, Ph.D.

Destiny Books
Rochester, Vermont

Destiny Books
One Park Street
Rochester, Vermont 05767
www.InnerTraditions.com

Destiny Books is a division of Inner Traditions International

Library of Congress Cataloging-in-Publication Data

Bluestone, Sarvananda.
  The world dream book : use the wisdom of world cultures to uncover your dream power / Sarvananda Bluestone.
      p. cm.
Includes bibliographical references.
  ISBN 0-89281-902-2 (pbk.)
 1. Dreams. 2. Dream interpretation. I. Title.
  BF1091 .B616 2002
  154.6'3—dc21
                                        2002014925

Printed and bound in the United States by Lake Book Manufacturing, Inc.

10 9 8 7 6 5 4 3 2 1

Text design and layout by Mary Anne Hurhula
This book was typeset in Bembo with Galahad as the display typeface

There is a Spirit who is awake in our sleep and creates the wonder of dreams.
He is the Spirit of Light, who in truth is called the Immortal. All the worlds
rest on that Spirit and beyond him no one can go.
                                        UPANISHADS, C. 800 B.C.E

Let us learn to dream, gentlemen, and then we may perhaps find the truth.
                                        FRIEDRICH A. VON KEKULE,
            FOUNDER OF MODERN ORGANIC CHEMISTRY, 1890

CONTENTS

ACKNOWLEDGMENTS

Writing a book is a strange process. On the one hand, it is one of the most solitary occupations on the face of the earth. On the other hand, the finished product represents a confluence of many streams and influences. Many people are helpful along the way.

One of the nicest things about getting a book published is being able to thank people publicly. It really feels good to do that. It's as though, for a tiny piece of time, an author can share his appreciation with the world.

First, I thank the campers at Appel Farm Arts Camp who participated in the "Dream Minor" during the summers of 1997 and 1998. In these dream workshops many of the explorations in this book were tested. Thank you Marisa Berwald, Daniel Blacksberg, Michael Dorwart, David Gershkoff, Alexandra Gerhsuny, Norah Hall, Rachel Kolster, Sara Radbill, Hannah Schulingkamp, Julia Slomin, and Sharon Zetter. Thank you Lori Adelman, Jessica Angelson, Allison Berwald, Marisa Berwald, Adam Bloch, Julia Brenner, Mark Castaldo, Jessica Engel, David Friedell, Steven Furlong, Jenny Gamell, Rebecca Ivory, Jackie Mott, Alexandra Peterson, Christopher Richards, and Eli Wing.

My thanks to Ellen Foreman and Claire Schmais of the dream group. They have shown the joys of dream awareness.

Thanks to Juhi Bendahan, who shares of herself so exquisitely and has provided several explorations. To Hira Bluestone—always a spark, always so new and yet so wonderfully old. To Helen Weaver, my beloved link to the wonders of being a Gemini, for her help in getting the chapter titles together. To Premda Wunderle for sharing her dreams and very good advice. To Hariet Hunter, who shared her wisdom on the way to the movies.

Shana Cutler, a fountain of ideas, provided valuable suggestions. To Christine Cunnar and the Human Relations Area Files of Yale University, this book simply could not have happened without them.

Thanks to Jonathan Kligler for providing information on Rabbi Hisda; to the librarians at the State University of New York at Albany; and especially to Greg Barron, who made things much easier. Thanks to Susun Weed for generously providing herbal advice.

Thanks to Arnie Weiner, who helped more than he can imagine. To Emma Shakarshy, who shared her dreams and interpretations and who reminded me that intelligence is ageless. To my dear friend Prartho Sereno, for whom the marriage of true minds has never admitted any impediment, but only continuing inspiration.

Thanks to Aseema Wunderle for saving my manuscript from the jaws of my jealous cat, Stella, and thanks to Stella for letting me amuse her and for providing necessary diversion from the monomania of writing. Thanks to Steve Larsen, who pointed me in the right direction. Thanks to Inner Traditions for giving this a chance and to Elaine Sanborn, who has been an author's vision of an ideal editor.

Last and certainly not least, love and thanks to Ralph A. Dale, who always provided me with a wonderful model of courage, curiosity, and chutzpah.

INTRODUCTION:
MEETING THE DREAMER

*To dream is to see the truth at night. If a man says something and you
dream about it at night and see it differently at night, then you know that
the man is misleading you. It is the dream that shows the truth, because
the shades never deceive their children.*

ZULU MAN

IN THE BEGINNING WAS THE DREAM

All that we see and feel around us—the mountains, the valleys, the streams—
was dreamed. The stars, the sun and men, the moon, the earth and women,
laughter, tears and children—all began with a dream. That's what the native
peoples of Australia have experienced. We are dreamed.

And we dream—each and every one of us. There is nothing more universal than dreams. Nightly, throughout the world, people close their eyes, drop
their daytime minds, and are carried away into a different land.

Can we fly? Can we leap across the chasm of time and visit long ago? Can
we change our shape in the blink of a thought or melt into an ocean or a
mountain? Can we meet and speak with those who have died and those who

have yet to be born? Of course we can. We do these things all the time in our dreams. We can build skyscrapers on a bed of clouds. We can travel beyond warp speed to the end of the galaxy. We can dance in the court of Queen Elizabeth or swim in a depthless sea. All this and infinitely more we can do in our dreams.

But dreaming is dreaming and waking is waking—right? We have, from the time we were little, kept these two very separate. Even in our language we recognize the difference between the two: A dream is "just a dream"; "You must be dreaming"; "Well, that's a nice dream"; "Dream on"; "What a dreamer you are!"; "It's only a pipe dream."

We in the West, in the culture of the industrialized world, have been taught that dreams are not actually real.* We have learned that they are projections of the waking mind, wish fulfillment, subconscious, unconscious, preconscious—definitely not conscious. But in this belief we are a distinct minority. Most of humanity has seen dreams differently.

In order to change our thinking, we first have to change our language a little bit. This is not about consciousness and unconsciousness. Nor is it about consciousness and subconsciousness. In either case there is a kind of implied judgment. Most of us believe that consciousness is related to the state of being awake. Similarly, we tend to see unconsciousness or subconsciousness as characterizing the dream state.

Think about it. Which is more evolved, *human* or *subhuman?* The prefix *sub* means "beneath," "below," "inferior," or "subordinate." Or how about *awareness* and *unawareness?* The prefix *un* simply means "not." So *unconscious* means "not conscious." By referring to dreams as either *sub*conscious or *un*conscious, we're stating that dreams are either lower than consciousness or are without any consciousness at all. This is a distinctly modern and Western notion of dreams, an idea that, despite its scientific trappings, has its roots planted firmly in the Middle Ages, when the dominant view was that dreams were the work of the devil.

We are taught to believe that dreams are either bad or unreal. But a belief is not necessarily truth. Beliefs are things we are taught. Truths are things we discover. Somehow we believe fervently that our eyes tell us what's real. "Open your eyes" is another way of saying "Look at reality"; telling someone to "wake up" is another way of saying "Accept reality." While our language indicates a strong belief that dreams are unreal, other languages do not, reflecting that other

---

* In this book I refer to the West as the industrialized world represented primarily by western Europe and the United States. It has also been called the "first world" and the "capitalist world."

cultures believe something different. In fact, some people hold that the waking state is illusion and the dream state reflects reality. Imagine that!

For most of the human race, the line between dream consciousness and waking consciousness is very thin and ever-shifting. For the Blackfoot Indians, as for many Native American cultures, dream consciousness *is* reality. For the Nyakyusa of Tanzania, reality is revealed to men in dreams by prophets who "go down thinking like the roots of a tree" to the world of the shades. The ancient Celts believed dreams took us to the places where we could discover the essence of reality—those places visited by the deities.

Of course, it would be silly to say that only dream consciousness is reality. You might jump off a skyscraper in a dream, but you wouldn't quite be in your right mind if, believing you could fly, you jumped off a skyscraper while awake. It's equally absurd, though, to assert that only waking consciousness is real. Both states are real. Each is truth in its own way. We don't have to choose—we can have our cake and eat it too. Yummy!

We all have two forms of consciousness. Our waking consciousness carries us from day to day, allowing us to drive cars and replace lightbulbs without killing ourselves. It allows us to accomplish tasks, learn from mistakes, and plan for the next day. Without our waking consciousness, we wouldn't survive a trip across the street.

But it is our dream consciousness that helps us see beyond our waking mind. It dissolves all the rules of logic and bends and twists time. It allows all our career programs and presumed talents to morph into something else. We become poets, singers, dancers. We are beyond boundaries. Without our dream consciousness, there would be no imagination.

Dreams, in part, are about imagination. Imagination isn't a luxury—it's the very essence of being human, enabling us to go beyond what we already know. Without imagination we wouldn't exist. It is what takes us into the unknown and into discovery. Without our imagination, we simply are not human, for it is what takes us beyond the limits of our experience. Without it we would go nowhere except where we have already gone.

Fire. Agriculture. The wheel. Think of where we would be without them. In the dark forests farther back than memory or even legend, fire was our enemy. Either through story or through experience, humans *knew* the deadly dangers of flames. And yet in fire lay our salvation: Someone had to see the power of the flame, to realize that fire could be tamed. Some person had to see the divine in a burning bush thousands of years before Moses, and then go beyond what people knew to a place where people had not yet been. It's hard to fathom now how frightened the little group of humans must have been when one of them held the first burning branch. But the fire has been burning ever since. Maybe the idea came in a dream. It certainly came from a place no one had visited before. That's imagination.

So important are dreams to imagination that they are its handmaidens. At night, when the waking mind relaxes and falls asleep, the dreaming consciousness arises. The visions we see then and carry with us into day—without them we would be dead. Albert Einstein stated it clearly when he said, "I am enough of an artist to draw freely upon my imagination. Imagination is more important than knowledge. Knowledge is limited. Imagination encircles the world." By definition, knowledge is limited to that which is known. Imagination penetrates the unknown. And dreams are the mother, sister, and child of imagination. Einstein himself traced the genesis of his theory of relativity to a dream he had at the age of fourteen. He took the world to the frontiers of space and time because he was willing to cross them—and to believe his dream was real.

Within each of us is an Einstein, a Mozart, an O'Keefe, an Edison. Our creative genius lies in the unexplored, in the land between waking and sleeping—in the world of imagination. And that can be reached through dreams.

Yet we in the West have downplayed imagination as much as we have downplayed dreams. How many times have adults responded to children who share their visions and dreams, "It's all in your imagination—it's only your imagination." *Only?* The conventional wisdom is that imagination, like a dream, is at best curious and at worst illusory and destructive. Of course, neither dreams nor imagination can be tested. But testing is surely not the only criterion for reality.

Every night we pioneers enter into the unknown, exploring new territory. No matter how many times we fly in our dreams, the experience will always be new. The dream journey is always a trip into the unknown. In our waking life, our mind likes to experience what it already knows, and so it tries constantly to put experience into familiar packages. While this may be comfortable, it's extremely limiting. Dreams and imagination smash this routine. They are eternally new.

A young child thinks that his small world is the entire world—but growing means seeing beyond this belief. To grow as a human means to expand our idea of the world, to know that there are unknown places, and to discover them.

A KALEIDOSCOPE OF REALITY

The West is not the world—what we here learn and see, what we think and feel do not define the world or the universe. In dreams there is a kaleidoscope of human experience. All people dream, and since the dawn of time all peoples have worked and played with their dreams.

What a rich tapestry we weave! The dream fabric of the human race is deeply textured and multicolored. For this reason, the exploration of the dream experiences of other cultures is an adventure for all of us. My own exploration has been a labor of love.

I am an amateur enthralled by the subject of dreams. My training is as a historian, not an anthropologist, but the work of anthropologists has been invaluable. It has allowed me to look through the eyes of those who have sought to understand the indigenous peoples of America, Asia, the Arctic, and Africa. The fascinating thing about seeing other peoples in this way is witnessing just how creative a species we humans are. Dreams are one thing that unites all of us over time, place, and culture. A young woman on the Irish coast two hundred years ago, a Mohave boy in the sands of the Southwest a hundred years ago, every man, woman, boy, and girl today—all of us dream.

We differ distinctly, however, in how we look at and deal with our dreams. In the beginning of my work in preparation for this book, I vowed to remain a detached observer studying exactly how different peoples viewed their dreams, but somewhere along the way I decided I could no longer be detached. At some point I was discovering for myself some new truths. My study of soul travel comes to mind: I found, much to my surprise, that I had recorded over one hundred different cultures that felt that the soul travels in dreams. My first impulse was to think of this as an interesting confluence of superstition. The idea of the soul traveling was a bit over-the-edge for me. Oh yes, I did have a dream once in which I visited a fancy party set in 1937. And when I woke up, I was aware that I'd attended the party—but it was just a dream.

Then I tried to see, for the sake of argument, just how soul travel could occur. After all, the peoples that believed in it were quite disparate—they hailed from all over the world and were not united in any religious way with regard to their beliefs about the soul. Some saw the soul as a spirit; some saw it as the life force; some saw it as one of the two identities that all humans have—there were a multitude of descriptions of the soul. But they all seemed to agree that, whatever it was, it left the body at night and traveled, experiencing all kinds of adventures.

I began to think that maybe all these peoples—most of whom have been around for a long time—knew something that I didn't know, and I figured if I was open long enough to what they were talking about, I might get to know it too. My notions of superstitions were shifting.

We are such materialists in this age. Most of us believe that if something can't be seen, it doesn't exist. If this isn't a superstition—a blind faith—I don't know what is. Because we fear the unknown, we explain it away. But not everything—including the magic of dreams—can be explained. A few days ago, I found the e-mail address of Bria, whom I have known since she was nine. I was one of her teachers back then. Bria is Irish and one of the most independent human beings I have ever met. She was the first person to get me thinking honestly about fairies. She knew them. She described them and told me what they did and what they were like and where they lived in the mountains. Because Bria never lied, I trusted her truth—and, for the first time in my life, I actually acknowledged the possibility of fairies.

Bria is now almost thirty and lives somewhere in Ireland. I haven't seen her since she was a teenager. When a mutual friend sent me an e-mail message, there, among the others who received the message, was Bria. So I wrote to her. She wrote back: "That was strange! I haven't thought about you in a long time, but last night you were in my dream, and when I got to work this morning, there was an e-mail from you."

There is a magic in dreams that can't be explained. Everyone knows that we fly in our dreams. Lots of us have done it. Meeting departed people in dreams is also common, as is soaring through space and time in an instant. We can do things in our sleeping state that we can't do in our waking state, and although they can't be explained, they are no less real.

Today's beliefs are tomorrow's superstitions. Conversely, today's absurdities are tomorrow's truths. For example, European physicians of the fourteenth century thought that wearing long black robes helped them resist the bubonic plague. It took another four hundred years before scientists discovered that the plague was carried on the saliva of fleas that lived on rats—and that the color black repels fleas. A superstition had stumbled upon a truth.

Our greatest superstitions are the ones we can't see, filtered through lenses in glasses we forget we are wearing. We think we are seeing what is—but we are looking through these forgotten lenses. Superstition is blind belief, conditioning, what we are told. And perhaps the greatest of them all is the one insisting that there is only one truth in every situation. This is so deep and seamless a part of the Judaic-Islamic-Christian cultures as to be invisible to the naked eye.

No matter what religious faith you follow—Christian, Jewish, Islamic, atheist—the main religion of the West is rationalism, the state church is the waking mind. But in other cultures, the world of spirits and dreams is as alive as the waking world. Very often we treat these other worldviews much the same way as we treat our own dreams. We try to impose on them our scientific, empirical "truth." We try to analyze our dreams and make sense of them. We try to put them in a rational framework that we can understand.

Believing that there is only one truth is an old habit, and old habits die hard. All of this is very understandable. We've been taught that venturing into the unknown is scary. Accepting the Mbuti pygmies' ideas of spirits and souls seems unlikely for many of us. Yet perhaps they know something we don't. There is no question that the technology of a nation like the United States can take us faster and farther in this world than anything that the Mbuti pygmies have created. But, perhaps, when it comes to the fall of night, we are the less advanced. As we step into the world of dreams with receptive minds, we find that there are many truths.

The study of dream consciousness is never ending. We will begin to know only if we first recognize that we don't know. Someday maybe technology will catch up. Perhaps in some future neurophysiology laboratory a machine will record something leaving the dreaming sleeper and returning upon the sleeper's awakening. Perhaps a Nobel Prize awaits the scientist who first measures the flight of the soul at night. At that time, the shades, shadows, and spirits of all those who have been will probably murmur an amused assent.

What we need is a gentle meeting of our waking consciousness and our dreaming mind. What we need is a respectful collaboration between the two parts of our being. Similarly, we need a gentle meeting of the experiences of other cultures with our own. In the history of the human race, so many societies—so many peoples—have embraced the gift of dreams. We can learn from those who respect dreams and allow themselves to be guided by them.

Last April, just as I was finishing the research for this book, I learned a powerful lesson from someone who had been dead for seventeen hundred years. Now if that sounds eerie, it really isn't. The lesson I learned was in a story.

In the fourth century in Babylon there lived a teacher named Rabbi Hisda. He started out in life relatively poor but worked his way up the rungs of Babylonian society to become a successful wine merchant. Then he dropped it and became a rabbi. Talk about going into the unknown.

One night Rabbi Hisda had a dream, which he took to various interpreters. Apparently everybody was interested in dreams in those days, and apparently there were a lot of dream interpreters hanging out their shingles on the streets of Babylon. Rabbi Hisda wrote that he took his dream to twenty-five different interpreters. Altogether he received twenty-five different interpretations—and, he wrote, *they were all right.*

When I read this story a little voice inside of me cheered, "YES!" Twenty-five different interpretations and they were all correct—it made such good sense. For much of my life I, like so many of us, had been concerned with finding out what's right and what's wrong, but gradually I was discovering that it was a pain in the neck having to be right all the time. A little more flexibility made life less stressful. It was a relief to find that I wasn't as all-knowing as I used to think I was.

Rabbi Hisda, however, reached across seventeen centuries to teach me something more: There are many right "answers," many truths—maybe even as many as twenty-five, or a hundred, or a thousand. Rabbi Hisda taught me that we can we experience many truths about dreams. And that's the point of his story and this book. Human beings can teach one another about dreams. My question, then, and the question of this book is, "What can I learn about dreams from other peoples in this world?"

There is so much to learn and there are so many teachers. In this book I have tried to provide a sampling of dream teachings from around the world and across time. At best this can be only a taste—a nibble here and a sip there. The Crow people will sacrifice a part of their finger if it means that they might receive a powerful dream. In this they teach the importance of the dream and the essence of commitment. The gentle Temiar of Malaysia encourage their children to face the beasts in their nightmares and in this way teach the importance of using our dreams to go through fear. The Naskapi hunters of Labrador follow their dreams to find caribou. In this they teach that our dreams can help us sustain our lives.

THE MEDIUM IS THE MESSAGE

If nothing else, writing this book has become an exercise in humility. I could spend the rest of my life—I could spend two more lives—working on a dream book and it would barely touch the surface. It is such a vast territory, such a mystery. I have come to realize that there can never be a definitive work on dreams. Perhaps any work on dreams must, of necessity, be a work in progress, as this is. The only certain assertion that I can make is that people can take back their own dreams—that we are all able to use our sleeping giant.

I have devoted much of this book to bringing together the two parts of our being—our waking consciousness and our dreaming mind. Like a true Gemini, I have been struggling within myself to make these two halves into one whole, so much so that I think I have written two books, as my perceptive aunt Charlotte has commented—here is the academic discussing the role of dreams in various cultures, and here is the intuitive playing with dreams. Marshall McLuhan wrote a book entitled *The Medium Is the Message.* In the case of this book, perhaps it is.

A whole number in mathematics is an *integer,* from which comes the word *integrity.* What is integrity but being wholly oneself? For me, bridging the gap between my dream consciousness and my waking consciousness—between my dream reality and my waking reality—is part of becoming whole, getting it together, respecting me in my entirety. It is integrity in the deepest sense. And getting there is more than half the fun.

This book is constructed to help you get there too. We in the West have created thick walls between our waking consciousness and our dream consciousness. In other cultures the border between these two is much more permeable. In the first chapter, "The Veil between the Worlds," we move back and forth between these two states to help blur the border between them.

Because we erect such strong walls between our waking and dream states, we often forget our dreams. Our waking consciousness takes over from the time we open our eyes. Our dream consciousness shyly retreats into the background. It was striking to me to learn that few cultures have techniques for remembering dreams. On the other hand, people all over the world have been interested in entering and inducing the dream state. In the second chapter, "Purging the River Lethe," we explore the rich cultural experience of inducing dream consciousness and some techniques for remembering our dreams.

Creativity, imagination, and dreams are sisters. In our dreams we are playwrights, artists, musicians, and inventors—our dream consciousness is a wellspring of creativity. We can access our dream creativity as countless people have. The third chapter, "Song and Dance, Mask and Lance," touches on the fountain source of dream creativity.

In the novel *Dune,* by Frank Herbert, there is a group of women who have faced their unconscious fears and turned them into power. Their motto is "Fear is the mind killer." Fear contracts us, blocks us. We humans have experienced fear in our dreams probably for as long as we have dreamed. Nightmares haunt many of us. Yet, as many cultures have found, we can transform the power of our nightmares. We can use our dreams to move through our fears. In the fourth chapter, "Saddling the Night's Mare," we join our ancestors in facing the darkness of our dreams.

Hundreds of cultures feel that the soul wanders during sleep. This nocturnal journey brings us in contact with other wanderers, with departed ancestors, with spirits invisible to the waking eye. In the fifth chapter, "On the Wings of the Night," we discover the adventure in this nightly travel.

Healers, shamans, and dreamers have been inseparable since the dawn of time. For many generations, people have been tapping dream consciousness to achieve health and healing. From ancient Greece to the top of the Andes Mountains today, healers and visionaries have recognized the healing power of our dream awareness. In the sixth chapter, "Dreaming Wholeness," we travel with these visionaries

To see the world with new eyes is the role of the diviner, the psychic, the intuitive—the dreamer. The vistas of dream consciousness pay no heed to waking rules of space and time. In our sleep we can see far and clearly. The seventh chapter, "Remembering the Future," helps us to realize the intuitive power of our dreams.

We are an impatient people today. We like to make sense of things right away. In fact, the phrase "to make sense" says it all. We make cars, videos, clothes, buildings . . . and sense. We are makers. We are doers. But dream consciousness is less aggressive. When we try to wrest meaning from a dream, we are violating a very gentle part of ourselves.

There is no one true school of dream interpretation. In the final chapter, "Making Love to Your Psyche," we learn that all of them carry a seed of truth that cannot be wrenched out of our dreams, but rather must be gathered gently and patiently.

A very wise educator once said, "Play is the work of the child." The child is parent of the dreamer. In our dreams we are like children, exposed and vulnerable, innocent and wondrous. It has been my experience that when we are allowed to play, we learn a great deal more than when we are chained to a desk and ordered to learn. As a teacher I have found that a playful lesson is one that lasts. We do not, in our dreams, work toward goals. We do that only in our waking consciousness. In our dreams there are no goals. Play is the work of the dreamer.

In this book I have created places where people can explore their dream consciousness and have provided exercises with suggestions for doing this. These Dream Explorations are sprinkled throughout every chapter. Many of them derive from the experiences of other cultures. None of them is ponderous or serious. None of them is a test having a right or wrong answer. These explorations are simply avenues for you to use to travel into the unknown and discover your own truths. They are meant to be enjoyable, interesting, even revealing.

On any given night, we have very little control over what we will dream, which is just how it needs to be. Control is the province of the waking mind and of our waking lives in which we need to determine, for instance, the direction in which our automobile turns or the time we take to get from here to there. In our dreams, this kind of control dissolves—but it does not necessarily have to. In fact, the control of our waking consciousness can meet our dreaming mind—but the goal is not a conquest of the dream state by the rational mind. The Dream Explorations help, in many cases, to achieve a meeting between waking and dreaming consciousness.

Of course, all the Dream Explorations and techniques in the world will mean but little if there is no intention. If we are committed to exploring our dreams, we will remember them and they will be helpful to us. The Crow people of the American Plains, whose lives revolved around the buffalo and the horse, felt very strongly about dream visions. Because their lives were mobile and uncertain, they needed all the insight they could get to survive their enemies and the difficulties of their environment. They would go to great lengths to bring about their dream visions. A Crow who desired one would leave his village wearing next to nothing and go to a lonely mountain peak. There he would neither drink nor eat for four days as he waited to be visited by a dream vision. Sometimes he would stick skewers into his body, or, as already mentioned, he might cut off one of his finger joints as a conciliatory gesture to the spirits. Clearly the Crow regarded dreams as more than curiosities.

We couldn't be further from the Crow. Most of us think the reality of being awake is more important than the reality of our dream state. Certainly some of us think dreams are interesting, and some of us think they're important because they can shed light on our waking state. But our dreams always seem to be at the service of our waking minds. It's an amazing level of dedication that spurs a person to cut off a finger joint in order to receive a dream.

We could be closer to our dreams too. Of course, we need not cut off our finger joints—but we can commit and dedicate ourselves to seeing and recalling our dreams. Without commitment, all such explorations and techniques are worth little. We must want to remember our dreams with our waking consciousness, and then remind ourselves to do it. Intention and commitment are enough.

Now, this book is quite relaxed and comes with no rules. People are not going to be tested on what it contains. In fact, you don't even have to read it from cover to cover. You can start in the middle and read to the end or start at the beginning and read to the middle. You can try out the explorations or you might want to stick with the narrative or the stories. It's up to you. But there is one strong suggestion, repeated over and over in the chapters that follow: *Whatever you do, keep a journal.*

Something happens when we put down our thoughts and experiences on paper. We take the act of writing for granted because we have been putting little squiggles on paper since we were in first grade. But writing a story is different from telling it or merely remembering it.

The written word is magic and a journal is an essential part of any dream play or work. Sometimes I get a bit repetitive about this, and I apologize in advance. However, let me say it at the start: When we write down something we change the world . . . really, even if that change is no more than the creation of those strange squiggles, which stand for words, which represent thoughts and experience and feeling.

Life being what it is, we do forget things, and dreams are easy to forget. They slip out of our waking minds softly but completely each morning. We need to hold on to them—that's one reason to keep a journal. Another reason to keep a journal is that it helps us play with our dreams. A dream journal becomes a meeting place for the dreaming and waking minds. Finding that meeting place is one of the themes of this book. Hanging out in that place is one of the goals of this book.

With that said, there are some important points to remember: First, in order for a journal to be meaningful, we must use it as a vehicle for free and honest speech. We are, after all, talking to ourselves—which means that journals are private. They need to be private. We need to know that what we write will be for ourselves alone.

A journal does not have to be an elaborate thing. Sure, you can get a leather-bound notebook and make it really classy. The important thing is that you keep it near the bed with a pen or pencil so that you can write down your dreams as soon as you wake up. The sooner the better. If we write down our dreams the moment we awaken, we are, in some ways, still in the dreaming mind, at the border between our two consciousnesses. I've found that remembering a few key words helps me to re-create my dream. In fact, the words we choose are still part of the dream. If we allow it, the dream will meet the waking mind on paper.

So keep a journal. It will repay you again and again. There will be times when you will look in wonder at what has happened that your ordinary waking mind has forgotten. A dream does not die. Each time we look back at our dreams—even if it is years later—new truths may emerge.

Finally, a word about dream interpretation: This is not a book that tells you what your dreams "mean." From ancient Sumeria through medieval Europe to the present, people have been telling other people how to look at their dreams. But both dreams and their symbols are profoundly personal. And their individuality has always been a threat to those seeking to impose a unified worldview. Thus the ancient monarchies of Sumeria sought to institute a text that would clearly and safely define the meaning of dreams. And thus the medieval church insisted that most dreams came from the devil and that only saints could distinguish between good and bad dreams. And thus books on dream symbols and interpretation abound today.

There is a conditioned part of ourselves that wants to be told what to think, but this book won't do that. Instead it will, I hope, help you to start on a new adventure all your own—your discovery of the richness of dream consciousness.

AND FURTHERMORE . . .

As I neared the finish line of this book, I had a curious dream. It was quite simple: a dream of somebody's last words. What were these last words? "And furthermore . . ." I awoke with a smile. All these years of doing psychic readings in the Borscht Belt hotels of the Catskills and here I was dreaming one-liners. "And furthermore . . ."—I thought it might be a nice epitaph.

There are several conspicuous absences in this book. Where is Sigmund Freud? Where is Carl Jung? They are not here.

This is by no means a commentary on the two founders of modern dream therapy. They are both pioneers and giants. However, there has been a great deal written by and about both men, while there hasn't been much written about the dream work of the Blackfoot Indians or the Pukapukans or the Hopi or the Mayawyaw. And these people have had a rich history of dream work and play.

In leaving out Freud and Jung, this book does not propose rejecting the rational mind. Rather, it's a call for the wedding of the rational mind with dream consciousness so that we can be whole.

Three and a half centuries ago the movement called rationalism was a beacon of light in the Western world. Particularly in France, the struggle to see the world in this light represented a reaction against a millennium of intellectual squalor, theocracy, superstition, and darkness.

In the old days in Europe people generally bathed once a year. Bath time was a big occasion. The woman of the house would fill a tub with heated water and each member of the family took his or her turn. First came the father, then came the older sons, then mother and daughters took their turns. Baby would be last. The families were quite big in those days, so by the time baby's turn came around, the water was opaque. Baby could be lost. It is said that from this experience came the admonition not to throw out the baby with the bathwater.

For the rationalists of the eighteenth century, the bathwater of a thousand years of intellectual torpor was filthy through and through. Baby in the murky depths be damned—the sediment of ignorance and religious repression must go!

Thus, in the centuries that have followed, the heirs of the rationalists, in the eagerness of purgation, have been throwing out the baby with the bathwater. In so doing they have created their own legacy of superstition and ignorance. They have simply substituted one "infallible" way of looking at the world with another. The new superstition is that unless we can explain something, it doesn't exist.

The left-brain analytical mode characterized by rationalism suited the industrialized world because it married well with the rise of the Protestant work ethic. In the United States, the industrializing Northeast spread its ethic with the same fervor that it spread its steamboats, textiles, and steel. As settlers moved from the established states of New England and the Middle Atlantic to the West in the first part of the nineteenth century, the gospel followed in the form of a practical Christianity, devoid of mysticism. Because history is full of ironies, the triumph of rationalism in the United States occurred in an environment of profound irrationality: civil war.

Now we stand at the twilight of rationalism. We are learning that orthodoxy, whether it be that of the medieval church or of the contemporary academy, is insufficient to answer the questions of the present. There is no returning to some golden day, yet we can move on. It seems that a society that can manage to send messages around the world with the speed of light or send ships to the stars can finally learn how to throw out the bathwater without throwing out the baby.

The baby is the mystery. The baby is the dream, the imagination, and the wonder. The baby is the multitude of truths, the thousand realities. The baby is within us, in our dreams. Let us keep the baby and realize the power of our dreams.

THE VEIL BETWEEN THE WORLDS: CROSSING THE BORDERS BETWEEN AWAKE AND DREAM

I believe in the future transmutation of those two seemingly
contradictory states, dream and reality, into a sort of absolute reality, of
surreality, so to speak. I am looking forward to its consummation, certain
that I shall never share in it, but death would matter little to me could
I but taste the joy it will yield ultimately.
ANDRÉ BRETON, *SURREALIST MANIFESTO*, 1934

Once I, Chuang Tzu, dreamed I was a butterfly and was happy as
a butterfly. I was conscious that I was quite pleased with myself, but
I did not know that I was Tzu. Suddenly I awoke, and there was I,
visibly Tzu. I do not know whether it was Tzu dreaming that
he was a butterfly or the butterfly dreaming that he was Tzu.
Between Tzu and the butterfly there must be some distinction.
But one may be the other. This is called the transformation of things.
CHUANG TZU, 399–295 B.C.

The only person in Germany who still leads a private
life is the person who sleeps.
ROBERT LEY, NAZI REICHORGANISATIONLEITER, 1934

THE VOYAGE OF THE METAPHOR

Our world is full of metaphors. The word *metaphor* comes from the Greek *metapherein*, "to carry over." The metaphor takes us to the heart of meaning by describing something other than what we are regarding. "Heart of meaning"— there's a fine example! It's impossible to communicate without metaphors; they are part of our everyday reality.

"To carry over." But where are we carried to? And where are we coming from? If a metaphor carries us from one place to another, where do we begin and where do we end up?

Even the definition of a metaphor is a metaphor. But "carried over" is quite apt for the world of dreams and waking reality. It is from the waking world to the world of dreams that we are carried or transferred each evening when we fall asleep, and it is back to the waking reality that we return when we wake up.

The description of this nightly journey abounds with metaphors. We do not simply sleep. We *fall* asleep. The verb *fall* reveals a key element of the dream state, as it does for the happy event of being smitten. We fall asleep and we fall in love—in both cases, there are circumstances beyond our conscious control. We do not recline in love, sit in love, or stand in love . . . we fall, sometimes head over heels. And we fall asleep, like Alice tumbling down the rabbit hole, entering a world where the logic and rationality of everyday life dissolve.

And then we wake *up*. We do not wake down or in between—we wake up. Here again is the metaphor: In our language of sleep and waking, the dream state is down and the waking state is up. We descend into the depths of our being and the netherworld in our sleep and rise to the light of day as we wake up. It's a vertical trip, falling into sleep and rising into waking.

The Greeks told of a mythical river called Lethe, the River of Forgetfulness. When a person left the body in death, his soul awaited its incarnation into another being. But before it could return to the earthly plane in the body of another, the soul had to drink from the river Lethe. In this way, it forgot its previous incarnation. Perhaps this leads to another sleep metaphor or two: Not only has the state of sleep often been seen as analogous to death, but many of us drink from our own river Lethe each morning before we awake, as we imbibe the water of forgetfulness.

What is it in a metaphor—or a dream—that moves us? The answer lies in the word *move.* Each can stir us. We are agitated, touched, provoked. We resonate. Each conjures feeling, and it is feeling that carries a metaphor or a dream. A nightmare is not a nightmare unless you feel scared. In a dream you may feel ecstatic while being chased or depressed while winning a million dollars. The feeling of a dream is every bit as important as the content.

Naturally, it's easier for us to look at content because it's more familiar. We are always looking at how things appear, at what things are *about,* in our work, on the television screen, in our millions of exchanges every day. But to see how things feel is often the province of the night and the moon.

In waking sight, things appear to be clear. Objects have definition in the light of day. In daylight we have the kind of vision that we associate with sight.

Dream sight is different. In dreams we see with our eyes closed. This means we have to use other tools of sight, one of which is feeling and another of which is imagination. Imagination is related to images, but not just those that are visual. The *American Heritage Dictionary* defines *imagination* as "the formation of a mental image of something that is neither perceived as real nor present to the senses."

The phrase "present to the senses" offers a telling assumption about the sense of sight, and ultimately about our Western notion of dreams. "Seeing is believing," right? Somehow we, in the West, have made sight the paramount sense—"Don't you see?" "See what I mean?" The English language regards *sight* and *perception* as synonyms. To see is to perceive. But perception is much broader than eyesight. There are, after all, millions of blind people who "see" quite well and millions of sighted people who can be quite blind.

Imagination is something that is really not at all connected with eyesight. There is no way that we can use our eyesight when our eyes are closed. The borders between perception and imagination are very fuzzy indeed.

⊚ Dream Exploration ⊚

See with Your Ears

One of the best ways to become aware of our habits is simply to watch them. Almost all of us use our sense of sight as the touchstone of truth. Here's a simple method for gaining awareness of your reliance on the sense of sight.

1. Note how many times you use *seeing* as an equivalent to *seeing*.
You might even want to keep a record in your journal for a day or two. It's amazing how many things come to light (!) when we keep our eye on them (!).

2. Change your vocabulary.
Every time you find yourself phrasing something in terms of the sense of sight, change the sense. For example, instead of saying, "I see," say, "I hear" or "I feel" or "That touches me" or "That smells right to me." See how that feels—whoops! Note how that feels and how that affects the way you perceive things.

3. Start paying attention to the other senses.
Take your time. Close your eyes. Remain alert to what your other senses are telling you, discovering what they reveal. What do you hear? What do you feel? What do you smell?

IMAGINING OURSELVES INTO THE UNKNOWN

While we revere eyesight as the source of perception, we dismiss imagination as trivial. Yet imagination is our prize heritage as human beings and dreams are the kingdom of the imagination.

We often tell children, and often heard as kids ourselves, "It's all in your imagination." Now it's time we accepted it—it *is* all in our imagination! Two things make us human. The first is that we can learn from experience—we can acquire knowledge, at school and at work. It's important stuff. Without it we would have to reinvent the wheel every generation.

The second thing that makes us human is that we actually invented the wheel in the first place. That's imagination, seeing the unknown, vision beyond our ordinary sight, and you need it before there can be any knowledge. If nobody had invented the wheel, there would be no information about it to pass on. It is imagination that has changed us from four-legged creatures with our faces to the ground to two-legged beings with our eyes to the stars.

It is imagination together with the intuitive sense accompanying it that allow us to see the world with new eyes. In flame, a destructive enemy that our ancestors had witnessed and feared for thousands of years, someone saw an ally. In the trees that had been around for millennia, someone saw a wheel. And these two humans changed the world forever.

Children can readily see wheels in trees. They use their inner eyes—their imagination. We can see with our imagination too. It's fun, and the easiest place to start is with our dreams.

We Westerners are very concerned with boundaries and the "black" or "white" they define: life or death, joy or sadness; reality or illusion; dreaming or awake. Yet such boundaries are the products of our minds. For most of humankind, such boundaries themselves have been illusory. People have found particularly that the borders between the dream state and the waking state are shifting, fluid, and ephemeral. Across these borders have come visits from those who have left the physical plane and serve as inspirations for healing. To cross these borders is to be transported through time and space.

Let's return to the metaphor: It's what allows us to go back and forth between the dream state and the waking state. It must "carry" us from one form of thinking to another, from the literal mind to the realm of dreams.

 Dream Story

A Metaphor Comes to Life

Her marriage was slowly falling apart. Or, as she put it, the foundation of her marriage was disintegrating. It had been a slow process—nothing sudden, just a gradual deterioration over the many years they had been together.

Her first impulse was to seek counseling. After all, that's the way to fix it, isn't it? Isn't the best way—the American way—to deal with a problem to confront it head on? Instead she decided to try a different approach. She and her husband had renovated their house years earlier. It was already an old house when they bought it. That was part of its charm. But now the foundation was deteriorating—just like the foundation of their marriage. So she decided to deal with the house.

She was handy. After all, she had done as much of the work on the house as anybody else had. With great zeal and focus she set about repairing the foundation: She buttressed sagging areas, repaired footers, poured cement. Slowly she brought new life to the old building. And slowly her husband joined her in her work, at first for an hour here or there, and then for whole afternoons and weekends. They began to talk again, about books and friends, about their life and their ideas.

Slowly, with each brick replaced, with each crumbling corner made new, their marriage began to quicken, come alive, become more solid. She had begun with a metaphor and ended up changing her life.

Dream Exploration

Sympathetic Magic 101

In dreams we live in metaphors. In our waking state we think we are living in literal reality. The story of the woman repairing her house would make a great dream. In a dream she could hammer and dig and pour, and then awake to realize that her house is a metaphor for her marriage. But it isn't a dream. It's lived as a waking reality.

In our waking state, we can work on one thing and, through the power of metaphor, feel its impact in another part of our life. We change something and that which it reflects also changes. Anthropologists have a name for this phenomenon when people create it consciously. They call it *sympathetic magic* and people have been using the strategy for thousands of years. So let's try it.

1. Think of something in your life that you would like to change.
But let's not be grandiose. We're not talking about completely changing your economic circumstances by winning the lottery. Choose from those perhaps small but significant everyday circumstances, those things that affect your daily activities. Something to remember: It's important that you play a major role in whatever it is that you want to change. For instance, the woman with the house and marriage knew that she was a major player in both.

2. Find a metaphor that applies and change it.
Here's a common example: Say your life is feeling hectic and disorganized. Perhaps you are experiencing a kind of chaos at work, at home, and in your relationships. The literal approach would be to deal with each of these. The metaphorical approach—the sympathetic magical approach—would be to change something that is representative of these. You might, in this case, clean out your car. Or you might organize the kitchen. In clearing and organizing one or two small areas, you might notice changes in other environments and in your relationships.

3. Keep up with the change.
Rome wasn't built in a day. See what happens over time. See how you feel. Watch what happens to the source of the change. And after you have tried one metaphor, you might try another. There is no limit.

4. Keep a record.
Writing is so important. Keeping track of our lives is one of the ways that both the waking and the dreaming states are enriched.

5. As always, take note of your dreams.
Maybe they will provide some insight about the metaphors in your life.

BLURRING THE BORDER

It is through the metaphor of the dream that our imagination can flourish. It is through dream consciousness that we go into the unknown—into the creative. Some anthropologists hold that the dream is the basis of all spiritual life, including the very notion of the soul itself. In fact, many have seen religion originating in the dream life of various cultures over thousands of years.

The border we cross between dream reality and waking reality is as arbitrary as the border between two nations. There is nothing "natural" or "eternal" about the border between Pakistan and India or the one between the United States and Canada. Human beings created those borders as they created the nations themselves. In a similar way, there is nothing fixed, eternal, or natural about the border between our waking and sleeping consciousness. It may shift, harden, or soften. As in the case of nations, we may allow a free flow across this border such as is allowed between the United States and Canada, or we may fortify the border, as India and Pakistan have.

For ages, humans have sought to make sense of our two kingdoms of consciousness. The Kpelle people have a simple explanation. Occupying part of Liberia and Guinea, the Kpelle are farmers and have been for countless generations. They mine the land for rice, cassava, and vegetables. It's a simple agriculture that sustains them, but not so simple is the Kpelle notion of dreams. They feel that everyone has two brains or spirits—one for dreams and one for waking life—and that dreams are as real as waking reality.

While the Kpelle may be unique in feeling that we all have two brains, they are not unique in their understanding that dreams are as real as waking reality. For many peoples the borders between these two states are not sharply defined.

The Jibaro people of eastern Ecuador and Peru are both fierce warriors and gentle healers. They have been headhunters and sophisticated observers of human consciousness for generations. The Jibaro feel that the experiences a person has during dreams are as real as the experiences he has when awake. In fact, they hold that only in dreams is true reality revealed. For them, everyday, conscious life is an illusion full of deception and lies. Only in dream consciousness do we see the real essence of things. In a dream, even our foes will tell the truth.

Other peoples agree. On top of the earth, near the Arctic Circle, are the indigenous people of Lapland. The Lapps, who live in darkness for half the year, also feel that the experiences a person has in dreams are as real as the those of his waking hours.

Likewise, the Azande people of Congo and the Sudan (man-made boundaries, like those that define the homelands of many of the world's indigenous peoples) believe that dreams are not fantastic but are instead real events experienced by the soul.

This notion takes us to North America as well. The Blackfoot Indians have long held that dreams have molded reality—as have the Australian Aborigines. The Blackfoot see dreams as the origin of material life. If a thing comes to your waking mind, it must be the consequence of a dream.

Lest we limit illustrations to the world's indigenous populations, the reality of dreams also finds expression in the Bible. Here, too, is the border between the two kingdoms of consciousness somewhat blurred. "For God speaketh once," says Job, "yea twice, yet man perceiveth not. In a dream, in a vision of the night, when sleep falleth upon men, in slumberings upon the bed; then he openeth the ears of men, and sealeth their instruction."[1]

There have been some Westerners who have recognized the truth of "primitive" cultures. Karl von den Steinen, a nineteenth-century German anthropologist, studied the Xingu people of central Brazil, who also felt that dream was reality. Von den Steinen made an important observation:

> We may not be too critical of the Indian's belief, based purely on the direct experience of the senses, if we remember that higher speculative philosophy does not find it at all simple to determine whether life is a dream or the dream is life, whether we experience reality while awake or during sleep, and we must not forget that, after we awaken, reality sometimes brings complete confirmation.[2]

In the West's cultural tradition, it was surrealism that captured the folk notion of dream reality and continued the blurring of the border between dream and waking consciousness. Probably the proponents of no other modern movement so clearly stated this as the surrealists. It was fitting that one of the leading spokesmen for this movement was a poet, Louis Aragon, for poetry unites the dream and the waking states.

In 1924 Aragon stated that

> . . . the real is a relation like any other; the essence of things is by no means linked to their reality, there are other relations besides reality, which the mind is capable of grasping and which also are primary, like chance, illusion, the fantastic, the dream. These various groups are united and brought into harmony in one single order, surreality.[3]

❖ Dream Story

Dream and Wealth Compete

Dream and Wealth were arguing. "I am the greater," said Wealth. "I can be everything to everyone. Everyone wants me. Everyone needs me. I am the most powerful."

"Ah," said Dream. "But I can pass through the world of substance into the world of spirit. I can disappear and reappear from the ends of the earth and—"

"Bah!" said Wealth. "Let us have a contest to see who is greater."

Dream and Wealth decided that each should hide in turn and whoever could find the other and yet not be found himself would win the contest.

Wealth hid himself first, taking the shape of a pot of gold and crawling into an anthill. Dream began his search going up to a poor boy who was lying asleep.

"Come out. Come out," Dream cried to the soul of the sleeping boy. When the boy's soul came out, Dream sent it to the anthill. The boy's soul returned and when the boy awoke he went to the anthill and dug up Wealth in the shape of a pot.

Then it was Dream's turn. Dream hid in the wind and was blown here and there about the world. Look as he would, Wealth could not find him. When the two met again, Wealth had to admit that Dream was the greater.

A STORY FROM THE MURIA PEOPLE OF INDIA[4]

◉ Dream Exploration ◉

Patching It Up

We stretch our memories to remember our dreams. Sometimes only a very small piece will remain in our consciousness when we awake. Certainly, there are ways to help us remember. But sometimes—often—all we have is small fragments of an experience. All memory is at best made of fragments and dream memories are no exception. How can they be anything else, given that they merely approximate the original experience?

Once we accept the fact that our dream remembrance is fragmentary, we have much more freedom. We can build on what we have. How? Improvise! In our waking state we can take over where the dream left off. After all, it's *our* dream.

1. When you wake up, write down as much of your dream as you can remember.

Yes, I've been harping on this one from the beginning. But remember: The very act of writing the dream brings our two consciousnesses closer together.

2. Give your dream notes a quick once-over, then retell the dream.
You may find it useful to use a small recorder. Or you may want to write down your retelling. Or you may simply want to tell it to someone. Whatever way you choose, you are to *expand* and *embellish* upon what you remember. This is a creation—it's not about "facts," it's not about accuracy. It's about imagination. Allow yourself to create situations, circumstances, happenings in your dream that aren't in your memory of it.

3. Start with little things.
At first, all you are really doing is patching up the remembrance. Treat it as if it were the original remembrance. Then begin expanding your dream. Feel free—it's your dream. As you do this, you are bringing your waking mind closer to your dream consciousness.

BORDERS WITHOUT PASSPORTS

It's a very delicate place—that border between dream and awake. There both worlds are present and there we are extremely vulnerable. There we are open and unguarded and our waking, rational mind is not in control.

Many cultures have given the greatest respect to the transition between dream and waking consciousness, being especially careful about waking people. Bringing people across the border is a serious matter. The Ainu people of Japan believe that a person can die if awakened too suddenly. The Bororo Indians of South America are extremely careful to wake people very slowly, if at all. The Maori people feel it a breech of etiquette to wake somebody who is sleeping. If it is done at all, it should be done gently at first, with very soft tones, gradually increasing in intensity until the person awakens. The Andaman Islanders will awaken somebody only in the direst emergency.

As so many of the world's peoples do, we must approach this border with the utmost respect. Straddling our two consciousnesses is a delicate maneuver and a vulnerable place, but oh, what a view!

⑨ Dream Exploration ⑨

Approaching the Borders on Tiptoe
We need to be gentle with ourselves in all aspects of dream play. As soon as we become heavy and overly serious, we are simply reinforcing the dominance of the waking mind. Again, the metaphor I use is the border between states. Peace and harmony between states can exist only if there is the mutual recognition and

respect of each state. If we approach the border of dreams with a notion of conquest, there will be no harmony. Our dream state is receptive and gentle. We must allow it to coexist with our waking state, approaching it on tiptoes. Otherwise, we will scare it away.

Every time we go to sleep we approach the border between waking and sleeping consciousness. We just haven't been paying attention to this up to now. So the first thing we need to do is pay attention.

1. Next time you are falling asleep, tell yourself that you are paying attention.

Intention, intention, intention! It's the most important ingredient in dream play, and it means telling ourselves what it is we want to do. This is the place where the waking mind can be our ally. Your intention here is to pay attention as you fall asleep.

2. Focus on an external stimulus.

If you have gentle music playing, focus on the music. If there is another sound around you, like a brook outside your window or the soft buzz of your refrigerator, focus on that sound. If there is a gentle breeze blowing, focus on that. Don't leave it; let it remain in the background.

3. Be a witness as you fall asleep.

Being a witness does not involve doing anything more than watching. But we have to tell ourselves to watch (intention again). We need to commit ourselves to witness what happens as we fall asleep. Continue to focus on something—music, an image in your mind's eye. The Tibetans focus on the dish of light behind the closed eyelids.

Be watchful and be aware. And remember: This is not a test. Don't worry about results, but try this process more than once or twice. After all, it takes awhile to turn around old habits.

4. Of course, check out your dreams.

See if there is any difference in your dreams when you witness falling asleep. Be open to what occurs. More often than not what we get is not what we expect. That is the nature and beauty of dream consciousness.

THE MAGIC OF NO-MAN'S-LAND

The permeable border between waking and dreaming is the province of shamans, visionaries, and seers. For many peoples the trance states of healing and divination take place on this border. There the visionary is aware and in a state of altered dream consciousness.

For most people, however, border visions are hidden. Interestingly, the Hungarian word for dream and trance is *regos,* which comes from the same root as *rejt,* meaning "to hide" something. Strange and wondrous things happen to those who "see" what is hidden in this way—that is, fall into a trance. They are able to communicate with both worlds—the wakeful one and the sleeping one, the living and the dead.

In the far north of the earth, on the Kamchatka peninsula, there are two kinds of seers: those who see when they are awake and those who see while asleep. The ones who see while sleeping are accessing the dream consciousness. They are at the border. And the Mandan Indians felt that waking visions were the most reliable, those from the conscious visionary who stood on the frontier and accessed them from the dream state.

What makes a visionary, a seer, or a shaman? Among the Caraja of Brazil, it is the ability to access the dream state at will, the gift of reaching that border with intent and awareness.

Native American cultures place great importance on visions and dreams. The Crow, the Mohave, the Blackfoot—all rely upon visions and seers. The Crow, for example, would undertake a military expedition only if it had been sanctioned in a vision. For the Crow it was intent that brought the vision. While visions might sometimes come unbidden, these were windfalls and not the norm.

Sleeping with care is the hallmark of the shaman. Among the Tarahumara of northern Mexico, the shaman is a healer, using his dreams to find cures for ailments. A large part of his power lies in his ability to sleep with great care and awareness, to exist harmoniously on the border between waking consciousness and dream consciousness.

The Selk'nam hunters of Tierra del Fuego also rely upon their shaman for healing. Here the healer uses a song to call his spirit and put himself in a dream state. Once in this state, the shaman occupies the border territory. He does not need to wait until nighttime and sleep to enter this state; he can enter this place at any time.

Recalling that intent and imagination are the key elements in waking dreams, it is easy to understand why the shamans among the Yahgan people of Cape Horn develop their power of imagination and auto-suggestion to put themselves in the dream state quickly, enabling ready access to that rich border between the waking and the dream.

The free flow between dreaming and waking, so important to the Selk'nam and the Yahgan and many other peoples, is certainly not new.

Countless cultures have been crossing this border. For us in the industrialized West, this may seem amazing—maybe even, to some, preposterous. But think about how many aspects of everyday life have qualities of the dream state, how many times things around us simply seem strange, part of the realm of the weird or bizarre. When we encounter the bizarre in our lives, we are jolted out of our sense of routine and the predictable reality that our lives so often seem to assume. In truth, however, the more we allow ourselves to see the bizarre, the more we are able to see it.

Now, the bizarre is not always flying soup spoons or ghosts swimming like jellyfish through the walls or caterpillars the size of elephants crawling down Main Street. The bizarre—the weird—is simply anything out of the ordinary.

The dream state is unique, weird, out of the ordinary. When we see these qualities in our waking life, we are softening the borders.

⑨ Dream Exploration ⑨

No Tricks, Just Treats

Next to Christmas, Halloween has become the most commercial festival in North America. But in actuality, the festival of Halloween is as old as Europe.

The ancient druids, who occupied what is now Great Britain, placed great importance on the passing of one season to another. The passing of fall into winter was particularly important, and the druids celebrated it with the festival Samhain (pronounced sah-win). It was the Celtic New Year, celebrated roughly on October 31, and marked the last gasp of summer and fall.

Most important, it was also the time when the veil between the world of the living and the world of the dead was the thinnest. The ancient Celts believed all laws of space and time were suspended on this day, allowing those of the spirit world to mingle with the living.

Later, the Roman conquerors of Britain incorporated the holiday into their celebration honoring Pomona, the goddess of fruits and trees, and much later, the Catholic Church incorporated this ancient holiday into All Hallows' Eve, the evening before Hallowmas, or All Saints' Day. Today, children dress as ghosts, ghouls, and witches and make their rounds of the neighborhood, collecting treats or creating mischief.

These child "ghosts" preserve the origins of this holiday, which celebrated the permeable veil between the worlds of the living and the dead. It may well be a wonderful time to explore the thin veil between our dream world and our waking world.

1. Pay attention to Halloween.
Of course, it comes only once a year, but that makes it all the more special. When it comes, tell yourself that you will celebrate it with more than just the consumption of candy.

2. Light a candle before you go to bed.
This is not about being spooky. Candles are an ancient source of light in the darkness of night. Almost every culture has some celebration of light within darkness. The burning of the candles on the Christian altar and the lighting of the menorah are just two examples of this.

3. Spend a moment or two silently thinking about those in your life who have passed away.
What relatives or friend are no longer with you? Think about who they were, what they were like.

4. Tell yourself that you will cross the border between living and dead as you cross the border between waking and sleep.
Stating this intention is about acknowledging life and the veil between life and death. If you start to make yourself frightened, remember that you are the one in charge and you can stop anytime. (But be sure to blow out the candle!)

5. Then check out your dreams.
As always, remain open to whatever may happen.

 Dream Story

Last Rites, Sukkoth, and Uranus in Whatever
This story is about farts, redheads, dead squirrels, Friday the thirteenth, and the full moon. But let me start with the dead squirrel.

It was Friday the thirteenth, the day of a full moon, and the beginning of the Jewish festival of Sukkoth when I pulled into my driveway to find a dead squirrel lying there. Do you think I would be crazy enough to make this up? And I've written a book on omens, no less.

It was just one of those days. Actually, it had been one of those days for about a week. The first thing I thought of as I very carefully parked my car was what to do with the squirrel that had chosen to depart on my neatly graded drive. The second thing I thought was, "What does it all mean?" But that question could wait.

At the moment, the squirrel was still whole and lifelike (at least, as lifelike as a dead squirrel can be). I decided that first I should see to it that the little fellow didn't get mushed by an errant car wheel—either my own or someone else's. It was time to dispose of the body of the deceased.

I don't know if you've ever had to dispose of a dead squirrel, but up until then, I hadn't. It's not exactly a daily challenge for most of us, and this was my first experience. To make my task even more significant was the fact that the appearance of this formerly alive squirrel in my driveway was simply the culmination of six or seven days of strange things happening.

For one thing, I was afflicted with some kind of cosmic gaseousness wherever I went. It wasn't I who was gaseous, mind you, but a large number of people around me who were. Wherever I went—bookstore, supermarket, the hotels where I work, even my own car after picking up a hitchhiker—someone was farting. Perhaps it was some astrological configuration—Uranus in Whatever. In any event, for that week or so before the squirrel, my sanctuary was the fart-free zone of my house in which only my cat, Stella, could grace me from time to time with her gaseous aroma.

But there were more than farts in those seven days. I had been as jumpy as a squirrel, so to speak, moving back and forth on writing projects, unable to do anything but distract myself. Of course, the payback was to get anxious and guilty. With such a payback, who needs creditors?

I spoke to my brother, Paul, in Chicago. Paul is a semi-reformed workaholic. He knows the meaning of drive and goals. His advice was that as long as I was doing nothing, I might as well relax and enjoy it. Instead of driving myself batty with the writing projects, I should simply play. It was good advice. I had given the same advice to others, from time to time.

My elevated anxiety could also be attributed to the fact that it was during those seven days that I found out that my first published book was to be remaindered, which meant to me that my literary baby was going to be passed on to liquidators, distributed to dollar stores, and sold alongside cheap spatulas.

All of this happened in the days B.S. (before squirrel): farts, the death of my book, my inability to produce anything constructive and my attendant guilt and anxiety. And then the dead furry creature blocks my path. Could have been a dream—but I was awake during the whole thing.

◉ Dream Explorations ◉
Becoming Familiar with the Weird

One way to help dissolve the border between waking consciousness and dream consciousness is to begin to be aware of the presence of the strange, odd, or seemingly alogical in our everyday life. Here are some ways to tune in to these elements of dream consciousness in our waking hours.

Is This a Dream, or What?

1. Think of a weird or strange experience you've had.
You may define *weird* and *strange* any way you wish. To me they mean anything that doesn't fit into our usual routine. It doesn't have to be spectacularly, over-the-top weird.

2. Write this experience as if you are describing a dream.
Keep it as close to your actual memory as possible. Write it from your waking memory, but thinking of it as a dream.

3. Continue this for a few days, with various experiences.
Write them down and keep on the lookout for more. Then give it a rest.

The Churkendoose Factor

Over forty years ago, Ben Ross Berenberg published his story of the churkendoose, a creature who was part chicken, part duck, part turkey, and part goose—very weird. Naturally, the churkendoose got a lot of flak for being so strange. It (we were never sure if it was a he or a she) definitely looked strange. The other animals in the barnyard—the chickens, the ducks, the turkeys, and the geese—saw this creature as too odd for words and definitely too odd to be part of *their* family.

The churkendoose was a hearty fellow (or girl). No matter how much it was teased and abused, its standard response would be, "Now, it depends on how you look at things." Soon the barnyard creatures realized that strange wasn't bad, it was just different—and they accepted the churkendoose for what it was.

What's the moral? It does depend on how you look at things. Our minds are making things "normal" all the time so we can handle them, but we can still see churkendeese all over. We can see the weird and strange in normal life, and when we do, once again we're approaching the realm of dreams.

Here's how to help yourself to see the weird and strange in everyday life.

1. Choose a normal situation.
What could be more normal than the checkout line at the supermarket? What could be more natural than the crowds of people trying to get to work, and then trying to get home again? These are examples of routine, "normal" situations.

2. Once you've chosen a situation, take a close look the next time you find yourself in it.
Watch it as if you were an anthropologist. You are watching the habits of the human species in all their variety.

3. Find the elements of this situation that could seem weird.

Approaching your situation as an observer from a place that does not have this particular routine, identify anything that appears strange. Remember: We have all kinds of assumptions about rush hour, shopping, watching television, and all of our other usual activities. But if we pretend that we don't have these assumptions and simply observe them, they can take on a different hue.

4. Write down a description of the situation from this new perspective.

We know that writing helps us see things more deeply, right? Here's an example: "We have discovered a world far beyond our galaxy. This extra-galactic world is marked by highly intelligent beings in whose living quarters are found small, furry creatures. Apparently these small creatures have a kind of symbiotic relationship with the beings who care for them; they are fed, though they are rarely, if ever, used as food. These small, furry creatures come in a variety of colors, brown and black, striped and solid-colored. Routinely the intelligent beings will pick up one of these small creatures seemingly for no other purpose than to elicit a unique motorlike sound from the furry being. Apparently this has a sedative effect on the intelligent beings. At this time the nature of the motor running these small, furry creatures is unknown. It does seem that these creatures are not always available to the intelligent beings, having an independence that defies explanation."

Sound familiar? Maybe not, but it pretty much describes every household with people and cats.

WAKING INTO DREAM

How do we bring our waking consciousness into the dream state? In our dreams we seem so distant from our waking mind. One student of dreams has commented that we seem to recall the world of dreams when we are awake, yet the waking world seems to disappear completely when we dream, vanishing in our dream consciousness.

The work of Stephen LaBerge and his colleagues has attempted to bring the waking mind into dreams. This has been called *lucid dreaming,* and while LaBerge's is the most formal effort, people have been doing this for centuries.

People have long recognized that what we do in our waking state can affect our dreams. A chief of the Tikopia people of the Solomon Islands in the South Pacific related a nightmare that he often had. In this dream, he was being chased and his feet were bound. The nightmare persisted until he did something about it by bringing his waking consciousness into his dream. If you sleep with your feet straight, he said, then you can run. His waking determination entered his dream state, and the nightmare ceased.

⊚ Dream Explorations ⊚
Bringing Waking Consciousness to Our Dreams

Lucid Waking: An Exercise in Clarity

There are no magic potions that bring us lucidity and no one technique that will bring our waking consciousness into our dreams, because each person is different. We each must find our own method of entering the dream.

Nevertheless, there is one common ingredient in a wide variety of lucid dreaming techniques: persistence. The longer we stick with the process, the longer we try to enter our dreams consciously, the more likely it is that we will succeed.

Sometimes, indirect approaches work best. What would happen if we started in the awake stage and then induced lucidity? Here's one possible practice.

1. Spend a day as if you are dreaming it.

Look at various aspects of the day, "normal" and otherwise, from the time you wake up until you go to sleep, as if they are part of your dream.

2. In the back of your mind throughout day, keep reminding yourself that this is a dream.

At the same time, remind yourself that you are carrying your waking mind into the dream, bringing this waking consciousness to bear upon the events that occur. Watch yourself brushing your teeth, eating, walking down the stairs, as if you are performing these actions in your dream.

3. In the evening, reverse everything.

As you are falling asleep at night, tell yourself that you are waking up. Try this for a few days, paying close attention to the results of your daytime and nighttime experiences.

Using Your Dream Hands

In 1867 a French scholar named Hervey de Saint-Denys published a book on dreams. For whatever reason, he published his book anonymously. Perhaps Saint-Denys was concerned about the response of his colleagues. Or perhaps he didn't want to be associated with the wide variety of hocus-pocus that seemed to permeate the discussion of dreams then, as it does now.

Mr. Saint-Denys had spent many years trying to bring his waking consciousness into his dreams and he had become a master of many techniques that allowed him to succeed in this. One of his favorites was simply to place his hands over his eyes in his dream to block out the existing scenery. He would then fix his attention on whatever new objects or events he wished.

Here's another technique to try to bring your waking consciousness into your dream.

1. Tell yourself that you will be aware in your dream.

As always, intention is the most important ingredient in dream play. Without it, nothing will happen. Remind yourself as you are falling asleep that you will be aware in your dream. You might say it out loud, you might write it down, or, best of all, you might do both.

2. Tell yourself that you will look at your hands in your dream.

Looking at your hands when you are awake is a very simple task. But if you tell yourself before falling asleep that you will look at your hands in your dream, and this actually occurs, you've successfully brought your waking consciousness into the dream.

3. Try this for several nights.

Sometimes we achieve our results swiftly; other times it may take longer. Remember, we've spent most of our lives with our dream state and our waking state existing far apart.

4. Be modest in your goals.

Simply bringing our waking consciousness into our dream is a great achievement. There is no need for us to expect that we could immediately fly, go through buildings, or change the course of human history in our dreams. Keep at it, but maintain perpective!

HUNTING A DREAM

For the Creek Indians, passing into the dream state is active, rather than passive. This is expressed in their very language: When a Creek is about to go to bed, he will say, "I am going to hunt a dream." Here the dreamer seeks the dream.

For many peoples, conscious or lucid dreaming is the practice of healers. Among the Cherokee, diviners and healers find the source of illness by means of controlled dreams in which the spiritual practitioner consciously seeks answers in the dream realm. Among the Plateau Indians, shamans are distinguished by their ability to dream at will.

Conscious dreaming is also a basic part of Tibetan spirituality, incorporated into a practice of meditation and divination for thousands of years. The Tibetan word *Ö-sel* describes this state in which the dreamer knows that he is dreaming, the sleeper knows that he is sleeping.

 Dream Story

Ö-sel *in Everyday—I Wake to the Dream*

It wasn't exactly a recurring dream. It was a recurring *place* in a dream. And I don't think it really existed in the way it existed in my dreams.

North of New York City there are many highways and roads that converge upon the city. In my dreams this became a vast spaghetti of arteries where I always got lost. If I was traveling by car in this dream territory, I lost my way. If I was walking through this part of New York, I got lost. Similarly, I got lost there if I was traveling by subway. It was a kind of dream Bermuda Triangle for me.

This time I was traveling by subway with three teenagers, and I carried a suitcase that was filled with valuables. The four of us ended up at the station where I always got lost. I left my traveling companions with the suitcase and went to ask someone for directions. When I returned, my companions and the suitcase were gone.

Now, some dreams have content that seems so real that we wake up feeling it's actually happened in the waking state. With these dreams, it takes a moment or two after opening our eyes before we realize that it was a dream and not a waking experience.

Not really nightmares, these are our anxiety dreams. When I was in college, my anxiety dreams usually involved me sleeping through an examination. I would wake up and realize that I hadn't overslept because there was no examination. When I was a teacher, my anxiety dreams involved having to teach a course that I knew absolutely nothing about, or taking a final examination in a course that I hadn't read or attended. In one set of such recurring dreams, I actually pursued an entire college degree program while missing all of the classes in some courses. Each time I woke up certain that this was a waking reality.

My dream of the subway and the lost suitcase was an anxiety dream. In it, I felt my anxious state building. My valuables were gone and my so-called companions had disappeared. I usually woke up sure that it had happened for at least a minute or so, bringing the anxiety of the dream into my waking mind.

But this one night something happened. In the dream I told myself something like, "There's no need to be anxious. This is only a dream." That's all. I didn't find my valuables. I didn't find my companions. I didn't even find my way. I simply reminded myself in my dream that it was a dream.

When I awoke, I had no residue of anxiety. I had discovered something. A few weeks later I experienced another recurring dream, a rather common one. I found myself at a public gathering and I was completely naked, which was acceptable as long as I could sit in my seat. After all, it was a large auditorium. But then I had to get up, go to the front of the room, and give a presentation. That was too much. Perfect material for great anxiety. So, as I had before, I reminded myself, when I rose from my seat, that I was in a dream. After this, my anxiety disappeared in the dream and upon my waking up.

☺ Dream Explorations ☺
Blurring the Border Again

Familiarity Breeds Awareness

Recurring dreams are not always nightmares or anxiety dreams. Sometimes they're simply things that we commonly do over and over in our dreams, and sometimes they involve dream places that we've visited again and again. There is something to be said for recurring dreams. They're familiar to us, and because they're familiar—and recurring—they allow us, perhaps, to be more aware. We can be more "awake" to the dream while we are still in it.

1. Choose one of your recurring dreams.
Actually, think of the recurring dreams you still have. If you think you don't have any recurring dreams, think again. Choose one of them—it need not be scary or anxiety-producing, but it does help if you have an incentive for being aware in your dream.

2. Write down the dream.
You have heard it before, but once again, when we write things down, they become transformed.

3. Decide that in your recurring dream you will be aware that you are dreaming.
Make this decision aloud. Make it in writing. Keep it at the back of your mind and at the front, too. But be gentle with yourself and the dream. This is not about conquest but about being aware in the dream.

Recurring dreams are like treadmills. We keep going over the same ground again and again. As soon as we bring awareness to them, we're in new territory and that's exciting. That's liberating.

Clear Waking: Creative Daydreaming

Let's blur the borders again. If we can bring our waking consciousness into our dreams, we can certainly bring our dream consciousness into our waking state. Are daydreams really dreams? If they are, they are more like recurring dreams. Most of our daydreams are repetitive—they have the same plot, the same characters, and the same endings. Really, they are an escape from boredom. Maybe we began daydreaming in school when we couldn't wait for the bell to ring. Perhaps they've continued into our work life. They are an escape.

But what about original daydreams? What about waking dreams that bring us to new places? We can experience these, too.

1. Find a place and time where and when you can do nothing.
This kind of daydreaming requires your full attention, so find a place and time in which you have no responsibilities. Unlike ordinary daydreaming, this is not about escaping from something. It is about going to something.

2. Close your eyes.
If you have your own way to relax, feel free to employ it, but definitely close your eyes. Our eyesight can be a distraction, and we don't want to be distracted from our daydreaming. You might want to take a few deep breaths, inhaling slowly through the nose and exhaling slowly through the mouth.

3. Think of something you have wanted to do and have not yet done.
Don't just think about it—actively *imagine* what you want. The more specific the images, the better.

4. Do what you have wanted to do.
Here's the key. In a dream we can do anything, we can be anywhere. We can travel through time and space. We are not bound by logic or practicality. We can visit the dead, speak to the unborn. There are no limits here other than those that you impose upon yourself.

Again, be as concrete as you can be. If, for example, you've wanted to visit France, be specific. France is a large place, but the waterfront at, say, Marseilles is more specific. I've never been there, but I can conjure up a breeze from the sea and the smell of fish. Which leads us to . . .

5. Pay attention to all of your senses.
The problem with visualization alone is that it focuses on one of the five senses—the sense of sight. We do more than see when we dream. We feel, and sometimes we smell and touch. Surely in our

dreams our sense of sight is foremost—that's how we've been trained. But in a daydream we can use all of our senses.

In my Marseilles daydream, I'd allow myself to imagine not only the sight of the harbor but also the smell of the fish, the feeling of the sea breeze on my skin, and the sound of the seagulls. The more senses, the merrier the daydream.

6. Let yourself explore.
Now that you've reached the place where you've wanted to go—explore. Walk, fly, swim. Explore.

7. Do this more than once.
Daydreaming takes practice. The more we do it, the better we get at it. Once again, most of what we call daydreaming is about getting *away* from a particular situation. In imaginative daydreaming we create something to go *toward.* It takes practice. The sky's the limit!

LETTING GO OF CONTROL

There is a difference between being aware in our dreams and being in control. Awareness is neither passive nor aggressive. Control is aggressive, something we *do,* something we try to make happen. As soon as we try to control our dreams, we're imposing our waking mind on our dream consciousness. And once we do that, we're no longer respecting both sides of the border.

We have to remember that our waking consciousness can often learn more from our dreams than our dreams can learn from our waking consciousness. Dreams are another truth, the continual reminder that we have two realities. They are teachers. There are times to be active in a dream, but control has no real place in one.

A German psychiatrist recorded hundreds of dreams of her patients during the first few years of the Nazi regime in Germany. Some of these people were so frightened that they dreamed in English to avoid being be discovered or exposed. Their fear had brought the Gestapo into their dreams. Other patients dreamed to find their source of strength and hope.

Perhaps, had the Third Reich continued for a longer period of time, people might have lost the very sanctity of their dream conciousness. The Nazis well realized the danger in people having their own feelings and ideas about reality. There could only be one truth. Ein Volk! Ein Kirche! Ein Führer! One people. One church. One leader. But what about dreams? They were private—people could still dream.

As we travel more often between the realms of waking and sleeping consciousness, the borders become more permeable. The veil of separation becomes more transparent. There is power at the border—new sight, sound, hearing, touch, and taste. For millennia, people have known the secrets of this borderland.

In our industrialized age, when the waking mind is king, it seems we have lost a part of our heritage. But both kingdoms still exist within us. And the more integrated they become, the more whole we will be.

Notes

1. Job 33:14–16.
2. Karl von den Steinen, *Unter den Naturvolkern Zentral-Brasiliens* [Among the Primitive Peoples of Central Brazil] (Berlin: Dietrich Reimer, 1894), 340.
3. Louis Aragon, quoted in André Breton, "What Is Surrealism?" Lecture given in Brussels on June 1, 1934. Posted at www.wlv.ac.uk/~fa1871/whatsurr.html.
4. Verrier, Elwin, *The Muria and Their Ghotul* (Bombay: Oxford University Press, 1947), 476. Retold by Sarvananda Bluestone.

Purging the River Lethe: Remembering and Inducing Dreams

*Whereas we think in periods of years, the unconscious thinks
and lives in terms of millennia . . . so when something happens that seems
to us an unexampled novelty, it is generally a very old story indeed.
We still forget, like children, what happened yesterday. We are still living
in a wonderful new world where man thinks himself astonishingly new
and "modern." This is unmistakable proof of the youthfulness of human
consciousness, which has not yet grown aware of its historical antecedents.*
Carl Jung, "Conscious, Unconscious and Individuation"

*Reveal thyself to me and let me behold a favourable dream. May
the dream that I dream be favourable, may the dream that I dream be true.
May Makhir, the Goddess of dreams stand at my head. Let me enter
E-Saggila, the temple of the Gods, the house of life.*
Babylonian penitential psalm

For the ancient Greeks, the river Lethe was one of the five rivers of Hades. As
we learned in the last chapter, it was also known as the River of Forgetfulness

or the River of Oblivion. All souls that were destined to reincarnate were required to drink of this river before they returned to earth to begin life again. Most drank so fully of the waters of Lethe that they returned to earth with no memories of their other lives.

It seems as if many of us drink each night from a River of Forgetfulness. No other culture has achieved such separation of dreaming and waking as we have, such forgetting as we move from dream consciousness to waking consciousness. But is this part of the human condition? "I don't have any dreams." "I don't remember any of my dreams." How many times have you heard these words? How many times have you said them yourself?

In researching this book, I was startled to find that for many cultures forgetting dreams has never been an issue. For most of humanity's history, people weren't concerned about remembering dreams—they simply remembered them. "Forgetting" dreams, or believing that we've passed through a night without having them, is undoubtedly a modern (and Western) phenomenon.

Scientists have determined that everybody dreams. In the early 1950s two physiologists at the University of Chicago, Eugene Aserinsky and Nathaniel Kleitman, made the startling discovery that during sleep people exhibited periods of rapid eye movement (REM). When the subjects were awakened during these periods, they could recall the dreams they were having. Aserinsky and Kleitman determined that rapid eye movement and dreams were connected.

Scientists around the world replicated Aserinsky and Kleitman's experiments. This further research showed that everybody experiences REM and that the bulk of normal sleep consists of patterns of non–rapid eye movement. In fact, almost three quarters of sleep time passes in this deeper state where dreams, apparently, do not occur. Scientists have divided non-REM sleep into four stages, which account for about 75 percent of total sleep. In each stage, brain waves become progressively larger and slower, and sleep becomes deeper. After reaching stage 4, the deepest period, the pattern reverses, and sleep becomes progressively lighter until REM sleep, the most active period, occurs. This cycle of stages and REM sleep typically occurs about once every ninety minutes in humans. All of us dream.

 Dream Story

Dreams on Demand

I hadn't had a dream for a whole week, or, to put it more accurately, I hadn't remembered a dream for a whole week. This was many years ago. I was working with an excellent Jungian therapist who was about sixty at the time. A white-haired Swede, he stood at least six feet tall, even when he was slightly stooped.

Every week I drove the tedious and tortuous forty miles of the Long Island Expressway from Huntington to New York City, where I would meet with Dr. Von Koch and, for an entire hour, talk about my dreams.

It was the night before my weekly trip into the city and I was appalled to realize that I had no dreams to report. I hadn't remembered a single dream in six days. As I lay down to sleep that evening, I faced the miserable possibility of driving eighty miles, paying a significant sum of money, and achieving nothing. Neither he nor I would have anything to say. The thought was chilling. I fell asleep dreading the next day, realizing the only way out of my dilemma was to have a dream. This was my last chance.

I did dream that night. I had not one, two, or even three dreams, but seven! And I remembered each of them in detail. I had definitely made up for lost time before I took that trip into New York and discovered that it was intention that gave me back my dreams.

INTENTION IS THE MOTHER OF MEMORY

Across time and civilizations people have remembered—and related—their dreams. Forgetfulness does seem to be a modern affliction. We, in the West, have achieved a pinnacle of technological development. At no other time in the history of our race has the left or analytical brain been so revered. Knowledge is available instantly with a few simple keystrokes.

Meanwhile, the right brain—the creative and imaginative side of ourselves—languishes. Dreams move further from our daily experience and, with them, memory. We don't remember our dreams because we don't think they're important and because the wall between our waking and dreaming consciousness has become so thick. But if Joshua could blow down the walls of Jericho with the blast of his trumpet, we, with the power of our intention, can bring down the wall that separates us from our dreaming self.

Merriam-Webster's Collegiate Dictionary defines *intention* as "a determination to act in a certain way" Here, the determination is to remember our dreams. Intention and determination can exist only in our waking consciousness. So what we must do is use our waking mind to bridge the gap that separates us from our dreaming mind. We must tell ourselves to remember our dreams. Without that intention—that determination—we will continue to forget.

But as difficult as it may be for us to remember our dreams, it is much more difficult for us, in our dream state, to "remember" our waking consciousness. Apparently, memory is the province of waking consciousness alone. In our dream state there is only now. One exception to this is recurring dreams—we can, and often do, remember our recurring dreams while we are experiencing them. In our recurring dreams we seem to have an awareness that we have been there before.

⊚ Dream Explorations ⊚
Being Awake to Our Dreams

Changing our current habits and programming new ones may help us to recall our dreams. Here are two new "habits" that might help.

Gentle to the Awakening

Our dream self and our awake self are both parts of who we are, but our waking self has been in top position for a long, long time. Wake up! Open your eyes! Lights! Camera! Action! Some of us even leap out of bed to start the day. Our waking self is impatient and full of the energy that carries us into the light of day in the material world.

Our dreaming self, however, is shy. It lives in the light of the night and the moon and shows us shadows and things of indefinite form. In the kingdom of dreams, boundaries of time and space disappear. Our dreaming self observes.

These two parts of us are closest to each other when we first wake up and when we just fall asleep, which is why these times must be treated gently. When we wake up suddenly, we are less like to remember where we've been. The light of day washes away the velvet darkness of the night. The moon at midday can sometimes be seen, but it looks very pale and insignificant. If we are to remember where we have been, we must linger a bit as we wake up. We must go slowly into the day, at least at the beginning. If we jolt ourselves into our waking state, it will be as though we are fleeing from our dreams.

1. Linger.
Don't even open your eyes when you start to wake up. Just stay a little longer in bed with your eyes closed.

2. Don't just do something, lie there!
If you linger, the dreams will remain for a bit. Let them. Just open yourself to whatever bits and pieces may come to you.

3. This is not a test. Repeat: This is not a test.
It's not a test.

4. Do go gently into this good day.

See how slowly, softly, and gently you can come out of sleep into awakening. Do this more than once. Do this again and again. See if you can slide into awakening instead of jumping into it, or if you are someone who already slides slowly into awakening, let yourself enjoy it.

5. Write down your experiences with this exercise as well as the dreams you remember.

I have to say that, of course.

Sipping the Water of Remembrance

The dream state, the nonrational, and the night have often been associated with the moon and the alchemical element of water, while waking consciousness, the rational, and the day have been associated with the sun and the alchemical element of fire. How appropriate it is, therefore, for us to sip water as a means of remembering our dream state.

We can program ourselves in many different ways. We do it all the time: We teach ourselves to put the keys to our cars in the same pocket every time so that we don't have to panic and hunt for them. We program ourselves to write appointments on the calendar. And we can program ourselves to remember our dreams. The kahuna of Hawaii and the aboriginals of Australia have used variations of this method for recalling dreams.

1. Before you go to bed, fill a glass with water.

2. Drink half of the water and place the glass next to your bed.

While you are doing this, state your intention: Tell yourself that you'll drink the rest of the water when you wake up and that after, you'll remember your dream.

3. As you fall asleep, repeat your intention.

This is about letting the waking consciousness program your remembering. The more ways that you establish your intention, the better. You could even write it down in your journal. By stating your intention clearly, you are affirming it—which is called affirmation.

4. When you awake, immediately drink the remaining water.

Remember that you are to remember and you will remember. But keep in mind that this may take more than one or two efforts—it's the determination that counts.

5. Write in your journal the dreams you recall.

Dreams evaporate as our waking mind takes over. The more quickly we put our dream memories on paper, the more we will remember. The longer we wait, the more difficult remembering becomes.

◈ Dream Story

The Rabbi Weeps for a Dream

Actually, it wasn't the rabbi; it was his student. The great Rabbi Simeon bar Yohai, a wise teacher and a learned man, had departed from the earthly plane, leaving behind some conscientious students. But alas, without the living presence of the good rabbi, some of these students became lazy and forgetful. Eventually one, a sensitive lad, realized that he'd forgotten almost all that he had learned from Rabbi Simeon bar Yohai.

In his sorrow, the student went to the cemetery where the rabbi was buried. There he was overcome with sadness and poured forth a flood of tears. His remorse at forgetting the beautiful lessons of his teacher found expression in his weeping.

Later that evening, while the student was sleeping, Rabbi Simeon bar Yohai came to him in a dream. "When you wail," said the dead rabbi, "throw three bundles and I shall come."

The student was so perplexed by this dream that he decided to see a dream interpreter. "Your weeping brought the rabbi," said the interpreter. "He is telling you to repeat whatever you learn three times and it will come back to you."

The student did as he was told—and the teachings of the rabbi came back to him. It was then that he learned the power of both tears and dreams.

TURNING AROUND TO FACE THE DREAM

Intention and affirmation make up the basis of dream memory. But there are other ways that we can assist our waking mind to collaborate with our dreaming mind. For example, people have called upon the ancient Chinese art of placement—*feng shui*—to aid in remembrance. One feng shui practitioner claimed that if we sleep with our heads to the north, we will more likely remember our dreams.

Any practice that supports our resolve to remember is worth trying. While a commitment to oneself is essential, a commitment to others can be helpful. Dream groups can play an important part in helping us to remember our dreams. Somehow, when we determine to share our dreams in a group or with a friend, we begin to remember more and more. Keeping a journal can serve this same purpose; with it we are dedicating ourselves to recording our dreams. This, in turn, strengthens our resolve, our intention.

Approach remembering your dreams with the spirit of experimentation. Anything that runs counter to your usual routine might well bring about better dream memory. For example, an elder of the Kaska people, who are nomadic Indians residing in northern British Columbia and the southern Yukon, declared that remembering dreams is simple: If you lie in one position, you will remember. If you lie in another, you will forget.

◈ Dream Story

Burps, Snores, and Groans: How Not to Record Dreams

I had been experimenting with many methods of dream recall, some of which are included in this book. Of course, none of them was foolproof—and all of them involved some work on my part. I began to think, wouldn't it be nice if a machine were all we needed to help us remember? After all, machines help us in so many other ways.

Then I found it—the perfect and painless way to remember dreams. A friend of mine had heard a famous author speaking about how he recalled his dreams without opening his eyes and allowing the dreams a chance to slip away. Instead of recording his dreams on paper, he used a voice-activated tape recorder, which he set up next to his bed before falling asleep at night. The following morning, with his eyes still closed, he simply described his dreams aloud. He didn't even need to turn on the machine!

Brilliant, I thought. I immediately sent away for a voice-activated microcassette recorder and within a few days was arranging it next to my bed.

The following morning it was all I could do to keep my eyes closed. I lay there and spent about two minutes recording the dream of the previous night, after which, greatly excited, I bounded out of bed and grabbed the recorder.

I looked at the machine and was a little bewildered. I'd spoken for only a minute or two but the tape appeared to be more than three quarters full. I couldn't imagine what had happened. I rewound the tape and pressed PLAY. Strange and mysterious voices issued from the machine—but the mystery was soon explained. I distinctly heard wheezes, burps, groans, and the creaking, rustling sound of every toss and turn I'd experienced the night before.

Needless to say, the tape recorder didn't magically help me remember my dreams—but it did offer me proof positive that two wives had been right: I snore.

◉ Dream Exploration ◉

Waking Up to Your Dream

As we've learned, we each go through at least four stages of sleep—from light to deep and back again—during the night. In the deepest part of sleep, where there is little or no rapid eye movement, we don't dream. Our dreams occur instead in a place that's nearer the waking state, in the lighter stages of sleep. It's been determined that the closer we are to the waking state when we have our dreams, the more easily we can remember them. Perhaps you've proved this yourself: How many times have you awakened early, then gone back to sleep and experienced vivid dreams that you could remember quite easily after awakening a second time? If it's been awhile, try it.

> **1. Find a way to wake yourself before you have to get up.**
> It's best not to use an alarm. If someone can wake you up gently, so much the better. Or you can simply program yourself to wake up earlier. If you have a CD player that doubles as an alarm clock, find some very soft and soothing music to use as your wake-up call.
>
> **2. Stay in bed after you awake.**
> Don't open your eyes. Don't move around. Just lie there with your eyes closed. The point is to go gently into the waking state and then to step back into sleep.
>
> **3. Let yourself slip back into sleep.**
> As you drift off, tell yourself that you will dream and that you will remember your dreams.
>
> **4. After you've awakened the second time, write.**
> Give yourself a few minutes to write down what you have experienced

 Dream Story

Rocking My Memory

A rock under the pillow? That does seem a bit over the edge. Yet I discovered that a crystal could bring me into a lighter sleep state. Of course, there's all kinds of hocus-pocus hype about crystals, but they're also the basis for our computer technology. One phenomenon of quartz crystals is called the piezo-electric effect: Pressure upon a crystal generates a small electric current. The story goes that in some South American cultures, the shaman would have to prove himself each year by taking a large sledgehammer to a giant crystal. If he wasn't electrocuted in the process, he was still in business.

Years ago I heard that if I placed a Herkimer diamond under my pillow, I'd remember my dreams. Herkimer diamonds are not diamonds at all; they're quartz crystals that are found only in Herkimer County, New York. These crystals are a bit harder than most quartz, are quite brilliant, and are double terminated, which means that instead of growing from a base, with a point on only one end, as most crystals do, Herkimer diamonds grow freely and have points at both ends.

From my collection of Herkimer diamonds I found the clearest and most brilliant and put it under my pillow. I tossed and turned for several hours. Forget about dreaming—I couldn't even sleep! Finally, I removed the crystal, placed it on the nightstand, and blissfully slumbered.

A few days later, I decided to repeat the experiment, only this time I did not use a perfect whole Herkimer diamond. Instead, I found a piece of one— a large, unclear stone, a fragment. I placed this chunk beneath my pillow—and the next day I remembered clearly my dream of the night before. I repeated the experiment the following night, and again I remembered my dream. In fact, I kept this piece of Herkimer quartz under my pillow for six months, and remembered my dreams almost every night.

There was no explanation for how the Herkimer diamond worked. I just knew that it did. Then a twelve-year-old boy at the arts camp where I worked proposed a possibility: "The lighter we sleep, the more we remember our dreams," he said. He then pointed out that the first Herkimer diamond I used woke me up but the second hadn't. "Instead the second one put you in light sleep mode, which meant you could remember your dreams."

It sounded like a reasonable theory to me. Putting things under our pillow is a useful way to affect dreams—whatever the explanation. Our conscious mind no longer controls things, and from there, who knows what can happen?

◉ Dream Explorations ◉
Recalling Your Dreams

Along with your intention, sleeping with these strange bedfellows may stimulate your remembrance of the previous night's adventures.

Crystallizing Your Memory

1. So let's try a rock first.
If you can find a place that sells Herkimer diamonds, great. They're available on the Internet, but in buying them this way, it's hard to determine their quality. It's likely, however, that any quartz crystal would have some effect.

2. Place the rock under your pillow.
Just make sure it's small enough so that it won't create discomfort when you sleep. The purpose of this exercise is not sleep deprivation.

3. Tell yourself that, with the aid of the crystal, you are going to remember your dreams.
No crystal in the world can substitute for your intention to remember the dreams. The crystal is an assistant, not a magic talisman.

4. Experiment with different rocks.
If you have a favorite little rock—especially if it's a quartz crystal—give it a try.

5. Experiment with this method for at least a week.
Keep track of the results. Be patient and don't worry if your expectations aren't fulfilled immediately. If you like, try objects other than crystals—photographs, a letter, anything that means something to you—and see what happens.

Smelling Your Memory*

The sense of smell is our most primitive. The faintest aroma can bring back a flash of our earliest experience. Our sense of smell does not require any middle receptors—it connects directly to the brain—and because of this it is the most potent sense for stimulating memory.

One way to stimulate our memories through the sense of smell is by using a dream pillow. People have for ages been making and using dream pillows—fabric envelopes containing herbs whose scent can be inhaled while a person sleeps.

Here are some simple directions for making one of your own.

1. Gather materials for the pillow.
Ideally, you'll have access to a sewing machine—but you can certainly sew your pillow together by hand (though it may take longer to complete). You will need a piece of clean fabric measuring about six inches by twelve inches; cotton is best. If you already have a small pouch of roughly these dimensions, then you can ignore the pillow making and skip to the part about filling it.

2. Now we're going to fold and sew.
Fold the fabric in half so that it now measures six inches by six inches and sew the two sides together, leaving open the end opposite the fold. A note about folding: The "wrong" side of the fabric should be facing out. Once the fabric is folded in half, you'll actually be looking

---

* I am most indebted to Susun S. Weed of Woodstock, New York, one of the country's top herbalists. She has been a great help in providing me with suggestions for a whole range of dream pillows.

at the inside of the pouch. A note about sewing: Make your stitches as close together as you can, if you're sewing by hand, so that none of the ingredients can sneak out. If you're using a machine, it takes care of this for you! And begin your line of stitches about a quarter of an inch in from the edge of the fabric.

3. Turn the pouch inside out.
The "right" side of the fabric will now be showing and the rough seams you've just sewed will be hidden inside. The top of your pillow will be open.

4. Gather your ingredients.
These are the dried herbal ingredients that help us to remember dreams: lavender, rosemary, mugwort, catnip, bay, and heliotrope.* Many or all of these are available at natural food stores and herb shops. If you can't collect all, get as many as you can.

5. Put about two teaspoons of each ingredient into the pouch.
More is not better. Enough to smell each is all that's necessary. You might want to crush the herbs in your hands before you put them into your pillow—this releases their aroma. And you may want to crunch the pillow a bit before you use it.

6. Sew up the top of the pouch.
You can make it pretty, if you want to, tucking in the rough edge of the fabric before you sew, but pretty isn't important with this pillow. Just remember to try to make the final stitches as close together as you can.

7. Put the pillow under your regular pillow.
Squeeze it and pinch it first, to release more herbal scent.

8. See what happens.
We sometimes get something different from what we expect, which is, of course, fine.

INCUBATING DREAMS

Through most of human history, people have taken dreams very seriously. Many of the world's peoples have long regarded dreams as a path to the divine. Remember the Crow man who happily cut off a part of his finger to induce a dream? Through time and across the globe, then, the question was not how to retrieve dreams, but how to induce them. People have always experienced

---

* With the exception of heliotrope, these are all readily available on the Internet from a variety of sources. Or you may order from the large and reputable Frontier Herbs, 3021 78th Street, P.O. Box 299, Norway, IA 52318, (800) 669-3275.

unsought or spontaneous dreams. But there is another class of dreams that can be quite different from those that simply come to us: those that have been sought or induced.

The purposes of inducing dreams are as varied as the people on the planet. Of course, healing has been a main impetus for dream visions. Guidance for the hunt has been another. Some have induced dreams to determine a course of action. In Ceylon (now Sri Lanka), when people were planning to found a new village, they first slept at the proposed site and saw what dreams might come to them. Others have induced dreams to ascertain future mates.

With the endless ingenuity of human creativity, people have developed countless ways to induce dreams. Probably the most universal method is that of *incubation*. In this practice, the dreamer goes to a special place to spend the night and there dreams are "incubated." Eggs are best incubated in warm places that encourage their hatching. In much the same way, dreams have been incubated by people for thousands of years in places and ways most suitable for their "hatching."

In ancient Babylon, the dream played an important role in life and religion. Dreams could be incubated in the temple of Makhir, the goddess of dreams, and she or another deity could appear in a dream and declare the will of heaven.

The practice of incubation in ancient Egypt can be traced as far back as 3000 B.C., to the temple of Serapis, a god of dreams. In fact, in ancient Egypt there was no single god of dreaming—Isis, Imhotep, Seti I, Thoth, Serapis, Ptah Sotmu, and Amon-Ra all had dream temples dedicated to them and open and available to everyone, regardless of age, status, health, or gender, as places for the inducement of dreams. The temple of the god Imuthese was in Memphis, while Thoth had temples at Khimunu and in Thebes. The goddess Isis had a sanctuary at Philae, and Hathor sent dreams to her temple near Sinai. Men would come to each of these with hopes of acquiring clearer vision through dream consciousness.

The practice of dream incubation passed from Egypt to Mesopotamia to Canaan, and, while there is no mention of incubation as such in the Bible, the great dreams of Joseph and Daniel certainly played important roles in ancient Israel.

But it was ancient Greece that experienced the greatest flourishing of dream incubation. Both the Greek Orphic religion and the philosophy of Pythagoras considered dreams to be divine. Healing sanctuaries established in Asia Minor in honor of Asklepios, son of Apollo, eventually spread to Greece. Asklepios, god, teacher, and healer, appeared to people in their dreams. At one time, in the vast territory from Asia Minor to Rome, there were more than three hundred healing sanctuaries dedicated to him. Many of these were in operation for over a thousand years.

The principle dream incubation sanctuary of Asklepios, located in Epidaurus, began being used around 600 B.C. Two hundred years later, an amphitheater was added that could accommodate fourteen thousand people. In this and other such incubation sanctuaries, the seekers were purified, which involved abstinence from alcohol and, sometimes, sacrifice of small animals. After purification, they awaited a dream that called them into the inner *abaton,* or sleeping chamber. Here in this narrow, womblike room the seeker would wait for hours or even days for the healing dream in which the god Asklepios would appear.

The power of Asklepios eventually passed to Rome, where he became Aesculapius. There emperors and slaves, soldiers and patricians, went to his temple to find their healing dreams.

But ancient Greece and Rome were not alone in their establishment of temples and special places where dreams could be induced. In China, from ancient times up to the sixteenth century, dream incubation was a matter of course. For several millennia incubation temples could be found in major cities and towns. Custom required that a visiting official spend the first night of his visit in a temple of the city's god to receive dream guidance. In addition, judges and other high officials were required periodically to seek dreams in these temples.

Independent of Rome, Greece, or China, the Celts developed their own form of dream incubation in which the seeker visited a special temple containing separate chambers. There he received a ritual bath and an anointing with oils, after which he was left to sleep and receive a dream visitation from a deity. The ancient site of Lydney in Gloucestershire, Britain, with its temple complex and sleep chambers, still suggests the incubation of dreams that took place there so many centuries ago.

Far from the British Isles, on the northwestern tip of Indonesia, live the Iban people, who have a long tradition of constructing and using special dream houses or *meligai,* in which they spend the evening awaiting the appearance of a guardian spirit in a dream.

Throughout the Western Hemisphere a number of peoples have practiced dream incubation from the dawn of time. Many Native Americans encouraged their children, from a very early age, to influence and embrace their dreams. Among the Chippewa (Ojibwa),* parents encouraged their children to think

---

* The Ojibwa and the Chippewa are the same nation. Generally speaking, in Canada they are known as the Ojibwa or Ojibway and in the United States they are known as the Chippewa. The variant of name used in each instance in this text is based on that used by the author of the material referred to here.

positively as they went to sleep so that they would have positive dreams. And children as young as five or six were often gently encouraged to fast for a morning or even an entire day to become more accustomed to accessing their dream consciousness and more available for significant visions. Parents hoped that by accessing their dreams, children would have a clearer idea of what to do with their lives. All Chippewa children were encouraged to remember and relate their dreams.

The Papago in the deserts of Arizona shared this believe in the power of dream visions. Papago boys from an early age tried to call great spirits to come to them in their dreams. A neophyte Papago healer was kept in seclusion in a special place so that visions might come to him in his dreams.

Among the southern Paiute, shamanic power came through dreaming. A shamanic hopeful often went by himself to a special cave, where he spent the night waiting to receive a dream—a spirit visitation.

Among the Plateau Indians, rather than going to a cave, those who were preparing to become shamans often incubated their dreams in a cremation place. A place of death fostered contact with the forces of life and death. In their dreams, the spirits of deceased shamans might come to them.

Similarly, in Java the grave of the ancestors was a dream incubation place. A man wishing to solve a particular problem, for instance, would take a mat and a pillow to his ancestors' grave site. There he would sleep, hoping to receive in a dream a visit and some guidance from his ancestors.

While the Yuman people of California were much less interested in dreams than were many other peoples, a man might occasionally visit a certain cave where spirits were known to dwell to induce dreams of them.

⊚ Dream Exploration ⊚

Incubation for Beginners

Most of us do not live near a dream temple; therefore, we need to create our own. To encourage our dream consciousness and access to it, there should be some special place where we go specifically to dream. Naturally, our regular sleeping place would not fit this bill.

1. Find or create a special place for dreaming.

For those of us fortunate enough to have more than enough rooms in our living space, the answer is simple: Make one of these rooms—perhaps a guest room that is rarely used—into a dream place. Furnish it sparingly, but make sure that the bed is comfortable.

For the majority of us, who don't have room to spare, we need to be a little more creative. Clear some space in a room you're comfortable in and designate it as your dream place. If you can partition it off somehow when you sleep there, all the better.

Another possibility is to find a church, synagogue, or mosque that allows people to remain overnight.

Still another possibility, when the weather is warm enough, is to find a meaningful place outside. If you really want to push the superstitious envelope, you might try sleeping in an old or little-used cemetery. The less adventurous of us might enjoy sleeping in a place that has some unique significance, such as an old battleground, the site of an old town, or near an unused train trestle. Most important is that the place you choose is in some way special to you.

2. Prepare the space.
All the time, keep in mind that you are preparing your sleeping space to facilitate your dreaming.

3. Prepare yourself.
You are going to be welcoming dreams in a way that you don't ordinarily—so treat the experience as special from the outset. You might want to take a long bath. Make yourself comfortable. Eat lightly, if at all, for dinner. It's probably best if you don't consume alcohol or smoke the day before your dream incubation. As you go through your activities, keep in mind that you are preparing yourself to welcome dreams.

4. Focus on dreaming.
Throughout your day, you are simply preparing yourself to be receptive to dreams. Focus on dreaming. If you have a particular issue in your life, you might tell yourself to ask for guidance in your dream.

5. Sweet dreams.
This is not a one-shot exploration. Try it for a few days or even a week—or as long as you like.

 Dream Story

The Voice of the Geese
He went into the woods alone. He pushed away his fear, and though it crept up behind him again, he kept ahead of it. He had been waiting for his chance and would not lose it. He was only fourteen, but that was old enough to hear, to see, to dream.

He went into the woods without food, prepared to remain there for ten days and nights. During that time he would not eat as he waited for the guardian spirits to come to him in his sleep.

For the first few days his stomach ached to be fed. No one could see the tears that came to his eyes, and he was glad of that. His throat was as parched as the dry air of a midsummer day, but still he waited. His stomach and throat cried to him, but he would not listen.

Seven days passed, and somehow it became easier than it had been at the beginning. On the morning of the eighth day, as he slept, he heard someone singing. He knew he was alone in the echoing hills, but still he could hear the voice.

As he uncovered his eyes, he saw a flock of geese, and their call sounded like men speaking. The goose that led the rest spoke to the boy as clearly as anyone ever had.

"We are your guardians," said the goose. "When you are fighting at war, you never need have fear, my young friend." The boy felt the voice of the goose both outside and inside his body. "Should you ever be in danger," the goose continued, "should you ever face darkness and destruction, only think of us and you will be unharmed."

His dream, his vision, had come. The quest was over. He stood and walked back to his village, carrying the guardian geese in his heart.

A STORY FROM THE CHIPPEWA[1]

HUNGERING FOR DREAMS

In the dream temples of ancient Egypt and Greece; in the urban temples of the Chinese gods; in the hills, deserts, and valleys of Native Americans, fasting was a means of inducing dreams. Fasting is simply the voluntary abstinence from food for any period of time beyond what is usual. For millennia it has been part of the spiritual tradition in countless cultures, and all of the major religions of the world have incorporated it into their spiritual practices—the Jewish fasting on Yom Kippur, the Islamic fasting during the holy days of Ramadan, the Roman Catholic fasting on Ash Wednesday and Good Friday.

Fasting can create in us a receptive state. When we fast, we suspend most physical activities. Some have suggested that this is a symbolic representation of the human being awaiting birth, with the receptivity created mirroring our time in the womb. In ancient times people fasted at the spring and autumn equinoxes, when their actions were thought to increase the fertility of the land

and the people. It wasn't until much later, within the context of the monotheistic Jewish, Christian, and Islamic religions, that fasting became associated with penitence and the purging of sin.

A fast allows us to let go of the routines and concerns of the conscious waking mind, enabling us to surrender to other forces and accept altered consciousness. We can't force them or demand that they come to us. We can only prepare ourselves for their visit—and fasting has long been a part of this preparation. Native American cultures, perhaps more than any other, have used fasting as a means of inducing dreams and visions. In many American Indian cultures even small children fasted to induce dreams.* Among the Crow Indians, for instance, anyone, regardless of age or sex, was free to seek a vision. Young, old, and middle-aged men and women fasted to induce a visitation, either in sleep or in waking. Likewise, the Blackfoot Indians regularly fasted to invoke dreams. When a Blackfoot wished to receive information beyond his normal perception, he went alone to a place where he fasted and prayed that he might receive a vision.

In many Native American cultures, dream fasts were part of the rites of passage from childhood into adulthood. For the Klamath Indians of the Pacific Northwest, a boy's deepening voice signaled the time to send him into the mountains to fast and receive his dream. On the other side of the continent, Delaware boys at puberty went through an entire fasting regimen so that they might have meaningful dreams.

Similarly a Chippewa boy or girl at the onset of puberty fasted for as long as ten days. A girl could choose to be in a separate hut or out in the open, in quiet solitude without food, in contact with only her mother, who might come to see her every day to bring her water. A Chippewa boy, however, usually around the age of fourteen, remained alone in the woods with nothing but a little water. Both spent their time waiting to receive a guide in a dream.

An important accompaniment to fasting has long been solitude. In many cultures, a person seeking a dream vision first sought time alone. The process of inducing a dream is highly personal and individual—it is not social; dreams do not come to a group.

Sometime in the years preceding puberty, a Sanpoil Indian boy was sent to an obscure place, such as a mountaintop or a hidden body of water, where he stayed alone for one night. He spent the time without sleep, in a heightened state of alertness. He might build rock piles or dive into the water, all the while remaining receptive to the visit of a spirit.

---

* In this I am including the vision as a form of dream. Even though a vision may come to its recipient while he is technically awake, the altered form of consciousness that attends it is like the dream state.

Such a Sanpoil boy was mentored by an old man who sent the youngster into the wilderness with his instructions to neither fall asleep nor interrupt activities. For a boy of eleven or twelve this, along with the requisite fast, was a difficult assignment, but the great social value placed upon dream visions no doubt offered him strength. Out in the wild, he would reach a level of exhaustion in which the waking consciousness was weak—and then the dream would come.

At times, fasting and solitude were combined with other forms of self-deprivation to assist the mind in its receptivity to powerful dreams. A Crow seeker, for example, might retire to a lonely mountain peak where, along with fasting and denying himself water, he would remain unclothed, even in the most inclement weather, perhaps using only a buffalo skin for a blanket, until he received his vision.

⊚ Dream Exploration ⊚

Appetite for a Vision

In our food-crazy culture, fasting is often associated with either eating disorders or diets. But many cultures have used fasting for generations as a spiritual practice far removed from any issues of weight and body image.

It's important at the start of this exercise to include some words of caution: Before you alter any of your eating habits, check with your health care provider. While for many of us missing a few meals is perfectly safe, for those of us who have any outstanding known or unknown health issues, the practice is unwise at the least and at most, dangerous.

1. Pick a day when you can miss a meal or two.
Some days are better than others. Obviously, a workday when you'll be surrounded by people is not the best—but a day off is just fine. Also try to arrange some time alone during your chosen day.

2. Miss a meal.
Probably the best meal to skip is dinner. Be aware that you'll go to bed feeling a bit hungry. Drink plenty of fluids, especially water.

3. Focus on dreaming—and let yourself dream.
Your focus—and, of course, your intention—helps you to be receptive to the dream. In a way, by missing a meal you're allowing your body to make room for a dream. Now you must begin making room in your consciousness as well. Tell yourself that you're fasting to allow more space for your dreams.

4. Explore other options.
You might try a daylong fast, or perhaps one that's a bit longer. Just be sure ahead of time that you and your body are able to safely handle it.

CHEWING ON YOUR DREAM

As people over the ages have denied themselves food in order to induce dreams, so have they ingested things—and, at times, both practices have been used together to create receptivity to visions. One North American herb specialist and author has maintained that people were using psychotropic herbs at least fifteen thousand years before the development of settled agriculture.* Perhaps nowhere else in the world has this practice been more widespread than among the native cultures of North and South America. The testament of a missionary traveling among the Delaware Indians at the beginning of the 1800s illustrates this use of ingested substances. He reported that a boy about to be initiated was "put under an alternate course of physic and fasting . . . swallowing the most powerful and nauseous medicines" in order to dream or see visions.†

Tobacco, specifically, has long been sacred among the Native Americans of both the northern and southern hemispheres—but their spiritual use of tobacco has nothing to do with our society's addictive perversion of the plant. To confuse the Native American use of tobacco with cigarette smoking is akin to equating the practice of taking wine in Roman Catholic communion with an alcoholic binge. The practice of ingesting it was—and is—sacred to these peoples, an aid to inducing visionary dreams.

Among the Yakut Indians of California, a person who wished to receive special dreams might drink a mixture of tobacco and lime. One of the most important goals for a Creek Indian boy undergoing his rites of passage was the receiving of a special dream. To induce the vision, he ate the leaves from *sou-watch-cau*, a very bitter root, and drank a tea brewed from them. In addition, he ate snakeroot, an emetic. After being purged in this way, he was ready to welcome his dream.

The use of peyote by Indians of the American Southwest—in our time the subject of debate and opposition by those not of these Indian cultures— was to induce dream visions. Similarly, the Yuman Indians of the Gila River in New Mexico have used jimsonweed to induce dreams.

In the western Amazon the Jibaro people, who find that waking

---

* From a conversation with Susun Weed. Among Susun's books are: *New Menopausal Years, The Wise Woman Way: Alternative Approaches for Women 30–90, Wise Woman Herbal for the Childbearing Year,* and *Healing Wise.*

† Quoted in John Heckewelder, "An Account of the History, Manners, and Customs of the Indian Nations Who Once Inhabited Pennsylvania and the Neighborhood States," in *Transactions of the Historical and Literary Committee of the American Philosophical Society,* Philadelphia: Abraham Small, 1819.

consciousness is illusion and dreams are the true reality, use a number of substances to enhance the dream state. On the evening of a wedding feast, for example, the bride and two other women repair to shelters where each can spend the night in her own place. A priestess follows and gives each of them a medicine called *savinya*. Taken while fasting, it produces intense dreams in which the Goddess and other spirits appear and speak to the women.

Another substance used by the Jibaro is *natem,* also known as *ayahuasca.* Derived from a native vine, ayahuasca is used to promote visions in the dream state. Like all native peoples who use them, the Jibaro approach the use of these substances very seriously. Meant, in part, to purify the body, ingestion of these psychotropics often results in vomiting and its attendant discomfort. If used without care and incorrectly, some can lead to death.

◎ Dream Exploration ◎

Take a Tea Break

For centuries, mugwort *(Artemisia vulgaris)* has been associated with women healers, due largely , no doubt, to the fact that mugwort has been used in the East and West to bring on menstruation. It also has been used as an appetite stimulant, in the bath as a treatment for gout and rheumatism, and topically in a poultice for the treatment of poison ivy and poison oak.

Perhaps its strongest association with women occurred during the dark period of Western history known as the Inquisition, when millions of women were burned as witches. Most of these were healers and midwives, and because the Inquisition occurred throughout Europe, many of these women went "underground." Because it was dangerous to advertise their healing skills, they often planted clusters of mugwort outside their houses to let people know. The association of this healing plant with these women healers gave it the nickname "croneswort."

Another use for mugwort is to stimulate dreams. When brewed in a tea and taken before bedtime, mugwort can render dreams more vivid. And it is totally legal and safe, if used wisely.*

---

* While mugwort is generally safe, it is an herb and needs to be respected. Do not use it if you are pregnant or breast feeding. Do not use it if you have a bleeding disorder or acid reflux or if you are allergic to hazelnuts. And do not use it if you are taking blood thinners, such as Coumadin. All of these contraindications may lean to the side of extra caution—but that's the right side to be on when deciding to ingest anything. I do, however, need to point out that definitive herbal guides also indicate side effects that could occur from ingesting cucumbers and dandelions. If you have any questions at all, consult your primary health care practitioner. Sources: Charles W. Fetrow and Juan R. Avila, *The Complete Guide to Herbal Medicines* (New York: Pocketbooks, 2000); John Lust, *The Herb Book* (New York: Bantam, 1983); Simon Y. Mills, *The Dictionary of Modern Herbalism* (Rochester, Vt.: Healing Arts Press, 1988).

1. Find some mugwort.

It grows as a weed throughout Europe, Asia, and North and South America. However, if you are not an expert herbalist or do not have the company of one, don't try to pick some yourself. Instead, find mugwort at any sizable health or natural food store.*

2. Boil one teaspoon of it in several cups of water.

Just simmer it for a few minutes.

3. Drink it before retiring.

Less is best. Try a little. While mugwort is safe, anything can be harmful in excess.

4. Notice if your dreams change in any way.

Be open to whatever happens. Note any changes in dream subjects or patterns or in your feelings.

TAKING A POSITION ON SLEEP

In what position do you most often sleep? There are cultures that associate sleeping position with dreams. In the heart of Libya, people believe that good dreams come from God and that bad dreams come from the devil. To escape a dream from the devil, we merely have to turn over onto our side opposite the one we were sleeping on when the bad dream occurred. Then the divine dream will come.

Koreans traditionally have paid a great deal of attention to the position of the body in sleep and, like those adhering to feng shui, the Chinese art of placement, believe the most auspicious sleeping position is to have the head directed to the south. A Western observer in Korea at the end of the nineteenth century claimed that the Korean habit of dreaming was due "to their mode of sleeping flat on their backs on the heated floor, which warms their spines and acts on their brains."

The Tzeltal people of Mexico pay close attention to sleeping position as well, lying with their heads toward the rising sun to avoid bad dreams.

◉ Dream Exploration ◉

Change Your Position on Dreaming

The waking consciousness is the consciousness of routine. When we change our routines, we change a number of things in our waking life. But what happens when we change the way we sleep? Let's change it and see.

---

* Frontier Herbs carries a large number of bulk herbs, including mugwort. Its number is (800) 669-3275. Glenbrook Farms Herbs and Such also carries almost all the herbs used in this book. Its number is (888) 716-7627.

1. As you fall asleep, notice you body's position.
Are you on your back? Are you on your stomach? Your right or left side?

2. When you wake up, notice your body's position.
We don't actually sleep all night in the position in which we fall asleep. We may shift our position a number of times during the course of the night.

3. If you regularly wake up in the middle of the night, notice your position.
It may well be entirely different from your wake-up and fall-asleep positions.

4. Change the position you normally assume when you fall asleep.
If you usually fall asleep on your side, try switching to the other side, or your back or stomach.

5. Fall asleep in your wake-up position.
If they're different, of course.

6. Notice your dreams—do they change at all?
Give it time.

To Every Dream There Is a Season

Dream researchers have found that during sleep, rapid eye movement varies with the time of the evening as a function not of mechanical clock time, but of our circadian rhythm or biological clock time. People from cultures around the world have long understood that the time of sleep—or even the seasons of sleep—affects dreams.

The Maricopa Indians of the American Southwest felt that different times of night provided different dreams. They believed that right after sunset was the worst time to sleep, for it was at that time that birds, animals, and even tree spirits were moving around. Sleeping at this time ensured that you would have bad dreams. Maricopa parents thus kept children awake until ten o'clock to avoid this inauspicious dream time. Dawn, when larger birds like the eagle and the hawk began to awake and kill smaller birds and insects, was similarly an unwise time to sleep—anyone sleeping in such an atmosphere would surely have bad dreams. For this reason, the Maricopa wakened children and young people before sunrise. In the Maricopa view, the middle part of the night was the best time to sleep. By then, animals, birds, and spirits had settled down, and dawn was still far off.

The Senegalese beliefs echo those of the Maricopa. For them, the best time to sleep and dream is when silence is deepest, from midnight to early morning and during the hour of the siesta.

The Javanese people classify their dreams according to the time of night when they occur. For them the most important dream, called *impén waskita,* is the dream that comes directly from God, occuring at about three o'clock in the morning. If it occurs before then, it does not have the same importance.

For many cultures, the time of year is also important to sleep and dreams. In the canton of Kahône in Senegal, people feel that April is the best month for dreaming. On the other side of the globe, the Bella Coola Indians of Canada consider dreams that occur during the winter solstice to be the most important. These people maintain that at that time supernatural beings are discussing events for the coming year, which means a spirit can inform us of what has been decided. Half a year later, the summer solstice, the longest day of the year, is also an auspicious time for dreaming.

The night of the summer solstice is also know as Midsummer Night. Historically, Europeans have also made a connection between this time of the year and spirits and dreams. After all, William Shakespeare immortalized this time in *A Midsummer Night's Dream.*

◉ Dream Exploration ◉

Hold It, Hear It, Smell It

Even what we sleep upon or with can affect our dreams. Healers, particularly, have been aware of this over time. An Iroquois healer would take an article of clothing belonging to a sick person, wrap it around an ear of corn, and place it under his pillow. This would allow him to receive dreams that would aid in the healing of the one who was sick. The Zuni Indians were careful to place a grain of black corn and a bit of charcoal under the head of a mourner to ensure that the mourner would not dream of the deceased.

In many cultures, great symbolism was attached to an object that accompanied sleep. A member of the Lower Carrier Indians, for instance, who wished a certain power to go to a particular spiritual leader, would sleep together with that leader under a blanket symbolic of the power. During the night the appropriate dreams would come.

In Ireland, a young girl knelt on the night of the first New Moon of the New Year, then took clay from under her knee, placed it in a stocking, and slept on it. In this way she hoped to see her future husband. Another tradition there involved wedding guests breaking a special cake on the bride's head, after which the young guests would place a piece under their pillow to dream of future partners. In Czechoslovakia, young girls placed a special garland under their pillow to dream of future husbands.

Holding or sleeping with a particular object can have quite an effect on dreams. For no particularly spiritual reason, over a period of several weeks I had been in the habit of holding a crystal ball while watching television at night. After about a week I noticed that while each of my dreams was different in content, they all had something in common. I couldn't put my finger on it until I put my finger on it—the crystal ball. There was a crystalline quality to the dreams, a kind of liquidity that reflected the qualities that I found in the spheres.

Here are a few ways to experiment with objects that might affect dreams. Each may be tried by itself or together with the others.

1. Find an object that has significance to you and place it under your pillow.

Obviously, it cannot be the size of a basketball or you won't be able to sleep. But size aside, your object might be anything. At first choose something with texture that you can feel. Later, it might be something as inconspicuous as a photograph. Experiment. See what happens. And do it for a few nights.

2. Try some more dream pillows.*

We've already discussed making pillows with the ingredients that help you remember your dreams (see pages 48–49). Here are a few more:

- For more vivid dreams, use dried mugwort, mint, lavender, and lemon balm.

- To dream of love, use dried yarrow, rose, dill, myrtle, coriander, and basil. Don't worry if you don't have all of the ingredients. And don't knock it if you haven't tried it!

- To dream of fairies (even if you don't believe in fairies), use dried thyme, catnip, and elder flowers.

4. Notice any changes in your dreams.

Remember, you might not get what you expect—and there's nothing wrong with that! The important thing is to be open to what arrives.

---

* Once again, my thanks to Susun S. Weed for her suggestions.

HEARTBEAT, DRUMBEAT, DREAM

What do drumming and mantras have in common? First, both are repetitive. Second, people have been using them for ages to induce dreams.

A *mantra,* in Hinduism and Buddhism, is a devotional prayer that is repeated over and over, and from ancient times people have been using them to alter their consciousness. The repeating of mantras and the recitation of specific sayings have also been used to elicit dreams.

Among the Javanese, a special dream mantra is used by lovers in a kind of magic called *asmara tantra* to bring together in dreams lovers who are separated in waking life. One of the lovers recites a specific mantra and then turns his pillow over. During the ensuing sleep, both the dreamer and his partner will have the same dream in which they will make love to each other.

In the Islamic tradition in Iran, in which dreams have been important from the time of the prophet Muhammad, Muslims have used the Koran itself in this way to induce dreams: Someone who wishes to receive guidance on a project writes certain verses from the Koran on a linen garment and places it under his pillow. During sleep a dream will result that will give him his answer. If, instead of placing the garment under his pillow, the dreamer binds these verses on his arm before going to sleep, he will see someone in a dream who will teach him marvelous things. Senegalese Muslims use verses of the Koran as a mantra to obtain favorable dreams.

Ibn Khaldun, the legendary fourteenth-century Arab historian, judge, diplomat, and scientist, spoke about inducing dreams that would guide him. He suggested that before falling asleep, you must speak the following non-Arabic words: *Tmaghis ba'dan yaswadda waghdas nawfana ghadis.* After this you have only to mention what you wish and what you've asked for will be shown you in your sleep. Said Khaldun, "With the help of these words, I have myself had remarkable dream visions through which I learned things about myself that I wanted to know."[2]

If repetitive chanting of a mantra brings about dreams, then, attest many in the world, so does the beating of a drum. The shaman's drum has been a vehicle to vision and dream consciousness for millennia.

The Chukchi of the northeastern tip of Asia let their dreams take them beyond their physical plane by means of the beating of a drum. By making this sound, the Chukchi shaman can transport himself into the vision of dreams. Slightly to the south, the Naskapi of Labrador use drumming, shaking, rattling, and a sweat bath in their sophisticated system of divination. All are meant to carry them into altered states of consciousness—to induce dreams—in which they can learn where the fish are running or the caribou are gathering.

Incubation, fasting and other forms of deprivation, the ingestion of psychotropic substances, seclusion, drumming, the investment of objects with dream-altering, consciousness-altering power—we humans have followed many and endlessly varied practices to invite dreams, those experiences that we have looked to for guidance, teaching, healing, love, and even a hint of the future.

Notes

1. M. Inez Hilger, "Chippewa Child Life and Its Cultural Background," *U.S. Bureau of American Ethnology Bulletin* 146 (1951). Retold by Sarvananda Bluestone.
2. Quoted in R. B. Serjeant, "Islam," in *Oracles and Divination,* Michael Loewe and Carmen Blacker, eds. (Boulder, Colo.: Shambala, 1981).

3

SONG AND DANCE, MASK AND LANCE: OUR SLEEPING ARTIST

If you could only hear what I dream.

BILLY JOEL

An artist is a dreamer consenting to dream of the actual world.

GEORGE SANTAYANA

The poet does not put the wild animals to sleep in order to play the tamer, but, the cages wide open, the keys thrown to the winds, he journeys forth, a traveler who thinks not of himself but of the voyage, of dream beaches, forests of hands, soul-endowed animals, all undeniable surreality.

RENÉ CREVAL, *L'ESPRIT CONTRE LA RAISON*

Appearing recently on a late-night talk show, Steve Martin, the comedian, actor, playwright, and novelist, discussed his latest work, a novella, and the process of writing. Paraphrasing a friend of his, Martin said, "Nothing creative comes from the conscious mind."

For most of the history of humanity, people have felt that creativity comes from a place of power beyond the familiar waking mind—which makes perfect sense. Creativity and imagination deal with the unexplored, with unfamiliar territory. And it is unfamiliar territory that defines them. To *create* quite literally means "to make something new," "to bring into existence," as in the words from the Bible in Genesis: "God *created* the heaven and the earth." Every creative act requires a leap into the unknown.

But what is the source of this creative leap? How does the spark of creativity burst into the flame of inspiration? Michelangelo painted this burst as the hand of God just as it's about to touch the reaching hand of Adam. Of course, he was representing the gift of life but he was, at the same time, illustrating his own creative source. For most of human history, people have seen inspiration as divine. People have regarded creativity, the imagination, and spirituality as interconnected.

And what better place to tap these forces than in the dream consciousness?

For tens of thousands of years, in countless cultural settings, the roots of art have been found in the dream state—the creative arts are the province of dream consciousness. One student of storytelling and dreams stated that dreams "constitute a private literature of the self."[1] Seventy years earlier, a French poet, Louis Aragon, in his book *Un Vague de rêves (A Wave of Dreams),* called the rich creative power of dreams "surreality—the common horizon of religions, magic, poetry, intoxications, and of all life that is lowly—that trembling honeysuckle you deem sufficient to populate the sky with for us."

Art has not always been what it has become in our contemporary society—a commodity, like everything else. Our culture has rendered art marginal, a plaything for the very rich. A complex maze of galleries and critics permit only a tiny handful of artists to survive.

The notion of the struggling artist, while trite and cliché, is also, sadly, very real. In Western history the last time an entire society supported artists was during the Renaissance over five centuries ago. The arts are simply not a priority for those who set priorities, especially in the United States. The president's proposed 2002 budget for the National Endowment of the Arts was 117 million dollars, while the proposed military budget amounted to 445 billion dollars. Or to put it another way, as indicated by these budget proposals, the priority of the arts in the United States is roughly .00026 of the military budget—a tad over one fiftieth of 1 percent.

This relegation of art to the unimportant hasn't always been the case, however. As exemplified by the climate of the Renaissance, for most of human history the arts have been an integral part of society and, in many eras, were thought to provide a connection to the divine. In fact, the idea of art and spirituality being separate is a distinctly contemporary one. For most of the time that we've been on this planet, spirituality, art, song, dance. and poetry have been one. Further, many have looked to the dreaming consciousness as the source of much of this expression.

 Dream Story

The Emperor Dreams a Prime Minister

It is recorded in the eighth book of the *Shu King* of the good and humble emperor Wu-Ting. For it was he, Wu-Ting, who used methods most unusual and divine to find a real guide for the affairs of state.

The old emperor, Wu-Ting's father and counselor, had died. He was an aged and wise man who had lived the fullness of his years, but his son was disconsolate. He mourned for his father for three years, remaining in solitude the entire time and refusing to speak even at the end of this period.

The ministers and officers of court were dismayed. "Your majesty," they implored, "knowledge and intelligence are necessary to the administration of the law. If you refuse to speak, your obedient and loyal subjects will be in ignorance of your will."

The good emperor was mindful of the needs of his ministers. Indeed, it was his very concern that had rendered him speechless, for he worried that his own capacity to reign was inadequate to the task.

It was then that Emperor Wu-Ting had a dream. In it heaven conferred upon him an excellent minister, one who would speak for him, advise him, and speak truth to him. And though it was no one of the court or of his acquaintance, the emperor was not dismayed—in his dream the face of his future minister was as clear as if he were standing in front of him.

The emperor described the minister as he had appeared in his dream and saw to it that a portrait was painted in that likeness. With this portrait, the agents of the emperor scoured the country. There, in the wilderness of Fuhyan, they found Yueh, a common laborer employed in the building of a dam.

They brought this worker to the emperor, who spoke to the subject of his dream and found that he was pleased at the wisdom and honesty of Yueh. Emperor Wu-Ting appointed him to be his prime minister, the "oar of the emperor's boat."

And so it was that through a dream that a common laborer became prime minister to the emperor of all China.

BOOK EIGHT, *SHU KING*, THE BOOK OF HISTORY[2]

THE DREAM SPIRIT IN ART

In the ancient East, dream, spirituality, and art have appeared together. In fact, the introduction of Buddhism into China came in a dream of the emperor Ming of the Han Dynasty in the year 61 A.D. The story goes that the emperor dreamed of a golden image that soared in the air above his palace, which was interpreted by the emperor's brother to be the statue of Buddha. As a result of this dream, the emperor sent a mission to India to acquire teachers and scriptures of Buddhism.

Eight centuries later, when Buddhism was firmly established in China, a Buddhist monk, Kwan Hiu, was renowned for painting pictures of saints. His technique was unusual and so were the results: Every time Kwan Hiu wished to paint a picture, he recited a prayer and then, in his dream, he obtained the picture. When he awoke he painted according to the guidelines of the dream and these dream pictures altered the nature of Chinese religious art. Far from being the exception to the rule, it is entirely possible that the majority of monsters and chimeras that populate Eastern art originated in dreams.

Beyond Asian cultures, many peoples have experienced the dream as the voice of divine spirits speaking to the dreamer and providing guidance in matters of artistic representation. For example, the Naskapi, a member of the Algonquin family in Labrador, receive symbols in the form of flowers or tree patterns from spirits in dreams. The Naskapi feel that the soul spirit residing in each of us often reveals itself to us in the form of a plant or animal in a dream. For an artist who dreams, the spirit communicates how these forms are to be rendered. The artist then executes the representation of these figures, and in this way his works become symbolic of the power of the spirit itself. The pictures revealed in a dream are power pictures; to ignore these figures would be tantamount to ignoring the soul spirit itself. The artist's representation of these pictures conveys to him their very power. These northern Algonquin assert that because each human has a different soul spirit, the representations of the soul spirit are extremely individual.

The Naskapi have not been alone in accessing in their dreams artistic representations of the soul. For the arctic Chukchi, even the designs of the knots in their amulets could be received in a dream.

◉ Dream Exploration ◉

The Shape of a Dream

Not all of us are accomplished artists, of course, but we can all make squiggles on a piece of paper. There is no "right" way or "wrong" way to do this exercise.

1. Find some drawing tools.

Simple is best. Felt-tipped pens are the most common and work just fine for this. Black ink is perfectly acceptable, but colors give you more choice.

2. Find something to write on.

Blank white paper will do the trick, but you might decide to use your dream journal.

3. Think about one of your dreams.

Usually this works best if the dream is recent.

4. Think of the shapes in your dream.

That's right, shapes. There are shapes all around us—a table has a shape, a door has a shape, and a window does too. How about a feeling? Does that have a shape? Are there more angles in the shape of anger than in the shape of, say, serenity? People also have shapes based on both their physique and their personality, presence, or the impression they give. In identifying people's shapes, try to keep them simple—for example, some people are more pointed and sharp, more like triangles, perhaps, while others are curved and rounded, more like circles and ovals.

5. Choose colors for the shapes you've identified.

An angry person, for example, could be red. A peaceful person might be blue. Of course, your choices of color are based entirely on personal impressions and experience. Again, there are no wrong answers. There is only what's right for you.

6. Using only shapes and colors, draw your dream.

Of course, you are not going to be able to draw the entire dream. You will need to focus on part of it or draw an overall impression of it. Remember, it's *your* dream. You can do whatever you want with it.

7. After you've finished, set aside the drawing and come back to it in a week or two.

See if it evokes the dream. See if you want to add anything to it.

DREAMS INTO EVERYDAY ART

While Western culture has tended to perceive art as something that is seen or observed, in most of human history art has been something to be used. For many peoples, inspiration for the design of such usable objects has come from dreams, and this dream guidance has endowed these everyday objects with something of the sacred.

The war shields of the Blackfoot—objects each warrior certainly made to be used—provide an illustration of this. Interestingly, warriors placed greater trust in the protective power of the paintings on the surface of these shields, designs received from spirits in dreams, than in the thickness of the rawhide from which they were made. The people considered them to be sacred.

Women have long played a role in this kind of "everyday" art. Next to the development of agriculture and the taming of fire, textile production was one of the greatest leaps in the growth of the human race, and, like agriculture, it was the province of women. From the beginning, from the British Isles to Africa, Europe, Asia, and the Americas, women's work included the nurturing of the young and the development of weaving. And the inspiration for many woven articles came in the form of dreams.

The Iban people of Borneo praised their women in ritual chants for their skills in weaving and dyeing. In these pursuits, spirit helpers called *antu nulong* guided the women, communicating designs to individual women through dreams. But not only were patterns passed on in this way—also provided was guidance to the women concerning technological innovation. Thus, the progress as well as the aesthetic of weaving and dyeing in Iban society originated in dreams.

The design of garments, the most common of items for many peoples, and ceremonial dress in particular, could be inspired by dream consciousness and invested with a spiritual element. For the Pukapukan culture residing on the most isolated island of the Cook group in Polynesia, the inspiration for their ceremonial garments came from the gods themselves speaking to them through dreams. These special *epa* garments were said to have been worn by the gods in the netherworld and revealed to the natives in dream visits.

In North America, the Arapaho Indians used dreams as a source for garment patterns and designs, as well as those of other everyday objects. A dream might inspire the changes in a little girl's beaded dress, the carving of a cane, or the design of a painted canvas tent. Among the Blackfoot, the owner of a tepee received guidance for both its construction and its design. Upon the owner's death, the tepee was usually destroyed.

The carved "false face" masks of the Iroquois, staring down through the centuries with their strange and twisted expressions, evoke nightmare images. And, indeed, they are monuments to hundreds of years of nightmares—each face appeared in a dream, and the dreamer, in response, carved it in wood.

For some American Indian peoples, even the designs painted on faces derived from dreams. Rather than following prescribed rules, the forms and colors chosen by a Crow woman painting the cheeks of another were those she saw in her dreams.

Nearly every Chippewa (Ojibwa) carried his dreams with him in the form of a dream object or *wadjigan,* which his spirit had shown him and had told him to replicate. Of value only to the person to whom it was revealed, the dream object might be as common as a knife or a pipe. A dream object, a symbol to be respected, was carried as a reminder of and a link to the power that resided in the dream.

THE DREAMING SINGER

Among the Klamath people of the American Pacific Northwest the word for spirit, as well as for song, is *swi'is.* For the Klamath, spirits are definite beings that live in the mountains and in the water. Song and spirit—where do they meet? In dreams.

The native peoples of Australia refer to the creation as the Dreamtime, the time when the gods dreamed the world. In Dreamtime, the aboriginal people declare, the world was "sung" into existence.

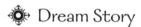 Dream Story

Eagle Hears the Thunder Song
He had been afraid of thunder from the time he was a child. At the first distant sounds of rumbling he would feel faint and his stomach would roll over queasily. When he was very little, he would run to his mother, who held him until the storm had passed and the thunder's roar had become a fading rumble.

This fear would pass just as a storm did as he became a man, they told him. He was a male of the Pawnee. He would be a warrior. How could he both cower at the peal of thunder and vanquish the enemies of his people?

But as he grew older, his fear did not leave him, though he could no longer run to his mother when the storm appeared. Instead he sat terrified in his tepee and wept with fear as the thunder beat loudly across the plains. Would it never end?

Then one night, as he lay asleep, he heard a voice in his dream. He knew whose voice spoke to him. It was no stranger. It was the voice of Thunder.

Thunder spoke quietly and slowly: "Do not be afraid. Do not be afraid."

And he was not. Thunder spoke again in his quiet, powerful voice: "Your father is coming." Then Thunder sang a song, and the boy learned the song that Thunder taught him in his dream.

He sang Thunder's song. Now Thunder was his ally. He sang Thunder's song when he went to battle, armed with Thunder's power.

His name was Eagle and he lived to be one of the old warriors of the tribe.

A STORY FROM THE PAWNEE[3]

Music is ancient—so ancient that it probably dates from the very origin of the human race. Song and dance, like art, have linked us to the divine. Like art, they have been part of our spiritual journey and an instrument of power—even today and even in the most industrialized countries—and have often been born in dreams.

The bull roarer, one of the oldest musical instruments on earth, is also one of the simplest. It consists of a slit board or a chamber attached to a board. When the board is whirled around in the air, it produces a whirring sound. From Australia to North and South America to the ancient Middle East and Africa, the bull roarer has been a popular and often sacred instrument. Many scholars believe that the very origin of the bull roarer lies in a dream. Among the Temiar and Senoi, dreams were the main source of music. For the Yuman, of the American Southwest, dreams were the source of all songs.

For some people, dream songs are a link with ancestors. The long gone souls of the Mundurucu of Brazil appear to their descendants and teach them songs. For other people, like the Crow, dream songs are the source of lullabies.

Long before the tunes of today, the world was alive with the sound of music. Insects, birds, animals, and even stones had their song. Among many cultures, these, rather than the songs deliberately composed by men, are the songs people sing. All Blackfoot songs, for example, come either from other tribes or from dreamers.

 Dream Story

What the Bear Brought in the Dream

It was the breaking of spring when the man went to sleep. He was a Ute in the land that the whites called Colorado. There had been nothing unusual in the day or time he lay down, but spring was in the air and snow was melting.

As he slept, he was visited; the voice of a bear told him to go to the mountains, to the places where the bears were waking from their long winter sleep, to a special place where he would meet a teacher.

On the wings of sleep, the man went to the place indicated by the bear spirit. There, outside his cave, was a large black bear shuffling forward and backward in a dance. The animal looked at the Ute and told him that he must learn the dance and bring it back to his people. The bear taught the man how to do the dance and how to sing the song.

And so it was and has been that every spring when the bears start to awaken from their winter sleep, each of the seven bands of Utes dances the Bear Dance.

A STORY FROM THE SOUTHERN UTE[4]

A dream begot a dream. Fred Mast, a Ute, received a song in a dream. He dreamed he was at a Bear Dance (itself conceived in a dream), where a crowd of people were singing a song. He learned the song from this dream crowd, sang it while he was asleep, and sang it aloud when he awoke.

Among the most sophisticated dreamers in the world are the Senoi people of Malaysia. The Senoi recognize that not all dreams are equally important—some are simply wish fulfillment—but a song can make all the difference. For the Senoi, there are two kinds of spirits. The *mara* is the spirit that causes illness, accidents, and mishaps. The only protection against it is another mara who befriends a person or a group. A mara who becomes friendly is called a *gunik*. This transformation occurs when a mara comes to a person in a dream and states a desire to be friendly. But there are deceitful maras who pretend to be friendly, yet will betray the person who trusts them. How can we distinguish between the two?

A mara can transform into a friendly gunik only through a dream, and it is only through a song that we can be sure it has truly changed. If a mara is sincere about changing, he tells the dreamer his name and gives him a song. The song then becomes the property of the dreamer, who can use it to summon the new gunik. The Senoi use the power of the gunik as presented in the song to protect themselves and their village. Thus the song becomes an instrument of power bringing protection from the benevolent spirit. Such a song can turn an ordinary dream into a power dream.

◎ Dream Exploration ◎

Sing a Bird

The Matako Indians of Argentina kill birds that sing well in order to eat them in a ceremony after the creatures have been made into a powder and mixed with the blood of the person conducting the ritual. They do this in hopes of dreaming about a singing bird and learning a song.

We hear birds all the time, but very often we don't listen to them. This exploration will not require you to kill a bird—only to be very attentive. The more we bring the song into our waking consciousness, the greater the possibility for it to affect our dream consciousness.

1. Choose a bird.
If you live in a northern temperate zone, it's pretty difficult to hear the sounds of birds during the winter. You might have to wait until spring to try this exercise, or you might go to the bird house at a zoo.

2. Listen to your bird's song.
Really listen—to the rise and fall of the pitches, to the tempo, and to which notes are long and which are short.

3. Whistle the song to yourself.
This will help you make sure that you've really heard it. Repeat it to yourself at various times during the day. If you wish, you can embellish it and go beyond the original song. Just make sure that the original melody is contained in whatever you create.

4. Sing or hum the song to yourself just before you go to bed.
There is no goal here. If you dream a composition while you sleep, wonderful. But the point of the exercise is merely to see what happens.

Rather than a source of entertainment alone, as it is here in the West, song has also long been the basis of ritual for many of the world's cultures. Often taught in dreams, they were sacred gifts of power. Among the Apache, for instance, a medicine man taught his songs and rituals to his students in order to convey his divine intelligence and wisdom. The student might then add his own dreamed songs, his own individual contact with the divine.

❖ Dream Story

The Song Returned

He had been only a boy when the vision came to him, just as it had to others like him. Though he was small for his age, he fasted, sitting near an old fir tree by the river. It was his place, near the bluff that hung above it.

He sat against the tree and closed his eyes, beginning this part of his quest. He sought the spirit and now the spirit, he hoped, would find him.

First he heard the sound, high pitched, like the whistling of the wind in the trees. But there was no wind; all was calm. He opened his eyes.

There in front of him was a spotted fawn. The deer was not timid but instead came up to the boy and looked him in the eyes. The sound he'd heard had come from the deer. His power spirit had come. The song had come from the fawn and, as he watched, the deer slowly disappeared. Yet the song remained.

Then, as the boy sat still as a deer himself, the song faded too.

Years passed. The boy became a man, a fine hunter of fish who was strong and swift as a deer.

One night, as he slept near the place where he'd slept as a boy, the deer returned in his dream—the same deer he had seen as a child. Then he heard the same song he had heard, his power song, and he listened well. The dream told him how to dance his first power dance and how to conduct himself as he did so.

Two decades after he first sat under the fir tree, his power spirit had returned. Now he took up the song and it became his own.

A STORY FROM THE SALISH[5]

A power song did not come to everybody. You had to be worthy enough to receive one. Because the power spirits would try to frighten the seeker, often the song came only to the dreamer who was able to go beyond his fears.

Among the White Mountain Apache, in order to receive a bear song, a seeker might have to grapple with a bear in his dream. To receive a snake song, snakes might crawl around his feet to frighten him in his dream. A collective wisdom showed fear to be the obstacle to the divine.

For many cultures through time, the world sang; it was alive with songs of life and power that were taught in dreams. The wind, birds, bear, and deer all sang, each to a specific dreamer. Among the Papago there were singers who dreamed a song of the wind. Others were famous for their ocean songs, cloud songs, or crane songs. The powers of the world sang and dreamers learned the songs.

Sometimes a song was a rite of passage through which a child became an adult. Among the Klamath people, when a boy's voice dropped it was a time to seek power. The boy went for as long as five days into the mountains , where he wandered at night, ran continually, fasted, swam in ponds and eddies, and piled up rocks. He constantly moved until, finally exhausted, he fell asleep and a song came to him in a dream. It was then that he arrived, his song serving as a sign of power and manhood.

Sometimes dream songs came to those in special places. The Nootka Indians of western Vancouver went to a large waterfall, where they slept for four days, receiving many songs in their dreams.

๑ Dream Explorations ๑
The Shape of the Dream Song

Dream Song, Dream Sound

Sometimes we need a little help in priming the dream pump. Once again, we need to use our waking consciousness to encourage our dream consciousness. If we want music in our dreams, we may need to create sound in our waking state. While it doesn't have to be music, some sound has to be programmed into our dreaming self.

1. Find a sound that you want to bring into your dreams.
It can be any sound—a clock that makes ticking sounds, perhaps, or maybe you have one of those machines that make nature sounds, like the chirp of crickets or the sounds of the sea or rain. Just be sure the sound is repetitive so that you can listen to it as you fall asleep, and don't use music at his point.

2. Play the sound in your bedroom while you are going to sleep.
Don't make it too loud. It should be just loud enough to hear.

3. Tell yourself that you will bring the sound into your dream.
Saying this out loud is always better than just thinking it.

4. Try this for several days.
We never know what's going to happen. As always, try to approach your exploration without expectations.

5. Switch your sound to music.
After you've tried sound for a few days, choose a piece of music that you love and play it softly as you are going to sleep.

Lullaby an Ear Worm

The marriage of sleep and song is as old as a lullaby. Mothers have sung their children to sleep from the dawn of time. Who knows how many dreams have resulted from the gentle crooning of mothers as their children drift off?

In an interesting twist on the lullaby, some people actually sing in their sleep. Apparently Laplanders often sing in their sleep, as indicated by one missionary to Lapland who, at the beginning of the eighteenth century, reported that Lapps were "frequently seen lying upon the Ground a Sleep, some Singing with full voice."[6]

In this exploration we sing ourselves to sleep.

1. Find a tune you've been known to sing over and over.
The Germans tell of a lovely little make-believe animal called an *ohr wurm*, or "ear worm." An ear worm is any tune that we sing, whistle, or

hum unconsciously, again and again. Everyone has at least one. Your choice for this exercise doesn't even have to be a tune you like.

2. Tell yourself that you will bring your ear worm into your dreams.
Say it aloud.

3. Sing or hum the ear worm.
Do it softly, as if it were a lullaby, just as if you were singing yourself to sleep. Try it for a few nights and see what happens.

THE POWER OF THE DREAM SONG

While people sang dream songs at celebrations, these songs were not considered frivolous. More often than not, they represented a purpose, a transfer of power.

Throughout the many parts of the world where singing and healing have been connected, healers have often received their songs in dreams.

Among the Senoi, healing adepts learned from those who had died. The spirit of a recently deceased healer appeared to a dreamer and gave her a healing song, which the living adept could then use in healing. Often the dreamer traveled through the jungle in waking life and there communed with the spirits of plants who brought their songs to dreams. Then, in his dream life, the spirits brought the dreamer a song. In the Senoi society the dreamer never asked for a dream or a song. It simply came.

 Dream Story

The Prophet of the Yellow Knives
There once was a man named Sinew Water, who, it was said, was a prophet. He saw clearly and spoke plainly and dreamed, it is said, about what was good. Through his dreams, he told the people where they were heading and what could befall them.

This man, Sinew Water, dreamed songs, it is said. He had songs about the many things that distressed or annoyed people and it is said that with his songs he was able to lessen the annoyances and afflictions of the people.

Because of these things this man became one who was very useful. It is said.

A STORY FROM THE CHIPPEWA (OJIBWA)[7]

In the Western Hemisphere from farthest north to south, dream, song, and healing go together. The healer dreams the medicine song, which then becomes his personal property. The world of the Blackfoot, for instance—

including their healing—is derived from dreams, and the key to healing is their song.* Blackfoot men of medicine dream songs that are essential to their healing rituals.

In Native American tradition, the spirits of all living things can instruct healers by passing on their power to humans. Among the Paiute, the healing power of the novice came from a supernatural spirit that appeared in his dreams, in the form of an owl, perhaps, or a bear, badger, sheep, coyote, or eagle, to give the novice a song. With this song, the animal spirit inducted the novice as healer and, in the dream, instructed him all night.

Dreams were a place to learn the healing arts, and sometimes the results were amazing. For example, the Cuna Indians of the Panamanian coast learned songs of healing from animal spirits in dreams, like healers from many other Native American cultures, but in addition, some Cuna Indians who spoke no Spanish learned how to speak it in their dreams.

The possibilities for learning, it seemed, were endless. In some cases, medicine men dreamed songs over their entire lifetimes. Among the Apache, for instance, an individual may have dreamed as many as ten songs. But the number learned by the medicine men apparently had no limit.

THE SPIRIT, THE DREAM, THE SONG

In dreams, we are closer to the divine intelligence of spirits and ourselves. All kinds of spirits might teach a power song in a dream. Among the Havasupai, shamans received their power through dreamed song. In fact, before he could practice the healing arts, it was necessary that a healing shaman receive a song in a dream. But other kinds of shamans received this divine instruction as well. Weather shamans obtained their power by dreaming of clouds or thunder, lightning, great rain-and hailstorms and, in turn, sang of what they had dreamed in order to affect the weather. One weather shaman among the Chiricahua Indians of Arizona stated it simply: "I received my ceremony through a dream when I was a young man. I just lay down and dreamed that I heard a voice, and the words of my song were repeated. The giver said these words of the song in my ear while I slept. I believe that this power came from Thunder."[8]

The dream song transcends healing—which is merely one of the ways it manifests—to transmit many kinds of powers. In their dreams, the Naskapi of Labrador receive the caribou spirits that give the hunter his personal caribou lure song. With it the hunter, in times of scarcity, may find the caribou.

* For more on this, see chapter 6.

Such a song ultimately acts as a link between the powers of the dream state and their waking beneficiary. But the ability to receive power songs from spirit guides during dreams is unique. Those who are able to receive a song from a spirit guide in this way become, through the song, the waking channel of that spirit.

However, implicit in this process between spirit power and dreamer is that the giving works both ways. For example, the Mescalero Apache, who feel that power and guidance come from various animals, plants, and natural forces, understand that the spirit of one of these appears to an individual in a dream and describes the power it offers. If the dreamer is willing to learn, the spirit then teaches him songs and prayers. In this way, power works through the Apache dreamer via the songs that are gifts from the power source. But the Apache dreamer must give as well—he is expected to be loyal to the power, creating a bond of mutual respect between himself and the power source, with song as its expression.

THE DANCING DREAM

Dance is the sister of song. In Greek mythology these sisters were two of the three Muses born of the union of Zeus and Mnemosyne, the goddess of memory. Terpsichore was the muse of dance, her sister Euterpe was the muse of music, and their sister Polyhymnia was the muse of sacred poetry, which was often sung, as poetry was in its early days.

Dance has always been an integral medium of expression for many of the world's peoples. The Papago Indians created elaborate musical performances involving song and dance. A singer among them who had dreamed a series of songs would then teach a number of girls and boys to perform dances based on them.

Every spring, as the snow is melting and the bears are waking from their winter sleep, the Utes do a Bear Dance, the origin of which was a dream. During the first day of this spring ceremony, the Utes also dance a Sun Dance for which the songs and the leaders of the dance have been dreamed. Even the costumes and painting worn by the dancers have been dreamed.

Invariably, dance and song were tied together in the dreams of the Utes. Sometimes, the dreamer would be at a dance in his dream and learn a new song. Sometimes the song and dance came together in the dream. Fred Mart, a Ute Indian, described a dream in which he was at a Bear Dance with a crowd of strangers. "All were singing this song," said Mart. "I sang it while I was still asleep and was singing it aloud when I awoke. After that I remembered the song."[9]

The Utes were not the only Native Americans to dream of song and dance. At the end of the nineteenth century, a Pawnee woman dreamed a modern form of the ancient Horn Dance. In many dreams she received instruction on everything from how to make a feathered lance and drum to where to get an eagle skin. In a series of dreams, this woman had received an entire ceremony. The Menomini Indians also connect dance and dream consciousness. Their ancient society of dreamers and dream dance is said to have originated in the dream of a little girl.

 Dream Story

The Devil Made Him Do It

In the year 1713 Giuseppe Tartini had a checkered career. He had entered the University of Padua as a law student three years earlier, but it was not long before he abandoned study of the law for his two true loves, music and fencing. He became a master of both.

In 1713 his musical career lay before him, though it would be eight full years before he received a meaningful appointment as solo violinist and master of the orchestra at the Cathedral of Padua. But now, all was uncertain; the field of music in eighteenth-century Italy was highly competitive.

One night, Tartini turned and turned in his bed—and then a visitor came to him in his sleep. It was none other than the devil himself appearing to him in a dream and offering Tartini an exchange: If the young musician would give him his soul, the devil promised to be at his service in all things.

It was an offer the violinist could not refuse. He agreed to the exchange and then handed the devil his violin: "Play—let's see what kind of musician you are."

The devil picked up the violin and played a solo so beautiful and executed with such taste and precision that Tartini knew it to be better than anything he had ever heard. So great was the artist's surprise and delight that he could not breathe.

When Tartini awoke, he seized his violin and tried to play what he had just heard in his dream. The result was the "Devil's Sonata."

Afterward, the young composer swore that, while he did approximate the dream sonata, the devil's performance had been far superior. Nevertheless, the "Devil's Sonata" became a keystone in the repertoire of violinists for the next four centuries.[10]

⊚ Dream Explorations ⊚
In the Beginning Is the Word

The Chant

Words are magical. First spoken and then eventually written, words have also been chanted and sung, shouted and whispered, wept and laughed. With a word we can smell a rose that has long since died and returned to the earth. As the Gospel of John tells us, the word is a source of creative and spiritual power: "In the beginning was the Word, and the Word was with God, and the Word was God." And, as Oscar Wilde wrote, a word can destroy:

> *Yet each man kills the thing he loves,*
> *By each let this be heard,*
> *Some do it with a bitter look,*
> *Some with a flattering word.*[11]

In rituals, the chanting of words is an ancient practice. The Hindu chant of *om,* for example, and the many mantras that are repeated over and over have, for centuries, brought people to an altered state of consciousness and even to the divine.

Here our mantras are only two words: *dream* and *sleep.* Interestingly, this exploration originated in a dream of mine as I was writing this chapter.

1. Think of as many combinations as you can of these two words.
This is one instance when you should *not* write down your thoughts. It's better to play with this step in your mind rather than put it down on paper. Note that it's fine to use variants of the words in your combinations. Some examples of combinations are dreamy sleep, dream sleeper, and sleepier dream.

2. Play with these combinations during the course of the day.
Repeat the variations to yourself, noticing their sound.

3. Repeat—chant—these variations as you are falling asleep.
Do this playfully, but be aware that chanting has impact.

4. Choose different combinations of these words—or others— another night.
Chant these too before you go to sleep and note what kinds of dreams you have. Other word combinations you might try include *dream* and *see, dream* and *hear,* and *sleep* and *see.*

The Dream Poet

Just as the imagery in dreams is not strictly realistic, the language of dreams is not logical. Poetry is the closest thing in our waking consciousness to the language of dreams. In fact, many poets, from William Blake to William Butler Yeats, have pointed to their dreams as literal sources of their inspiration.

Often our dreams are themselves poetry. All we have to do to allow the poetry to emerge is to describe them simply and clearly.

1. Close your eyes for a minute and let your mind wander over your most recent dreams.
This is best when you use as little focus as possible. Simply let your mind wander. If your memory needs some help, you can go to your journal.

2. Pick one dream and think about it for a moment or two.
Let it sink in.

3. Bring up all of the dream's details—color, action, feelings.
This is like conjuring. You are conjuring the dream.

4. As simply and directly as possible, write down the dream. Think of this step as writing a very simple, straightforward story.
If you have used your dream journal to jog your memory of the dream, simplify and clarify as much as possible and add in new information.

5. Underline all the verbs and circle all the nouns.
Remember, in general, a noun is a person, place, or thing and a verb is an action word or any "state of being" word (such as *is, are, was,* and *am*).

6. Write the story using *only* the nouns and verbs.
As a variation, you may also write the story using only nouns or using only verbs.

7. Arrange the lines on the page in any way you choose.
It's up to you.

8. Voilà! You have a dream poem.
Read it aloud.

Here's an example. Several years ago I was teaching a dream class to a group of kids at an arts camp. One of the kids in the class was a girl named Amanda. During the second week, I had the following dream:

I was standing outside of my bunk. It was late at night and the moon was casting a grayish silver glow on the path. I thought I was alone, but then looked to see that Amanda was standing next to me with a faint smile on her face.

She didn't speak to me directly, but intruded in my thoughts. "I am going to the dance platform," she thought to me. I looked at the dance platform and then back to Amanda, but she was gone.

With the speed of thought my bunk became a cottage that whirled around until it rested partly on the dance platform, facing toward a small clearing in the woods beyond. There, in a pit, a fire was burning. A large log hung out of the firepit, burning furiously from end to end. I was certain that this log would start a dangerous fire.

I looked around to find other people. There were none. I knew that the log would spread the fire to the woods, to the dance platform, to my cottage. And yet I merely watched.

After underlining the verbs and circling the nouns, and then writing my dream using only these words, with some punctuation for embellishment and effect, here's what I came up with:

> *I was standing bunk it was night*
> *Moon was casting glow path*
> *I thought I was . . .*
> *Looked Amanda was standing*
> *Smile face speak intruded thoughts*
> *Going dance platform thought*
> *I looked dance platform Amanda*
> *She was . . .*
> *Speed thought bunk became cottage*
> *Whirled it rested dance platform*
> *Facing clearing woods, platform*
> *Pit fire was burning*
> *Log hung firepit burning end*
> *I was certain log would start fire*
> *I look find people—were none*
> *I knew log would spread fire*
> *Woods, dance platform, cottage*
> *I watched.*

Play with leaving out some nouns or verbs for effect, and experiment with adjusting the tense (change past tense to present tense, or vice versa, depending on your original telling). But be sure you're still conveying the essence of the dream.

Dream Haiku

Haiku is a form of poetry originating in Japan. Now, many people freeze when they hear the word *poetry,* but this is a kind of poetry that anybody can handle. Children understand the rules of haiku and write it with ease. As proof of haiku's approachability, here's an example of a haiku poem written by a middle school child. The theme was Halloween:

> *Fall is a big ball*
> *always bouncing up and down*
> *leaves flying around.*[12]

It's not difficult at all. There are just a few rules: A haiku has only three lines; the first line has five syllables (fall is a big ball); the second line has seven syllables (al-ways bounc-ing up and down); and the last line has five syllables (leaves fly-ing a-round).

Keep in mind that haiku is simple. It describes things as clearly as possible. It's not about complicated philosophical concepts—it's simply about what *is.*

Here's another one that was part of a children's world haiku project:

> *In early morning*
> *My Dad goes out for seafood*
> *From the ocean rocks.*[13]

And another from an elementary school girl in Colorado:

> *Golden aspen trees*
> *Tingle lightly in the breeze*
> *In the high mountains.*[14]

Haiku helps us to focus and to be specific—and it also helps us in playing with our dreams. In this exercise we're going to explore writing a dream in the form of haiku.

Not long ago I dreamed I was supposed to be selling tomatoes, but I worried in the dream that I would not have any tomatoes to sell. Then, lo and behold, I had a wheelbarrow that was filled with luscious, ripe red tomatoes.

Here is the haiku describing this dream:

> *I lacked tomatoes*
> *What could I do about it?*
> *But wait! There they were.*

Now it's your turn to give it whirl.

1. Choose a dream.
At first, select one of your dreams that's simple, not complicated. The more accessible your dream is, the better. You want to be able to capture its essence.

2. If you haven't written it down, write it down in narrative form, as you would usually.
But you already have written it in your journal, right?

3. Write the dream in haiku form.
Don't be intimidated by the fact that haiku is poetry. If a six-year-old can do it, you can too!

4. Write the haiku in your journal and read it from time to time.
See if there is a change in the way you view your dream.

Dream Juxtapoetry*
Often, the feelings and events in dreams occur in strange and out-of-the-ordinary juxtaposition. It's this unusual positioning of feelings and situations that makes dreams so interesting. Here, using writing, we bring unusual dream connections into our waking consciousness.

1. Choose a dream.
Find a dream in your journal that you can recall. It need not be an "important" dream, but it should be one that has some substance, one with which you resonate.

2. Write down all the objects that you can remember in the dream.
"Ordinary" objects are fine: People, horses, houses, trees, pencils— any like these may be included if they appeared in your dream.

3. Fold in half a blank 8½″ x 11″ piece of paper (your average sheet).
Lined is best. Fold on the long side and keep it folded.

4. On one side of the folded paper, list all objects in your dream.
Give each its own line and number.

5. Turn over the paper —still folded.
You now have on one side of the sheet the list of objects, facing down.

6. On this blank half of the paper, using the same dream, write down all the feelings you can recall from it.
There may be obvious feelings, like sorrow, joy, fear, and so on, and

---

* I am very grateful to my friend Prartho Sereno for suggesting this exploration. Poet, writer, intuitive, artist, Prartho has used a variation of this when teaching poetry to children.

there may be those that are a bit more abstract, like wonder and confusion. Both sets of feelings can be included—as long as they're true to the dream. Once again, write one feeling to a line and number each of them.

7. Open the piece of paper.
The objects should now be on one half of the paper and the feelings on the other. If, for some reason, that has not occurred, just use the numbers. Object number one will relate to feeling number one.

8. Starting with an object, read it aloud, insert the word *of* after it, then read the feeling whose number corresponds to the object.
For example, if the first object is a chair and the first feeling is misery, you would read *chair of misery*. Do this with all the objects and feelings.

9. Anything new?
See if your view of the dream has changed. You may want to rewrite the dream with these new object/feelings.

EINSTEIN ASLEEP: THE DREAMING SCIENTIST

Human creativity encompasses the whole range of imagination, including both art and science, and it is imagination that carries us beyond the known. Imagination is dream consciousness—as one author has suggested, it is "only in sleep that true imagination ever stirs within us."[15] In our waking consciousness, we do not imagine. Instead, we vary what we already know, turning the pieces of our knowledge this way and that like pieces of a puzzle. Only in sleep, however, do we actually create the pieces.

Nowadays we tend to equate science and technology, but they are not the same. Technology is the application of science, which is creative. And, once again, creativity exists in the domain of dream consciousness. There is a story that Albert Einstein at the age of fourteen had a dream in which he saw a train and the place the train was passing. In that dream, he later asserted, was the foundation of what became the theory of relativity.

As we draw the line between dream and waking consciousness, so do we draw the line between art and science. In most cultures this boundary does not exist. Dreams inform both art and science. The Kiwai Papuans received from their dreams new methods of spearing dugongs. The Melanesians of the Solomon Islands saw in their dreams how to craft more-efficient war clubs.

But even if we draw a line between the two, dreams have always been an engine of science in the West. Mathematics has been one of the greatest beneficiaries of dream consciousness. The life of renowned eighteenth-century mathematician René Descartes was entirely changed by his dreams, which helped him decide to become a mathematician and to unite Euclidean geometry with algebra. It is ironic that the very rationalism that Descartes created, Cartesian rationalism, was born of dreams, for it rejects the notion of dreams as reliable sources of knowledge. Other mathematicians from East to West were inspired by their dream consciousness. The Indian mathematician Srinivasa Ramanujan was visited in his dreams by the Hindu goddess Namakkal, who gave him formulae that he could verify upon waking. And it was in a dream that the mathematician Condorcet was able to complete the final stages of a particularly difficult calculation.

This relationship between the power of dreams and mathematical creativity was likewise revealed in a questionnaire about the role of dreams distributed at the beginning of the twentieth century by one mathematician to others who had been practicing their discipline for at least ten years. Some of the respondents described dreams in which they found actual solutions to problems they were addressing, some learned the beginnings of solutions, and a significant number reported they could solve problems they had been working on immediately upon awakening.

Dreams have led to leaps in other fields as well, including chemistry. In 1869, Dmitri Mendeleyev, a professor of chemistry in Saint Petersburg, Russia, dreamed the atomic elements, the periodic table of elements, and three new elements that were yet to be discovered. At roughly the same time, Friedrich A. von Kekule, a professor of chemistry, dreamed the first model of what was to be the basis of organic chemistry. So profound was this experience for him that he declared, at a convention of scientists in 1890, "Let us learn to dream, gentlemen, and then we may perhaps find the truth."[16]

Some scientific dream epiphanies have had lasting benefits for all people. Jonas Salk apparently kept a copious daily record of his dreams and let his dream consciousness inform his waking consciousness in the development of a vaccine against polio. The seminal ideas that helped in his research came directly from his dreams.[17]

❖ Dream Story

The Euphony of Dreams

It was June 2, 1789, and there was change in the air. The known world seemed to be going through the agony of birth. Across the ocean in the American colonies, a band of farmers had defeated the British, the most powerful army in the world. In just over a month, in France, Germany's neighbor, a revolution would erupt.

On June 2, Ernst Chladni, a twenty-three-year-old German, went out walking. The son of a lawyer, Chladni himself had briefly studied the law, but his true vocations were music and physics. He eventually combined the two and began to study sound waves, which would lead to his recognition as the father of acoustics.

But on this June evening, after tiring himself on his walk, Chladni came home and sat down in a chair to take a short nap. He had scarcely closed his eyes when an image appeared to him, an image of an instrument, exactly the kind of image he had wished to receive.

Chladni awoke and felt as if he had been electrified. He was bursting with excitement. In the next nine months his dream project gestated as he worked to create his dream instrument. On March 8, 1790, he completed his work and the instrument was given the name *euphon,* meaning "pleasant sound." The euphonium was born in his dream.

In the Western creative arts, dream consciousness has informed multitudes. The list of those whom it has inspired is as endless as imagination itself. Samuel Coleridge, the eighteenth-century English poet, after taking medication containing opium, had a vision of Kubla Khan and his palace. Upon waking, he wrote the poem "Kubla Khan," which has been read by generations of students ever since.

Robert Louis Stevenson, in trying to write his story *The Strange Case of Dr. Jekyll and Mr. Hyde,* found he had the basic theme but could not come up with a plot. He racked his brains for two days, but could not put it together. Then, on the second night, his dream brought him the plot and the solution to his dilemma.

The poet William Butler Yeats dreamed a play, Robert Penn Warren dreamed a large part of his novel *All the King's Men,* Graham Greene and Katherine Mansfield dreamed some of their works, and Charlotte Brontë found that dreams helped her to realize sensations such as opium smoking that she would never encounter in her waking life.

And not just writers access the help of dreams. The film director Ingmar Bergman declared that all of his films were dreams. Other contemporary directors like Orson Welles, Robert Altman, Federico Fellini, and Jean Cocteau all used their dreams in their films.

The sculptor Jean Depré saw his *Pieta* in a dream, though, like Tartini with his "Devil's Sonata," felt he was unable to reproduce the splendor of what he had dreamed. George Frideric Handel dreamed the last movements of *The Messiah* and Richard Wagner dreamed his opera *Tristan und Isolde.*

And there is the dream of Fon Njoya of the Bamum people. The Bamum tribe of Cameroon had a stable monarchy for several hundred years, with their king, or *fon,* ruling from the capital city of Fumban. In 1880, Fon Njoya, an educated and creative man, succeeded his father, who had fallen in battle. In his wisdom, he knew that his people must have a written language. Njoya had studied Arabic and Latin scripts, but they did not suffice. And so, at the end of the nineteenth century, the king dreamed a written script for the Bamum people.

The stories of their guidance are innumerable; the discoveries they've prompted have been limitless. In dreams we receive so that in waking consciousness we may create.

Notes

1. Quoted in Bert O. States, *Dreaming and Storytelling* (Ithaca, N.Y.: Cornell University Press, 1993).

2. Translation reprinted at www.wisdomworld.org/additional/ancientlandmarks/ OldChinaAndNew.html. Retold by Sarvananda Bluestone.

3. Alexander Lesser, "The Pawnee Ghost Dance Hand Game," in *Columbia University Contributions to Anthropology,* vol. 16 (New York: Columbia University Press, 1933). Retold by Sarvananda Bluestone.

4. James Jefferson, *The Southern Utes: A Tribal History* (Colorado, Southern Ute Tribe, 1972). Retold by Sarvananda Bluestone.

5. Walter Cline, et al., *The Sinkaietk or Southern Okanagon of Washington,* contributions from the *Laboratory of Anthropology* 2, General Series in Anthropology 6 (Menasha, Wis.: George Banta, 1938). Retold by Sarvananda Bluestone.

6. John Scheffer, "The History of Lapland," quoted in Rafael Karsten, *The Religion of the Samek: Ancient Beliefs and Cults of the Scandinavian and Finnish Lapps* (Leiden: E. J. Brill, 1955).

7. Fang Kuei Li and Ronald Scollon, *Chipewyan Texts* (Taipei, Taiwan: Academica Sinica, Institute of History and Philology, 1976. Retold by Sarvananda Bluestone.

8. Morris Edward Opler, *An Apache Life-Way: The Economic, Social, and Religious Institutions of the Chiricahua Indians* (Chicago: University of Chicago Press, 1941).

9. Quoted in Frances Densmore, "Northern Ute Music," *United States Bureau of American Ethnology Bulletin* 75 (1922).

10. Brian Hill, compiler, *Gates of Horn and Ivory* (New York: Taplinger, 1968). Retold by Sarvananda Bluestone.

11. Oscar Wilde, "The Ballad of Reading Gaol."

12. MidLink Magazine, http://longwood.cs.ucf.edu/~MidLink/haikus.html.

13. Agnes Thomas, age thirteen, in *Haiku Written by Children of the World,* www.jal-foundation.or.jp/html/haiku/html/english/EFa Sato.htm.

14. Sarah Mayhew, Red Rocks Elementary School, Colorado, in "Children's Haiku Garden," The Poet's Corner of the Little Red Schoolhouse, http://suzyred.com/poetry.html.

15. Jerome Klapka, "Dreams," ftp://uiarchive.cso.uiuc.edu/pub/etext/gutenberg/etext97/jjdrm10.txt.

16. Robert Van de Castle, *Our Dreaming Mind* (New York: Ballantine, 1994).

17. From a conversation with Helen Weaver, February 28, 2002. Ms. Weaver's father, Warren Weaver, was a scientist, author, and member of the board of the Salk Foundation. It was at her parents' house that she met Jonas Salk and afterward, she recorded this in her journal.

SADDLING THE NIGHT'S MARE: AWAKENING TO OUR SLEEPING FEARS

From ghoulies and ghosties and long-leggety beasties
And things that go bump in the night,
good Lord, preserve us.

OLD CORNISH PRAYER

Sleep lives face to face with death.

YAKUTAT TLINGIT SAYING

Nightmare! The very word is strange and mysterious, conjuring the terrifying image of a wild horse riding through our dreams. But the "mare" in a nightmare is much darker than a mere horse. It is a demon, a succubus, an evil spirit that takes possession of the sleeper and suffocates him.

Nightmares are the dream embodiment of fear. In them we are out of control, powerless in the face of danger—or, more to the point, we *feel* powerless in the face of danger.

It is the feeling of fear that makes a dream into a nightmare, fear that is not the subject of the dream, but its effect. Whatever we may see in a dream is made nightmarish if we feel fear as we see it. If, for example, I am chased in my dream by armed men who are shooting at me and I reach a place from which there is no escape, the dream is not necessarily a nightmare. It is only when I feel fear or feel the terror of being cornered and shot at that I am experiencing a nightmare.

All dreams have two parts: the visual, or what we see, and the visceral, or what we strongly feel. Nightmares are always visceral as well as visual.

Fear is part of the human condition. Of course, all animals experience fear in the face of danger. It would be silly to deny the importance of this emotion. Without fear, we would still be trying to put our fingers in light sockets or walk in front of moving cars. As is true for all animals, there are definitely some things that we have to fear in order to survive. In fact, teaching our children a certain amount of fear is part of parental responsibility.

When my daughter, Hira, was two years old, we rented a house in southern Vermont that came with a pond that we had all to ourselves. Hira, her mom, and I went swimming often. One day, Hira simply walked off the edge of the dock and splashed right into the water, where she lay facedown. She was fearless—at two years old, many of us were. She also might have drowned. A little informed fear was definitely in order. Young, small human beings must be taught the meaning of danger.

This teaching trades on the fact that we humans are probably the only species who can fear danger that does not yet face us. Other than those domesticated animals that have associated with us for so long, we are uniquely capable of generating our own fear and anxiety.

It's a fact that we all need a little fear. After all, we come into this world unprotected and unguarded. We need to learn the parameters of danger. For this reason, fear has been a part of education for ages. The tales from the Grimm brothers are merely a collection of various instructional tales from their part of western Europe. Through stories like these, apparently grandmas have been scaring kids into safety for centuries.

There are very few situations that require the basic survival response of flight or fight, a fear response connecting us with our ancient animal nature. How many times do we face such a necessity in our everyday lives? As we grow older, presumably we grow more aware and the fears instilled in childhood no longer apply. After all, what sane adult would put his finger in a light socket?

In our waking consciousness, we can often deal rationally with our fears. More often we are able to push them down. But in our dream consciousness, our rationality is of little help, and our submerged fears may rise.

.◎. Dream Exploration .◎.

Having Fun with Fear

We take fear too seriously. In fact, fear feeds on seriousness. Can you imagine fear being light and humorous? We don't associate it with butterflies, rainbows, and flying (except, of course, airplane flying). More likely we connect it with spiders, earthquakes, and running from something or someone.

We humans are a very creative species. Imagination is what has enabled us to survive. However, as they say in the East, as above, so below, or, for every upside there is a downside. The downside of imagination is anxiety and fear, for it is through our imagination that we can conjure monsters, demons, and things that go bump in the night.

More than five hundred phobias have been recognized by therapists, ranging from *ablutophobia* (fear of washing or bathing), the familiar *agoraphobia* (fear of open spaces) and the more common *claustrophobia* (fear of enclosed spaces), to *zemmiphobia* (fear of the great mole rat).

Regardless of what we fear, fear itself thrives in darkness, whether it is the dark of night or the darkness of denial and repression. If we keep it down, it only grows, which may help to explain nightmares. They provide a stage where our fears may play out. If we are not aware of them in our waking consciousness, our fears emerge in our sleep. In this way they provide a way for us to become more aware of what makes us tick.

Consciousness is like the light from a candle. If we become aware of our fears, we can watch them and witness them, and the darkness begins to recede.

Now, let's play with our fears.

1. Create a fear.
Make up one. The only rule is that it cannot be a fear that you really have. It can be as far out as you wish and you may be certain that some of the phobias on the list are pretty far out. (How about *epistemophobia*, fear of knowledge, or *genuphobia*, fear of knees?) The more far out it appears to you, the better. I actually met a woman once who was terrified of New Mexico license plates. Now, that one didn't even make the list.

2. After you've created your new fear, explore it fully.
How would you experience it? Create a worst-case scenario for the fear.

Let's say that your new fear is a fear of basketballs lying on the ground. Let's call it *ponerepilacanistrophobia* (everything sounds so much more official in Latin). As a confirmed ponerepilacanistrophobe, you might imagine the worst to be finding yourself locked in a large room with basketballs rolling all over the floor. What would you do? How would you react? Carry this as far as you can.

3. Finally, create a nightmare in which this new fear is the star.
What might be the "perfect" nightmare to highlight this fear? You make up the story, characters, change of scenes—the works.

4, Write it down in your journal.
You're used to this by now.

5. Wear your fear for a while.
You might want to adopt this new fear for a day or two and see how it plays out. After a couple of days, create a new fear, a worst-case scenario, and a nightmare in which the fear is featured.

All of this exploring is really playing with fear—and it hasn't been scary at all.

OUR LITTLE DEATHS

Perhaps it is our surrender of control in sleep that makes the dream state such a fertile ground for fear. We do not take deliberate steps into that land of dreams. We pass to another shore, much as we do in death. We leave the familiar and go into the unknown. In both death and sleep we have no control.

The Yakutat Tlingit Indians express the nature of sleep as death. In their language, the phrase meaning "he's sleeping" or "he's falling asleep" is translated literally as "by sleep he was killed." Among these people a common saying is, "Sleep lives face to face with death."

From the time that the first child or adult woke up screaming, people have been trying to find the root of nightmares. Where do they begin, these nightly messages of terror? They begin in broad daylight. Nightmares allow us to process things that we have been unable to process in our daily waking lives. The attack on the World Trade Center on September 11, 2001, illustrates this. A young woman witnessed the first moments of the attack. Walking to a subway less than a mile from the site, she heard the roar of the first plane and turned to see it tear into the tower.

The immediate aftermath of the attack was a waking nightmare for her. Twenty blocks away from the event, the scene was surreal, with two distinct groups of people: those who had heard or experienced the disaster, who were screaming and running or walking aimlessly; and those who were unaware of the event, who were going about their business as if nothing had happened.

For ten days she coped, attending her college classes, coming home on the weekend and resting. And then the nightmares started. She dreamed of little boys carrying bombs. She dreamed of her mother, shot by an angry woman who was aiming at someone else. She had carried on in her waking life in the midst of a quite real nightmare, which meant that her fears could emerge only in her sleep.

This example presents one Western interpretation of the origin of nightmares, but humans everywhere have been watching their nightmares for a long time, trying to understand where they come from.

In some cultures, ancestors are blamed for nightmares. In the language of the Konde people of Tanzania, the word *minyenya* means both "ancestors" and "nightmares," indicating that for the Konde it is the action of ancestors that creates nightmares. The Kiwai of Papua New Guinea also believe in this connection, seeing the occurrence of many nightmares as the attempt to escape a pursuing dead father.

The Araucanos of Chile considered the spirits of nightmares—very often the spirits of the dead—to be real beings who attack us. Sometimes, according to the Tikopia of the Solomon Islands, a spirit can come and sit on a person's chest or belly, where it pushes and presses, giving the unsuspecting dreamer unpleasant feelings of being crushed—nightmares. The Tikopia believe that nightmares are caused by such spirits, or *atua,* who have never held human form or lived on earth, but who may counterfeit familiar forms to confuse and deceive the dreamer.

The Western Shoshone and Hopi Indians saw dreams and nightmares as part of the positive life energy, or Buha. Eastern mystics call it *chi.* For the Shoshone and Hopi, it is the energy of the Great Spirit, and without Buha, a person dies.

With positive life energy, however, there must be negative energy. That, for the Shoshone and Hopi, is Diji Bo, the energy that destroys life, stunts creativity, and disrupts relations among people. It is part of our dual universe that the presence of good is mirrored by the presence of evil. Spirits of evil, the Tsoavite, appear in the form of human beings or possess human beings. They are the bringers of bad dreams. Thus nightmares, to the Hopi and Shoshone, are part of the scheme of life. As such, we need not judge them, but must be aware of them.

Sometimes it is simply nasty spirits that are to blame for nightmares. In Malaysia, these nasty spirits are ghost hags that haunt kitchens and bring bad dreams. The Bella Coola Indians of Canada hold one creature responsible for nightmares, a supernatural being called Sllimsila. This manlike creature has a black face and an enormous head, which he constantly scratches. Frequently, he will descend to earth for the sole purpose of frightening people and bringing about nightmares. The Tamil of southern India blame evil spirits for the symptoms of mental illness, including nightmares. In northern India, people blame witches—male and female—for nightmares. The Azande of the Sudan and Congo also hold that nightmares are the result of bewitchment.

The work of evil spirits, nightmares, and illness in the body have long been connected. The Korwas of Mirzapur in northern India believe that a dangerous female ghost named Reiya attacks them at night under the orders of a witch. Reiya gives both nightmares and rheumatism. The Senoi of Malaysia believe that both bad dreams and disease are due to disease spirits, and that disease spirits are brought about by projected emotions.

Some cultures feel that there is a connection between bad dreams and the direction our head points to when we sleep. Many cultures associate the east, where the sun rises, with life and good fortune, while they see the west, where the sun goes down, as the direction of death. In central Thailand, monks place the head of a corpse in a westerly direction. But a living person would have to sleep with his head to the east. If a living person slept with his head to the west, he would invite nightmares.

As we learned in the second chapter, the Maricopa Indians associated specific times of night with the dreams we experience. They divided the night into four quarters and believed it was during the first and fourth quarters that nightmares occurred. Because children were affected most by nightmares, they were kept awake during the first part of the night and were awakened before dawn, the last part of the night, to avoid dreaming during the nightmare times.

Some people hold that not witches or evil spirits or the times or positions of sleep produce nightmares, but rather that certain foods are the culprit—especially if they are consumed just before bedtime. Many of us have grown up with the warning that eating bananas before bedtime will bring nightmares. In Malaysia, people believe that some nightmares are caused by eating meat before sleeping and that others are caused by the sleeper meeting with agents of illness. And how many of us have had a night of disturbing dreams after eating too much pizza too late in the evening?

It makes sense—foods that disturb our physical comfort or digestion result in more fitful sleep, which in turn results in a greater chance of having bad dreams. Usually, the less peaceful our sleep is, the less peaceful our dreams will be.

Even when the cause of bad dreams is as common as the food we eat, a great many people hold that nightmares don't come to us; rather, we go to them. Scores of societies believe that the soul wanders abroad during sleep. As the soul goes traveling, it will meet noxious influences along the way. The Pukapukans of the southern Pacific held that in the nocturnal travels of the dreamer, noxious spirits would interfere and cause nightmares.

The Kol tribe of central India believes that a very thin and fragile thread connects the dreamer with his waking soul. If this thread were broken during sleep, the sleeper would die. A kind of bio-spiritual telephone wire, this thread allows the soul to remain in constant contact with the dreamer, no matter how far it wanders. If, on its nightly journey, the soul is attacked by an evil spirit, the ensuing struggle is communicated to the sleeper through this thread. Nightmares are this communication of the soul's struggle at some distant place. The sleeper shouts or groans or thrashes about, depending on the severity of the attack upon the soul. At such times the sleeper should be gently wakened to force the soul to return to the body and out of harm's way.

PASSING THROUGH FEAR

Regardless of the origin or cause of nightmares, how do we go about purging the demons of the night?

It is the feeling of helplessness and powerlessness—the certainty that no matter what we do, we are doomed—that is most characteristic of nightmares. There is no question that our dream feelings of powerlessness can emanate from our experience in our waking lives. It follows, then, that as we feel more empowered in our waking lives, we will feel empowered in our dreams. But it can work the other way as well. If we are empowered in our dreams, so are we empowered in our waking lives. The border is permeable and the traffic goes both ways.

The Temiar people of Malaysia recognize the connection between waking consciousness and dream consciousness. In their understanding, people can use the strengths of their waking lives to aid them in their dream lives. If a person is generous and caring and helps others in his waking life, he may call upon his friends and neighbors to aid him in his dreams. In his nightmares, the Temiar adult is able to rely upon a network of support. In fact, dream support is a keystone of Temiar society. Adults encourage children to advance against dream monsters, and if a child defeats a dream monster or ghost, it becomes his slave. If the child runs away, however, the dream monsters will pursue him until he finally faces them. Say, for example, a dream lion is pursuing a Temiar child. The youngster will tell his family and friends, who will encourage him to turn and face the dream beast. In this way, the power of the lion is transferred to the child.

For the Temiar people, the only real adversary is fear. If a Temiar child dreams of smoke, he need not avoid it, as he might in his waking state to prevent the stinging of his eyes. Instead, he must go directly into the dream smoke, for inside he might find the spirit of the smoke, which he can overcome and make his own. If a Temiar child dreams she is falling or soaring, she must let herself go, for this represents the effort of one of her souls to break free of her body. If, however, she is afraid of going too high or of hurting herself, she will impede the soul. Courage allows the child to gain power, while fear makes her soul withdraw deeper into the body, paralyzing her.

On the surface, the Temiar approach to nightmares and fear is very simple: As we enter into nocturnal fears, we can transform them from enemies into allies. But beneath the simplicity of this lies a wise understanding of the blurred line between waking and sleeping consciousness and an acceptance that what we do in one directly affects the other.

There is intensity to a nightmare. Its fear is alive and electric. On one level the Temiar suggest that our fear is simply energy that doesn't feel good. But if we can turn this energy around, it can feed our power instead of feeding on our powerlessness. We can transform it. After all, our fear is ours and we can do with it what we will.

For the White Mountain Apache, a dreamer's fearlessness in the presence of fear allows him to have elaborate visionary experiences. The Senoi of Malaysia believe that there is no such thing as a bad character in our dreams. Only if the dreamer is afraid and retreating from them will dream characters seem bad.

The Jicarilla Apache believe, as do the Senoi, that dream fears are a testing ground, especially for those who will be shamans. A Jicarilla child receives from the spirit creatures a power representation of an animal, bird, heavenly body, or natural phenomenon like thunder, lightning, or whirlwinds. For the child who is destined to become a shaman, this guide leads him through terrifying experiences that have been set out to test the child.

Among the Paiute Indians, a nightmare is actually a positive sign that a child is receiving power from his dreams. In fact, if a child rejects his dreams, he is considered to be rejecting their power as well, and will soon become ill. This belief is true to some extent in the psychology of the West: Unless we face the fear in our nightmares, it can make us ill. At the same time, the fear can become the source of our power.

☀ Dream Story

Reclaiming His Voice with a Scream

He hadn't spoken for as long as he could remember.

He couldn't speak . . . but he could drink. Late one evening, after stagger-ing out of the tavern, he tried three times to mount his horse, but each time fell in a drunken heap. A neighbor, taking pity on the poor mute, took him home and put him to bed.

After falling asleep, the man had the most horrible dream. He was falling—a long, terrible fall—into a furnace of boiling liquid. And as he fell, the fear inside him boiled too until he struggled to scream out for help. So great was his dream agony that he succeeded in screaming, there in his bed, thus recovering the use of his voice, which he retained from then on. His nightmare had set him free.

The feeling of powerlessness in nightmares takes many forms: A beast or mur-derer pursues us and we are unable to move, or we move too slowly; the world explodes around us, loved ones are killed or dying and we can do nothing. If we can bring our power into our dreams—if we can transform our night-mares—we can transform our lives.

◉ Dream Explorations ◉
Four Ways to Reclaim the Night

It is always a child who has a nightmare—whether that child is seven years old or seventy—because the fears in nightmares are primal, the kind that have been with us a long, long time. Of course, no matter what we do to rid ourselves of them, nightmares often don't disappear overnight. There are no quick panaceas in this world. But we may address the root of bad dreams—fear and powerlessness—in our waking lives and thus transform them in our sleeping lives. Here are some practices that may help.

Embracing the Beast

This exploration follows the practice of the Temiar people. Fear holds us back. Once we face it in our dreams, we bring ourselves to a place of power. Remember, the border between waking consciousness and sleeping con-sciousness is blurred. The resolutions we make in our waking state help us when we are asleep. Our intention is of primary importance.

1. Determine the nature of your nightmare.
Is something pursuing you? Is something happening to you? What is the fear?

2. Once you have determined the source of the fear, write it down.
Make it as simple as possible. For example, "A murderer is pursuing me but I can't run." Or, "Monsters are behind the door and will leap out at me. I try to run but can't." Or, "I am falling and will crash."

3. Choose a fearless course of action and tell yourself you'll follow it.
What would be the fearless thing to do in your dream? After you have figured out the essential fear of the nightmare, then decide on a fearless course of action and tell yourself each night before sleeping that this is what you will do. If you are running from a pursuer, for example, the fearless thing to do would be to turn toward the one who's chasing you. If you dream you're falling and you fear crashing, facing the fear in the dream might mean you accept the fall, you embrace it.

Be patient with yourself, keep at it, and remember that even changes with strong intention don't happen overnight.

Learning About the Fear

Fear is the mind killer.

FRANK HERBERT, *DUNE*

For thousands of years people have been struggling with ways of dealing with nightmares. Here we've explored facing our fear as a means of vanquishing it and the nightmare, re-creating the dream to empower ourselves and speaking directly to the dream to banish it.

But what of the fear itself—so powerful in the story above that it could bring back a man's voice? Here we look more closely at the fear we encounter in a nightmare, to see if maybe, by understanding exactly what it's made of, we can eliminate its scary power.

1. Find a comfortable place where you won't be disturbed.
Give yourself some space for this exploration.

2. Recall the last nightmare you've had.
For those who've never had a nightmare, remember the last really scary thing that happened to you. If you've never had a scary thing happen to you and you've never had a nightmare, skip this exercise.

3. Write down briefly and clearly exactly what happened in that experience.
Write this as if it were a story. What happened—and what exactly occurred the moment you first felt fear?

4. Write down how you felt during the experience.
Be as specific as you can be when writing about your feelings. In

which part of your body did you feel the fear? Was your stomach tight? Did your head pound? Did your back or neck tighten? Emotions resonate in different parts of our body.

5. If you've had this dream before . . .
If it is a recurring dream, do you feel the same way each time or do your feelings and your level of fear vary?

6. For a few days, note if the feelings and fear in your dream occur at all when you're awake.
Are they in the same part of the body? What's happening around you when you notice these feelings—what situation or environment surrounds you?

7. Note and write down any changes in your dreams.

Look at It from the Monster's Point of View*

In our nightmares we can get so caught up in our own vantage point that we can't imagine there's another perspective. If we are being pursued in a dream, for example, we never think about what's going on with the pursuer.

The fact is, we're dreaming the whole dream—the pursuer as well as the pursued. Let's see what can happen if we change our point of view.

1. Choose a nightmare.
It can be one you had a while back, one that's recent, or one that's recurring. It would be best to pick one with other people or creatures that are in some way creating the fear in the dream.

2. Write down the dream.
You may already have written it in your journal If you have, write it again as you remember it and as you remember feeling it.

3. Now rewrite the dream from the perspective of the creature or person causing the fear.
If there isn't another creature or person in the dream, then create one and write it from that perspective. What's that character's reason or justification for his actions?

4. Next, see if there's any change in the way you experience the dream.
Does some of the fear go away? Do you have a better understanding of it?

---

*I am indebted to the work of Jeremy Taylor, particularly in *Dream Work: Techniques for Discovering the Creative Power in Dreams* (New York: Paulist Press, 1983), for the idea of changing the vantage point in a nightmare.

Transforming the Past, Creating the Present

Time doesn't follow a straight line from past, to present, to future; it is full of curves and twists. The ancients knew this well—in fact, high-energy nuclear physics has caught up with notions that are thousands of years old, and recently, modern psychology has caught up with the physicists. It is the genius of neurolinguistic programming and Gestalt psychology, for example, that encourages people to rewrite their past—to take incidents from childhood and re-create them in their own way. We can do this with our dreams, as well.*

The Navajo, who are very respectful of dream consciousness, understand the power of altering dreams that frighten. One Navajo man kept having dreams in which he was falling, and every time, he woke with a start. Finally, he found an answer to this persistent nightmare: When he dreamed he was falling, he simply spread his arms wide. Then he would land lightly.

To accomplish altering a bad dream, we must first bring the nightmare to the light of day by talking to a friend about it, for instance, or by writing it in a journal. Once we have brought the dream to waking consciousness, we can then mold it and transform it. In a nightmare we are powerless, passive victims in the face of forces that whirl around us. By becoming active, though, we are empowered to make allies of our dream antagonists—to rewrite our dreams.

It's a simple technique: While you are awake, take the elements of the dream that are fearsome and, bringing your imagination to bear, turn them around; then write down the nightmare in its changed form.

Do this exercise shortly before you go to bed.

1. Recall a nightmare that you'd like to change.
Close your eyes and think about it, allowing yourself to feel the feelings it inspires. Try to visualize the dream and see it in detail. Then write it down.

2. Now think of ways that you can change the dream.
Remember, you can do anything in a dream. Your powers are great—if you wish, you can fly or have great strength, you can have the power to become invisible, or you can have powerful friends to guard and help you.

3. Imagine your new dream.
Visualize it as completely as you can, awaken all your senses to it—see the colors, hear the sounds, smell the aromas.

4. Write down the new dream.

*Many thanks to Patricia Garfield, particularly for her work *Your Child's Dream* (New York: Ballantine, 1984).

If you wish, you may also draw the new dream. Drawing can be a particularly effective form of expression for a child you might be guiding through this exercise.

Here are two examples of experiences with this exploration.

Pete described his nightmare as follows: "I was walking along a mountain path. I knew there was something behind me, following me, but I didn't know what it was. I could hear it there, but I kept climbing up the path. When I reached the top, I realized that I was at the edge of a cliff with a drop of thousands of feet and no place to run. At that point a screaming tiger burst out of the woods and raced at me. I awoke screaming."

Here's Pete's nightmare rewritten: "As I walked along the mountain path, I could hear the tiger behind me. Still, I kept climbing. When I reached a clearing, I called the tiger to me—I was able to speak to and befriend him—and he came to me and let me touch his fur. He purred like a giant kitten and licked my hand. I rode the tiger to the top of the mountain and there, at the edge of the cliff, he turned into Pegasus. Together we flew off to discover new lands."

Sometimes we have to revise our nightmares more than once. That's what Jenny had to do. Both she and her boyfriend, Jon, were about fifteen. At summer camp they'd grown very close and shared a number of interests, including music. Though the summer session lasted only one month, Jenny had never grown quite so close to someone as she had to Jon.

Despite her happiness, however, Jenny began to have a recurring nightmare. In the dream she was at a concert and was told that Jon was dead, but she knew that if she were with him, he would be all right.

We discussed the dream and how she wanted to change it. First, she altered her dream so that Jon was with her in the car, but she discovered that though this would prevent her from being told that Jon was dead, he still died in the dream.

In her next re-creation, she placed him not only in the car, but also away from the concert. That did the trick. He was saved and the nightmare was over.

A girl's recurring nightmare was that the devil was chasing her on the beach, coming closer and closer to reaching her. She could not run fast enough—her legs felt like lead. Each time she experienced this dream, she would awaken in a cold sweat, heart pounding, just before the devil caught her. The girl worried that soon he would succeed; he came closer and closer to reaching her each time she had the dream.

When she told her grandmother about the dream, her grandmother replied that rather than running from the devil, she should turn and face him. The grandmother then gave the girl a poem that she could recite in her dream to tell the devil to "return from whence you came."

Each night before she went to sleep, the girl repeated the poem, preparing for the return of the nightmare. And finally it arrived.

Once again, she was running across the beach, and once again the devil followed behind her. Suddenly, she remembered her grandmother's words. She stopped, turned, pointed her finger at the creature, and shouted the poem. Poof! He was gone. She never dreamed of him again.

This girl had succeeded in talking to the dream, simply carrying her statement from waking consciousness into dream consciousness. In her favor was the fact that, because she was a child, the line between the dream state and the waking state was a bit more blurred than it is for adults.

When my daughter Hira was four, she learned to talk to herself and her dreams to rid herself of nightmares. One night, she called fearfully from her bedroom. When I ran into the room, I found her sitting upright in bed, her eyes wide with fear.

"There's a bad witch coming out of that picture," she sobbed, and pointed to a small picture on the wall.

"Let's both tell her to leave," I said. So we both turned to the picture and told the witch to leave, that she was not welcome, and she must never come back again. Hira knew that we had taken gotten rid of that witch, and she never came out of the picture again.

We can deal with nightmares when we are awake often by talking directly to the dream or to the forces that bring it to us. The Havasupai, or "people of the blue-green water," have lived in and around the western end of the Grand Canyon for over one thousand years. For these people, a nightmare usually comes from visiting in sleep a land where there are bad people. A man who had such a dream immediately awakened and sang what he had dreamed. He then spoke to the dark, saying, "I do not want to dream this way. When darkness is here, I want you to make me dream pleasantly."[1]

The Japanese also awaken to call upon aid against nightmares. For them, the good spirit Baku, "eater of dreams," helps to rid them of the nightmare. When a person awakens from a nightmare, she may call upon Baku, who has a lion's head, a tiger's feet, and a horse's body, and say, "Baku, eat my dreams." Baku obliges, turning a bad dream into good fortune by eating up the evil.

⊚ Dream Exploration ⊚

Talking to the Dream

Before we can talk to our nightmares, we have to know what we're going to say. This really isn't so difficult, if we keep in mind that we want to change what it is that is haunting us in our dreams.

1. Decide what you need to say and to whom you must say it.
Sometimes the words can be as simple as "Go back from whence you came" or "Go away and never come back."

2. At bedtime, tell yourself what you have decided to say, being as clear, precise, and direct as you can be.
You are consciously altering the pattern of your dreams simply by talking to them. If someone is chasing you again and again in your dreams, you might say, "Go away and don't ever bother me again." Of course, it's up to you to choose the statement that's going to get the desired results.

☀ Dream Story

Blink and You're Awake

I always liked crowds, though my mom and my grandmother used to warn me against running to follow them. My grandmother, particularly, belonged to the Brothers Grimm school of child rearing, in which scary stories served to control kids and teach them lessons, especially uncontrollable kids like me. She often told me of little boys who were hit by cars and run over as they tried to follow a crowd. In waking life, there were plenty of crowds in those days. There were marching men in uniforms and brass bands—it was The War, and the excitement sometimes rippled through the streets.

I dreamed of a crowd, but it was different somehow. All the people were gathered around something in the middle of the street, but I couldn't see what it was. Grown-ups were so large sometimes. I found myself having to slip between the legs of the big people—it was easy, for I was small even for my age—until I came out at the inner edge of the circle. There, lying on the ground with all those people around him, was the body of a little boy. The boy was me.

"He's stone dead," somebody said.

I looked at myself lying stone dead in the middle of the street. I didn't like this dream at all. I had to get out of it, so I told myself that if I closed my eyes, I would wake up. So in the dream I closed my eyes and the next thing I knew I was fully awake. I had given myself an exit from the dream. I was five years old and it was the last nightmare I ever had.

There is no reason to hold on to bad dreams. Many peoples have found ways to get rid of them by passing them on to inanimate objects. The Tlingit people of Alaska have a specific method of dealing with bad dreams: On the morning following a nightmare, they simply kill the dream by talking it into a glass jar.

Dream catchers—essentially a hoop of wood with a net in its center—have long been part of Native American tradition. Originally created to protect babies from bad nighttime spirits, the bride's mother-in-law would begin making one as soon as it was clear that a baby was on the way. The hoop was fashioned from honeysuckle, buck brush, or willow, and animal sinew was used to weave the net in the center of the hoop. The parents hung the finished piece above the cradle to catch dreams as they came on moonbeams to the baby's head. The woven net caught bad dreams, which were always larger, while the fine dreams, which were smaller, could slip through. While fancy dream catchers are somewhat ubiquitous today, the originals are quite simple, without feathers or other ornamentation.

The earth's bounty has always provided human beings with tools for dealing with nightmares. Because science has yet to discover the reasons why many remedies work, people will often dismiss these curatives as superstitious hokum—and in some cases, they may indeed be hokum. Yet one person's silly superstition is another person's proven remedy, and we must be careful in letting the fact that there is no scientific explanation for them be the sole reason for denying the existence of certain realities.

Recently, people have discovered crystals as a source of energy. Of course, this is no discovery at all. People have long recognized the beauty and usefulness of stones, and in our time the unique electrical qualities of quartz crystals have been harnessed for use in the development of computer technology.

Hematite is another substance from the earth that is thought to have unique power. Found throughout the Western Hemisphere, hematite is a metallic, earthy gray in his natural state—really little more than a shiny lump. Chemically, its two main ingredients are iron and oxygen: an element of earth and an element of air. The appearance and chemical composition of hematite do not tell the entire picture, however. After it is tumbled and polished, a piece of hematite looks like metal, with the gray sheen of a ball bearing, but when its surface is scratched, a redness clearly shows through. Ancients imagined the stone as bleeding and thus gave it the name of blood *(hema)*. Since it was first discovered, many have felt that it is a remedy for blood disorders. Hematite has also been known as a remedy for nightmares. Placed under a pillow, a small polished piece of the metal can effectively alleviate or eliminate bad dreams.

Another ancient stone remedy for nightmares is amber, a substance that lies in a strange limbo between stone and plant. Amber is the petrified sap of trees, which connects it to the world of plants. But the process of its creation—petrification (literally, "rock-ification")—makes it more like stone. The ancient Greeks used amber to ward off nightmares by placing a piece under their pillows.

⊚ Dream Exploration ⊚

Spit It Up, Throw It Away, Burn It

The ancient Mesopotamians had a ritual for dealing with dreams. The dreamer first rubbed clay over his body, saying, "Lump, to your substance my substance has been fused, and to my substance your substance has been fused!" Then the dreamer would tell the clay all his dreams and say, "As I throw you into the water, you will crumble and disintegrate, and may the evil consequences of all the dreams soon be gone, melted away, and be many miles removed from my body." Alternatively, the dreamer could tell his dreams to a reed and then burn it.

This exploration duplicates the practice of giving your dreams to an object, rather than carrying them in your body.

1. Find an object that appeals to you as a receptacle for your nightmares.

Make sure it is something that you can get rid of—water in a paper cup, for example, or a piece of paper. Don't use that priceless vase that has been in the family for three hundred years.

2. "Talk" the nightmare into this object.

Tell it the dream in great detail, and then tell it what you want to have happen. For example, you might say, "My nightmares are with you and with you they will stay."

3. Get rid of the recipient of the nightmare.

For example, if you were to use a glass of water, you would speak the dream into the water, throw away the water, and clean the glass thoroughly (to avoid having to throw away the glass as well). If you were to use a piece of paper, you would write down the dream in great detail, then burn the paper.

4. Try a variation of the Mesopotamian lump of clay.

If you have access to real clay, great—otherwise, an old-fashioned mud pie will do just as well. For those who have forgotten how to make one, you simply get some fresh dirt, mix in a little water to make a paste, and—voilà!—a mud pie. Talk your dream into the clay or mud. If you wish, you can rub it all over your body, as the Mesopotamians did, or you can simply throw the lump into a body of water, such as a pond, lake, stream, or the ocean. If no natural body of water is available, fill a pool with water and let the clump dissolve.

❖ Dream Story

A Lullaby for Jamie

Jamie was less than a year old, yet almost every night he awakened screaming and clearly terrified.

His parents felt helpless. They couldn't even talk about his dreams with him—he was a baby with no vocabulary, no means to carry on a conversation.

Jamie's father was one of my oldest friends. When he told me about his son's experience, I thought of hematite. Earlier that year, at camp, I had given a stone to a student who was having persistent bad dreams, and after she slept with it under her pillow, the nightmares stopped.

I gave Jamie's father a piece of hematite, which he tucked under his son's pillow. Jamie's nightmares ceased immediately.

Peoples of the world have long used plants even more than stones to heal and to nurture—and to dispel their bad dreams.

Smudging, a technique found extensively, though not exclusively, among Native American peoples, is an ancient method used to cleanse an area of spirits and negative energy. It involves the burning of certain dried plants in the area to be cleansed. The Ojibwa Indians, for instance, burned cedar to cleanse a house and also used it as an aid to dispel the negative energy represented in nightmares. Thus an adult could avoid unpleasant dreams by the use of cedar smoke and prayer and a child who had bad dreams could be sprinkled in bed with water in which cedar boughs had been soaked. Sage, with many varieties that grow throughout the United States, is another plant often used for smudging. Burning sage to cleanse an area is nearly as American as apple pie.

Other botanicals have been suggested by herbalists over time for the treatment of bad dreams. One eighteenth-century herbal suggests that placing rosemary leaves under the pillow alleviates nightmares, and another suggests taking catmint tea. The ancient Roman scholar Pliny asserted that an anise plant hung over a bed would prevent bad dreams, while wood betony in the pillow is offered as another curative. In times gone by, Scottish Highlanders drank a tea made of wild thyme for strength, courage, and the prevention of nightmares.

As far as using any of these remedies today, it's extremely important to be as careful about ingesting herbs and plant materials as you would be about taking any other medication or substance. That something is "natural" does not mean it is safe to take internally. (Arsenic, for instance, is natural—but, of course, it can kill you.) A good rule of thumb is this: If the directions for use say you have to eat or drink it, DON'T.*

Susun Weed, a renowned contemporary herbalist, has suggested a very safe way to banish nightmares—placing a dream pillow near or beneath your regular pillow, where the power of its scent can work its wonders. The herbal recipe to enclose in your pouch that we made in chapter 2 includes the following dried herbs: rosemary, anise, valerian, and lemon balm.[2] Remember to crush the herbs a bit to release their scent.

Smudging, sleeping on a dream pillow, and burning incense all involve the use of smell, our most primitive and basic sense. Together with taste and touch, it is one of the proximate senses that precede our conscious thought and which develop before the senses of sight and hearing. Odors and aromas can stimulate long-buried memories and can evoke feelings from the depths of our being. In addition, we can use their power as we confront our nightmares.

◎ Dream Exploration ◎

Smell Your Way Out of Your Nightmare

1. Identify the aromas in your life.
For one day simply pay attention to all that you smell in your everyday life. Which scents attract you? Which repel you? Which scents bring back pleasant memories, and which conjure memories that are unpleasant? Make a note of these in a journal or notebook explicitly designated for this purpose.

2. Once you have determined the scents that are pleasant and soothing, see if you can find ways to bring them into your bedroom.
Sometimes this will be quite simple. For example, if the scent of roses is pleasing to you, you can easily place some roses in a vase near your bed. Obviously, we can access spices and flowers without any trouble, but you might have to use your ingenuity for other scents. Be creative. However, remember that with the flood of chemical odors on the market, our sense of smell has been clouded and manipulated. For this exploration, it's good to have scents that are as natural as possible.

---

* Exceptions to this rule are the vibrational remedies, which we discuss later in this chapter.

3. Experiment with different scents as you are going to sleep, and note their effect on your dream.
You might try one odor for a while and then try another. As usual, write down the results in your journal.

One scent alternative you might try in this exercise is essential oils, highly concentrated oils that result from the steam distillation of flowers and plants. There are several hundred essential oils available for purchase in the United States, from rose to cedar wood, lemon to chamomile, and jasmine to nutmeg. Only a few drops are needed to send fragrance throughout a room—they are highly potent substances and must be handled with great care. Essential oils are *never* to be ingested and *never* to be put directly on the skin. If you find a scent that is right for you, put a drop or two on a tissue and place it under your pillow.

Incense is another form of scent that is easily distributed, and one you might use in this exploration. People have been burning plant resins for thousands of years. Today, many people burn incense for relaxation, meditation, or simply because it smells good. Once you find an incense that smells good to you, try burning it for a few minutes before going to bed. Then put it out. The smell will permeate the room. Note how this affects your dreams.* As we take in scents that soothe and relax us while we drift off to sleep, we carry these feelings into our sleeping consciousness. Nightmares, then, may no longer be able to rear their ugly heads.

On the other end of the spectrum from essential oils are vibrational remedies, which have also been used to heal nightmares. Among these are homeopathic remedies and flower essences in which the very energy of the flower or plant is captured in the medium of distilled water—the stock solution. In homeopathy, a drop of the stock solution is mixed with one hundred drops of water, and a drop of the resulting solution is mixed with another hundred drops of water, and so on until the desired strength is reached. In homeopathy, the more a solution is diluted, the more powerful it becomes.

For those of us who are most familiar with traditional or allopathic med-

---

* There is a great deal of hype today about both oils and incense. Some claim that oils relax and cause euphoria and the like, and incense has proliferated to the point where there are many on the market that are cheap and artificial. It's important that both oils and incense be completely natural, not synthetic. When you purchase incense, make sure it is made from natural resins. For both oils and incense, stay away from blends and choose the simplest scents—it's hard enough finding the perfect single scent, let alone the perfect blend! Also, while very inexpensive oils are almost always inferior, it does not follow that the very expensive ones are the best. Trust your nose and not the hype. One source for essential oils is Tisserand Essential Oils. They are invariably fine. You can reach them at (800) 227-5120. Another source is Aroma Vera, American Brand Labs, 5310 Beethoven Street, Los Angeles, CA 90066, phone: (800) 669-9514, e-mail: www.aromavera.com.

icine, vibrational remedies sound a bit mystical if not downright silly. We are used to medications that slam us, bang us around, and produce noticeable results fairly quickly with the usual physical side effects. But homeopathy has been around as a healing modality for over two and a half centuries and is recognized in Europe as a valid school of medicine. In this country, homeopathy is gradually achieving recognition as a valid form of healing, though skeptics argue that its effectiveness can be attributed to the placebo effect: If you want it to work and expect it to work, it will work. Interestingly, though, more and more veterinarians are using homeopathic remedies with their animal patients. Surely horses, cows, dogs, and cats are not responding to these medicines because they believe in them and expect them to work!

Children and animals respond most dramatically to homeopathic remedies and flower essences. And the beauty of these treatments is that they generally have no side effects. It is virtually impossible to take too much of a given homeopathic or flower remedy.

Modern vibrational flower remedies are the child of an English homeopathic physician named Edward Bach, who, having practiced for many years, wanted to find remedies that were simpler to use than the vast panoply of homeopathic remedies. The result, in 1936, was the thirty-eight flower remedies that could be taken to cure a variety of conditions.

Unlike homeopathic remedies, flower remedies generally address the mind and emotions rather than physical conditions. Similar to homeopathic remedies, they have no harmful side effects, do not interfere with any medication, and do not need to be prescribed. In most cases, only a drop or two of flower essence is taken in a glass of water several times during the day and particularly at bedtime.

Of the Bach flower remedies, the two that can help in alleviating nightmares are Rock Rose, which is used for extreme fears or terror—to alleviate, for instance, nightmares of annihilation and death;* and Aspen, which helps to balance anxiety, hidden fears, and nightmares, and is particularly helpful for children. A third flower remedy, St. John's wort, a product of the Flower Essence Society rather than a Bach flower remedy, helps to alleviate nightmares. These three remedies may be taken individually or in combination.†

* There are several sources of flower remedies in the United States. One of the largest is the Flower Essence Society, P.O. Box 1769, Nevada City, CA 95959, phone: (800) 548-0075. The Flower Essence Society carries its own essences (several hundred of them) as well as the Bach Flower Essences.

† There are other flower remedies recommended for nightmares. They come from various parts of the world and are available through the World Wide Web. Among them are Rose of Sharon (the Amazon); Green Spider Orchid (Australia); Pa-nini-o-ka and Passion Flower (Hawaii); and Swallow Wort (India). I found all of them within six seconds each, using the Google search engine.

Nightmares are an important and universal part of both our dream consciousness and our waking consciousness—a part that can tell us a great deal about what we feel. Whatever your beliefs about the origins or causes of nightmares, and whichever method you choose to use in dealing with them, it is sure that in journeying through these nighttime fears, we access a great deal of power and blur even more that border between our waking and dreaming beings.

Notes

1. From Leslie Spier, "Havasupai Ethnography," *Anthropological Papers of the American Museum of Natural History* 24 (1928).
2. From correspondence with Susun Weed.

5

On the Wings of the Night:
Soul Searching and
the Searching Soul

*My dreams are of architecture and of buildings—cities abroad, which
I have never seen, and hardly have hoped to see. I have traversed, for
the seeming length of a natural day, Rome, Amsterdam, Paris, Lisbon—
their churches, palaces, market-places, shops, suburbs, ruins, with an
inexpressible sense of delight—a maplike distinctness of trace—and
a daylight vividness of vision that was all but being awake.*

CHARLES LAMB

*When the shadows of this life have gone,
I'll fly away
Like a bird from prison bars have flown
I'll fly away
I'll fly away (O glory)
I'll fly away (in the morning)
When I die, Hallelujah bye and bye,
I'll fly away, fly away.*

AMERICAN SPIRITUAL

*Sleeping is like dying, but smaller. That is why we
call it* hisk'a hiwa, *"little death."
In sleep the soul leaves, just as in death.*

AYMARA INDIAN OF PERU

We human beings are bones and flesh, muscle and brain. We live, reproduce, and die. We eat and excrete, just as fish, reptiles, birds, and other mammals do. And, ultimately, we return to earth as minerals and chemicals. But we are much more.

We also think and plan and love. We create, hate, and remember. We dance and write and sing. No other animals do these things. We *are* special—and for a very long time we humans have sought to put a word to what it is that these unique qualities and abilities add up to. Some call it *consciousness,* these collective parts of living beings that connect us to something larger, to the divine. Some have called it *soul.*

In our death-denying culture, the effort is often expended to make the dead look as if they were alive. The mortician applies makeup and funereal cosmetics until the lifeless body looks as if it were merely asleep.

But it is undeniable that in death, something has fled. Many of us have had the experience of seeing a loved one who has recently died. Many of the words and phrases that we use to describe the state of death imply that something has left—such as "passing over," "passing on," "leaving the body," "passing away." In fact, anybody who has been with a person who is no longer alive knows that though the body is there, the person is not. What has left? The life force? The soul?

The Seneca Indians have an expansive notion of the soul, which includes the beliefs that nature is conscious and that all living creatures have souls. The important connection their outlook establishes is the link between consciousness and soul.

It's likely that every language group in the world has a word for what in English is called the soul. And it's likely, too, that each word provides a slightly different shade of meaning. On Tikopia, one of the Solomon Islands in the South Pacific, every person possesses a single vital principle called *mauri* or *ora*—the life force, the root of life itself. Similar to the Chinese notion of chi, it is also echoed by the indigenous Ainu people of Japan, who call it *ramat.*

In the northeastern corner of India, near Nepal, Bhutan, and Tibet, live the Santal people. Long independent of the dominant culture of the country, the Santal have their own worldview. For these people, human beings are composed of two substances: *hormo,* which is the body, and *jivi,* which is the soul.

Hundreds of years ago, some slave ships wrecked off the east coast of South America below Mexico and next to Guatemela on what was to become the nation of Belize, and the Africans transported on them, instead of becoming slaves, became the fiercely independent Garifuna people. The Garifuna had their own notion of what characterized humans. They called it *iuani,* or "the spirit that is in the body," and believed that every person had this spirit, which was imperceptible to the senses and unable to be controlled by the mind.

In the Ituri rain forest, deep in the Democratic Republic of the Congo, the Mbuti pygmies use the word *boru e'i* for soul. It is also the word for pulse, for life and soul are one. For the Bambara of Mali, a force called *ni,* though not at all bound to the body, animates it and also represents the breath and the beating of the arteries. But for the Bambara, this is not the only "soul" we have. There is also the *dya,* a kind of fluidlike shadow that emanates from the body and can be seen only by reflection.

The ancient Chinese, like the Bambara, held that there were two souls in every human being. The material or animal soul, called *p'o,* represents life and is attached to the body and dies with it. The spiritual soul, called *hun,* can leave the body without endangering its life. The Semai and Temiar people also see two psychic entities in each human—one behind the center of the forehead and the other in the pupils of the eyes.

Interestingly, the words *shadow* and *soul* are synonyms in several cultures. The Algonquin Fox Indians use the same word for both. The Andaman Islanders, eight hundred miles off the coast of west Bengal, use the word *ot-jumulo* for both "reflection" and "shadow." It's telling that their word for a dream is *ot-jumu*—for them, the world of the soul is seen through dreams, while a person entering a dream world is entering a place of shades or reflections. In central Nigeria, the Tiv people also equate the soul and a shadow; they believe that everybody has a *jijingi,* a shadow or shade.

For many of the world's peoples, the world of souls, of our shadows and reflections, is the world of dreams. In our waking state we are rarely aware of more than our material boundaries. Our bodies and our minds tie us to the physical plane. But the soul—our shadow, the *chi,* the *p'o,* the *inunga* and *kapix* and *dya,* the *ruwaay, remat,* and *jiwa,* the *mouri* and *ora,* the *ampo* and *jijingi* and *ni*—is not the province of the physical world.

Soul Travel, Dream Journey

Where do we go in sleep? And what part of us goes there? We fly to distant places. We soar over landscapes that are both unfamiliar and very familiar, transcending time and space. This is the stuff of science fiction—yet it is the everyday (or everynight) material of dreams.

 Dream Story

Dreaming out of Prison
He was of the Muria, a people who loved to dance and sing. The last place for a Muria man was in prison, but here he was and here he would be for a long, long time.

Physical walls, though, could not keep him completely. After all, Muria shamans traveled to the Otherworld on eight-legged horses and returned to speak of it. Could he not escape from this prison in the same way? After all, he had his soul, his *jiwa,* and they could not imprison that.

So at night, the bars of the prison dissolved and his soul would fly. As his body lay in his cell, asleep, his soul went wandering abroad. It flew to his house and saw all his friends and relations there. For the duration of the night he celebrated, no longer a prisoner.

Sometimes people would come to him. His wife came and slept with him in his dream. Other times, he was able to see all that was going on in the world beyond the bars. His dreams had set him free.[1]

When we enter our dreams, our body stays put, but a part of us journeys out of our body on the wings of the night. From the beginning of time, we human beings have tried to understand our nocturnal journeys. For many, if not most, it is the soul that provides the visual landscape of our dreams. In fact, as astounding as it seems, given the endless variety of human experience, the overwhelming consensus of hundreds of cultures is that our soul can and does leave us in sleep. Some scholars have even suggested that this understanding of dreaming is the origin of religion itself. Robert Van de Castle, in his monumental book *Our Dreaming Mind,* claims that the notion of soul travel was introduced to the West from India in the fifth century B.C. It seems that the notion of the soul journeying in dreams, wherever it may have originated, is nearly universal.

And what a trip! At night we leave the prison of our bodies and travel unencumbered by weight or density. We see though our eyes are closed. For eastern European Slavs, "[I]t is nothing more or less than that the soul comes out of a man and goes about the world and only blood remains in the man to keep him alive."[2] From eastern Europe to Malaysia the vision is the same— the Senoi and Temiar people see dreams as nothing less than travel and the accounts of dreams as traveler's tales. In fact, a standard Temiar greeting of family members in the morning is *"Ma-loo,* "Where have you been to?"

Where have you been to? The Bella Coola Indians of British Columbia speak of the *xix-mänoäs,* or spirit, which leaves the body every night and travels, unrestrained by any barriers, to the scene of the dreams. Thousands of miles to the south, the Mundurucu Indians of central Brazil also feel that the souls of sleeping people travel abroad and that their experiences are the substance of dreams. On the other side of the world, in South Asia, the Miao and Akha people hold an identical view of dreams, as do the Fang people of west Africa. The Tucuna people of the Amazon hold that during a dream, the soul *(naa'e)* leaves the body and has its own adventure. Even on the island of Pukapuka in the isolated Cook Islands, people see the soul as a mobile unit that leaves the body at night and wanders freely about the world, engaging in nocturnal experiences that constitute the fabric of dream life.

Once freed of the body, we can go anywhere—perhaps, in the future, even across galactic space and time. It's sure that here on earth, our restless souls can party. The Bambara of Africa eat, drink and chat with friends while they are asleep—and this is as real as waking reality. However, it's only the spirit that drinks and eats during these evening parties. The physical dreamer will wake up with an empty stomach.

꩜ Dream Exploration ꩜

Close Your Eyes and Drive

There is something very Einsteinian about the travel of the soul. For here, too, time and space collapse—clock time loses its meaning and we can travel to places long gone and yet to be. The Mohave Indians of California placed great value on what they called power dreams, those dreams that carried the dreamer backward in time into the presence of the creator. For them, time travel was a recognized dream experience. Farther south, the Tapirape of Brazil see dreams as the journey of the *iunga,* the soul, which can move as freely through time as it can through space.

In this exploration, we take a trip that we have taken many times before— but this time, with our eyes closed.

1. Right before you go to sleep, close your eyes and think of a trip you've made many times.

It might be a trip that you've taken only once or twice a year, for a special occasion or a vacation, or one you make much more frequently. For our purposes, the trip should be one that involves driving or train travel rather than travel by plane.

2. Take the trip in your imagination.

Call up every detail that you can—what do you see from the windows? What can you hear and smell? What environments do you travel through? Be aware of all the sensations you feel as you take the trip in your imagination.

3. Note your perception of the trip—including any changes in your perception.

If the trip feels different to you in your imagined travel, how does it differ from the actual journey? If it feels exactly the same as the actual trip, take note of these strongly rooted feelings.

4. Let yourself drift into sleep while you are still traveling, and recall and write down any dreams you have.

You will not necessarily dream about the trip. However, be aware of those dreams that do come to you while you're exploring this exercise. You might try this for several nights in a row.

❖ Dream Story

It Takes One to Tango

Emma's earnest intelligence made her seem at times like an old woman, though she was actually only eleven years old, with glasses and a giant, infectious grin. This combination of youth and wise age made for an unusual appearance—when she wore pigtails, she looked like a fairy with attitude.

I met her while I was directing a play at the arts camp—*The Bad Seed*—and Emma was auditioning for the lead role of Rhoda. In the play Rhoda is an adorable ten-year-old psychopathic killer. Emma won the role and was, in fact, so terrifying as Rhoda that her little sister didn't want to sleep in the same room with her any more.

After camp, Emma and I kept in touch by e-mail. Her correspondence was never boring and, knowing that I was writing this book, she occasionally sent me a description of one of her dreams, complete with proposed interpretations, which always struck me as right on.

Because of this continued interest in dreams and her astute observations about them, I decided to include Emma in a dream experiment: I wanted to investigate the ability of two people to choose an evening and actually meet each other in a dream.

Neither Emma nor I had any expectations that anything would happen, though both of us were open to whatever might occur.

On the evening we had agreed to, I brought Emma to mind before going to sleep. During the night I had two dreams: The first was short and I didn't feel her presence there at all, but she was very present in the second dream. I couldn't see her or hear her, but her presence was quite clear. It was as if she were occupying the same space that I was. It was obvious to me that our beings had met, our souls had traveled in tandem—and all from our intention.

Of course, that's not the end of the story. Things are always a bit more interesting than they appear. I hadn't yet found out what Emma had experienced. A day or two later she wrote, somewhat apologetically, that she had completely forgotten about the experiment on the night that we had agreed to meet. Strangely, I didn't feel any less excited about the results. In fact, I still maintained that I had indeed experienced a connection, even if Emma hadn't made the trip. After all, I reasoned, if people can travel solo on planes and in cars, then certainly souls can travel by themselves in dreams.

A month or so later I visited my daughter, Hira, in Seattle. She, her fiancé, Todd, and Joe, a mutual friend, all agreed to participate in another experiment of dream meetings. This time, I took a page from Susun Weed, herbalist, healer, and intuitive extraordinaire. Susun had told me that often, when she teaches live-in groups, she gathers the members of the group around the campfire in the evening and tells everyone to meet at three o'clock in the morning—in their dreams.

So Hira, Todd, Joe, and I all agreed to have a dream meeting at four in the morning for two consecutive nights. I didn't experience much—I suppose I might have been too tired; Todd and Joe didn't experience anything. Hira, however, arrived at the meeting place, though she was late, so she left. The next evening she arrived early. But at least she did show up on both nights.

Conclusion? I had taken a solo trip with Emma, and Hira had taken a solo trip with the four of us.

⊚ Dream Exploration ⊚

Meeting with Eyes Wide Shut

The idea of traveling through space and time in the hours of darkness smacks of witchcraft, which is interesting considering that witches were not accused of flying through the air at midday. Perhaps some "witches" in the West—those women who were healers—were, like shamans all over the world, able to leave their bodies and fly in dreams.

If our soul travels at night, we might as well go along for the ride. In this exploration we try meeting someone after we've fallen sleep.

1. Gather a group of two or more people willing to try the experiment.
Remember, this is not a test. The lighter and more playful we are, the more likely that something interesting might happen. But the most important things, as always, are commitment and intention. To put it another way, people need not be serious, but they need to be sincere.

2. Be wary of expectations.
As soon as we define what we think is going to happen, we set ourselves up for disappointment. Simply allow things happen as they will. Any result will be just fine.

3. Agree on a time when you will meet in your dream.
Obviously the meeting time you choose must be a time when all participants are asleep, but that's the only limitation. Those involved do not have to be geographically close to each other.

4. As you are falling asleep, keep in mind your intention.
And keep in mind the meeting time and the other participants.

5. When you wake up, record your dream experience.
If no meeting occurred, no problem. This exploration is best practiced over a period of time rather than as a one-shot attempt.

LEAVING OUR BODIES WHILE WE'RE AWAKE

To travel in sleep throughout the night, for the soul to leave our body, meet people, and observe and participate in events, is the experience we all have in our dreams. But to be able to do this in a waking state is the province only of great healers and shamans.

In the tundra of the arctic north, a great Chukchi medicine man can beat his drum and send himself into a state in which his soul sees whatever he wishes. The steady rhythm of the drumbeat relaxes his conscious mind and allows his dream consciousness to take over. Thousands of miles to the south, a Hungarian healer beats his drum repeatedly, and then he too enters into a waking dream state in which he soon travels beyond his physical body.

If we can travel outside of our bodies in dreams, why can't we do so in our waking state? In this kind of travel, the line between waking consciousness and sleeping consciousness is entirely blurred. This is the province of trance. From time immemorial people have attempted and achieved this waking flight of the soul, sometimes using psychotropic substances to facilitate the journey and other times, like the Chukchi, Lapp, and Hungarian healers, simply using the beat of the drum.

At the root of such an experience is changing consciousness, allowing our everyday, waking consciousness to take a backseat so that our dream consciousness can emerge and our soul can take flight.

Dream Exploration

Drumming Out the Soul

> *And it will happen, when you have come there to the city,*
> *that you will meet a group of prophets coming down from the high place*
> *with a stringed instrument, a tambourine, a flute and a harp before*
> *them; and they will be prophesying.*
>
> I SAMUEL 10:5

From the North Pole to the tip of South America, from Africa to Labrador to Woodstock, New York, drums are used as a vehicle for transporting the human soul. For many lifetimes around the world they have succeeded in freeing the spirit and taking us to places far away from the everyday.

1. Today drumming groups exist in many major urban areas and in a number of rural areas, too. Join one.
Usually these are informal groups of people who gather to drum on specific occasions, such as those represented by the phases of the moon. Find out if such a group meets in your area and ask if you can attend. Once there, let yourself go—move and dance to the drumming.

2. If you have a drum, use it.
Drums played directly with the hand, like bongo and conga drums, are best. If someone you know has a drum, plan a time to meet and drum together. Remember, this is not a test of musicianship. Let your rhythm emerge. Repetitive patterns are easy, and for drumming out the soul, easy is best.

3. If you have no drum, use a table or board.
"Play" it with your bare hands until the beat takes over and simply happens.

4. Give it some time.
Whether you are in a drumming group, drumming with a friend, or playing a drum on your own, keep at it for a while, with no expectations. You may begin to find that as your mind relaxes, you are transported, with new thoughts and images passing through your mind. Or your experience may be altogether different from this. Whatever you find, it's worth keeping.

◈ Dream Story

The Spirit Finds the Wealth
One day two men, Kamal and Prakash, entered a blacksmith's shop to rest. It was a hot day and both men were tired. Almost as soon as they sat down, Kamal fell asleep, his mouth relaxed and wide open.

Prakash, who sat by his friend's side, was about to fall asleep as well when he saw something amazing. He was both alarmed and astounded and had never seen anything like it before: From out of Kamal's mouth came his *jiwa,* his soul, in the form of a lizard, which soon began walking in search of something to eat.

Prakash watched as a dog saw the lizard and chased it into an anthill—but the lizard saw more. In the anthill it discovered a pot full of rupees, hidden in the recesses of the wall.

Prakash knew nothing of the rupees—witnessing this lizard was strange enough. The sight of it affected him deeply—truly it did—but he was a practical joker and even the appearance of a soul lizard did not dampen his desire to trick Kamal. He decided that while his friend was sleeping, it would be a good joke to cover Kamal's face with dust from the blacksmith's fire. Then, when Kamal awoke and saw his reflection, they would both have a good laugh.

The plan, however, backfired when the lizard returned from its journey into the anthill. It did not recognize the blackened face of its sleeping host. Kamal's soul could not return to him.

The lizard ran frantically back and forth, trying to find the body of its owner. Soon Prakash noticed it darting to and fro and realized what had happened. He quickly cleaned Kamal's face, and then the lizard, recognizing Kamal, entered his body and became Kamal's jiwa again.

Kamal had been sleeping, of course, during this adventure of his jiwa, but he saw his vivid dreams through the eyes of the lizard. When he awoke, Kamal told his friend what he had seen in the anthill. They both went to the hill then, where the lizard had hidden himself. And behold, they found a pot full of rupees.

A STORY FROM THE MURIA PEOPLE[3]

JOURNEYS TO THE SHADES

At night we close our eyes to release our spirits to fly and meet the spirits of others. What's more, in this night flight the spirits of the dead and living commune with each other. "We live with the shades," said an elder of the Nyakyusa people of Tanzania. "Continually, the fathers come to us, and also a wife who has died. The shades rise and come to us."[4]

The Tikopia people of the Solomon Islands call living spirits *mauri*. When a Temiar sleeps, her "head soul" leaves the body and in its travel meets the detached souls of other beings, including those of trees, flowers, animals, and other humans, both living and deceased. Some of these spirits might be either positive or negative *guniga*, or familiars, that actively provide guidance to the dreamer. The dreamer, happily, does not lose her ability to discriminate—with both helpful and hurtful guniga, she needs her powers of discrimination more than ever.

The form that the dream spirit takes is that of the body—but only to a degree. The Nupe people of Nigeria call this image of the soul *fifingi,* or shadow.

For these traveling night souls, time and space collapse; they have no dominion in the world of dreams. Among Puerto Rican spiritists there is the belief that in the nightly meeting with other spirits, our own spirits can travel anywhere, to any time. The Rwala Bedouins likewise feel the sleeping soul moves among spiritual beings from which it can learn hidden things of the past, present, or future. In our dreams, time and place can shift.

This transcending of time allows us to meet the spirits of the deceased. The Araucuno Indians of Chile often meet the dead in their dreams, and for these people, as for many others, such meetings are as real as those that take place in the light of our waking lives. Similarly, the Teda people of the east-central Sahara believe that dreaming about a deceased person means that the dreamer's soul has, in fact, encountered the deceased. If a Tarahumara Indian dreams of the dead, it may be that the soul is helping the dead with the planting. On the island of Truk, if a person dreams of another, it means that the souls of both people have flown away and met in the gathering of the spirits of the deceased. In an interesting variation of all these notions, if a Navajo dreams that he himself is dead, it means that in his dreams he has been in the next world with the spirits of the dead.

For all of these peoples and others, the telescoping of time and space in the nightly travels of the soul blurs even more the line separating the living and the dead.

◈ Dream Story

Antibelle Visits Me (and Leaves)

As far as I could recall, I had never dreamed about my aunt Belle. She was my first mother's younger sister and she lived in Glasgow, Scotland.

When I was a child, my aunt Belle and my grandparents would board the *Queen Mary* or the *Queen Elizabeth* and sail across the ocean to visit. I was quite young when we began to correspond and, somewhere along the way, she became Antibelle. It was our own special name for her.

In her middle age, Antibelle married Joe. When I was fifteen, I visited them for a rainy summer in Glasgow, and over the next few decades, she and Joe came periodically to the United States. After Joe died, my daughter and I took a trip to see her in Scotland.

In between these comings and goings, we mostly connected through letters—and it took years for each of us to stop apologizing for what terrible correspondents we were.

In my dream it was evening and Antibelle and I were at a party, which even in my dream I found to be somewhat odd. I was, however, happy that she was there.

The party took place in a large house with many rooms. For some reason or another I had to leave the room that Antibelle and I were in, and I told her that I wouldn't be long, but when I returned, my Antibelle was gone. Even in my dream I knew there was more to this than meets the eye.

When I awoke I immediately placed a call to Antibelle in Glasgow, but there was no answer. I dialed again later. Still no answer. I tried several times during the next week or two and finally gave up, thinking she was probably on vacation. It was winter, after all, and she and Joe had always taken winter vacations in Blackpool, though that was several decades ago.

Winter receded into spring when, four months after my dream, I received a letter from Glasgow. Joe's niece, who had been taking care of my aunt over the years, wrote to tell me that Antibelle had died. She had been ill for quite some time—in fact, she'd entered a coma from which she never recovered.

After a bit of figuring, I realized the coma enveloped her just about the time that she disappeared from the room in my dream.

⊚ Dream Explorations ⊚
Visiting with the Dead

Crossing the River

I once heard a story in which all those who had lived and died inhabited a place on the other end of time and space. In this place there was a river, and these people who had left earth dwelled along its banks, where any number of communions and interactions could occur between any combination of souls. For instance, Shakespeare could hobnob with Abraham Lincoln, or Beethoven could play duets with John Lennon.

In a similar way, we, the living, can meet the dead in the places of our dreams. These meetings are usually not at all scary. All people—even deceased ones—seem just like people in the world of dreams, where the boundaries between waking life and dream life, between life and death, can so easily dissolve.

In our waking lives spirits reside mainly in memory. Many of us have lost people who were close to us. To perhaps meet these people again in our dreams, memory is the first place to which we turn.

1. Choose someone who is no longer with you.
It may be someone who has died or someone who is simply no longer in your life. It's important to choose someone who is no longer a part of your life in order to force you to rely on your memory.

2. Write about this person in your journal.
Describe this person as clearly as you can—how he or she appeared and behaved, his or her mannerisms and personality. Include everything you recall to create as vivid a picture as possible.

3. If you have pictures of the person, spend time looking at them.
Then keep them somewhere near your bed.

4. Just before you go to sleep, close your eyes and imagine this person—picture him or her in your mind.
Be as clear as you can be—see the person's face, eyes, hair, and body. Visualize physical expressions that characterized this person. Then see if you can remember the voice of the person—the tone, inflection, and particular verbal expressions.

5. Visualize any interactions you had with this person.
Recall them as clearly as you can. Note your feelings. Then write down the memories very briefly in your journal.

6. Do this for several nights—a week is ideal—just before you go to bed.
Make sure these recollections are fresh in your consciousness as you drift off to sleep. Make sure this is the last thing you do before you fall asleep.

7. Note your dreams, recording them in your journal.
Once again, set no expectations.

Remembering to Remember

We've all probably had dreams of people who were no longer with us. Take time to recall them

1. Recall a dream you have had of someone who is no longer in your life.
Remember as much as you can about the situation and its circumstances. What happened? What was the setting? Very often we meet people in entirely different places from those they were connected with in waking life.

2. Note how you felt in this dream.

Were you happy or scared, sad or confused—how did you feel? Did these feelings correspond with how you felt when this person was in your life?

3. What was the nature of your exchange with this person in the dream?

Sometimes we exchange words with people in our dreams and sometimes we don't. But remember that words themselves are not that important in dreams because we often know or intuit what is said.

4. What was happening in your waking life at the time of the dream?

Are there any similarities to what occurred in the dream itself?

5. Write down the dream experience in no more than fifty words and put it under your pillow.

Those things placed under our pillow can have a powerful effect on us.

Try to practice this exploration in conjunction with "Crossing the River," above. And try to do them both for at least a week.

SLEEP, SPIRIT, BODY, SOUL

Sleep is an avenue for liberation of the spirit. But with this flight there are dangers. If the spirit is in one place and the body is in another, can the connection between the two be permanently severed? After all, death and sleep—death and dreams—are siblings. Many peoples have expressed this connection in their very language. The Tlingit Indians of Alaska declare that "sleep lies face to face with death."[5] And there are indeed clear similarities between the two states. In both death and sleep we surrender control. In both death and sleep we leave our bodies. In both death and sleep the spirit and body are separated—permanently in the case of death and temporarily in sleep.

For millennia people have struggled to harmonize body and spirit, to increase awareness of their connection. Humans have seen the nature of this connection as relating directly to a person's very health and well-being. To claim that the spirit influences health is another way of saying that the body, mind, and spirit are joined, if not one and the same. While some believe this is strictly a theological issue, traditional Western medicine more and more accepts the connection among the body, mind, and spirit, and the notion that when these are split, illness can occur.

Some people, like the Kol of central India, visualize the connection between the soul and the body as a thin thread. No matter how far a soul may wander in sleep, this thread remains intact. If the thread were to break, the sleeper would die. What's more, how this thread of connection is maintained and honored directly affects the physical health of the dreamer.

Many cultures believe that if the voyage of the dream spirit is disrupted, there will be illness, or even death. Much healing is connected with soothing and facilitating this connection between the wandering soul and the dreamer. In the southern Himalayas people believe that a thread in a dream can descend from the heavens as a call for the sleeper to become an intermediary between God and man. If this thread is cut, the dreamer will die. The Hmong people of Southeast Asia believe that illness can occur if the dream spirit, in leaving the body to wander at night, becomes lost. A healer must then locate the spirit and reunite it with the body. If this is not possible, the dreamer will die. In Korean folk culture, if a piece of paper is placed over the face of a sleeper, he will die, for the soul will not be able to find its way back into its host.

The Tarahumara of northern Mexico believe that the most common cause of illness is an ill-fated wandering of the soul. In their understanding, not all of the soul travels at one time, for if it did, death would surely result. What is left in the sleeping body, however, is not strong enough to resist attack or molestation. It is the job of the Tarahumara healer to find the lost, captured, or injured soul and return it to the compromised person. If the soul of the ill person has been captured by other spirits, it is the job of the shaman's soul to agree to a ransom.

The Iban people of Malaysia also fear the soul's loss or capture. They speak of the *semengat,* or soul, wandering abroad and becoming lost or the victim of a malevolent spirit that ensnares it. For the Iban, this is the most common cause of illness and a healer must attempt to recover the imperiled soul. And for the Southern Ute Indians of Colorado, the healing of illnesses consists of recovering the soul lost in dreams.

To our Westernized, rational minds, all this talk of soul travel and its potential perils must sound very suspect, even silly. But our language can sometimes indicate beliefs we never knew we had. How many times, for instance, have we heard the expression *lost soul*—"Poor fellow! He's such a lost soul." Perhaps our notions do not lie so far from those of so many of the world's peoples.

❖ Dream Story

The Cat, the Boy, and the Butterfly

The villagers couldn't help but notice that Jacobo was sleeping as if he were dead. Was he breathing? Yes, but his breath was ever so light.

Certainly the boy was no saint. At nine years old, he had gotten into his share of mischief, though nothing serious. Whatever you may say about him, Jacobo was not lazy. Indeed, his mother, Marguerita, often tried to curtail the boy's energy. He never seemed to stop moving, she said. He never wanted to go to sleep. In fact, she said, it was his little catnaps during the day that kept him so energetic.

This particular sleep, however, seemed like more than a catnap. Jacobo was not moving. He simply lay there, his mouth open, his eyes shut. Several of the villagers gathered around the boy. It was Jacobo's best friend, Felipe, who noticed the white cat. No one had ever seen it before. It was exceptionally large, well groomed, and wild.

The cat walked around and around little Jacobo, keeping a distance of several yards, then seemed to move closer. Felipe reached down and picked up a large white stick. When it grew nearer the sleeping boy, Felipe struck the animal.

The giant cat howled and a large white butterfly flew out of its mouth and into the open mouth of Jacobo. The boy's eyelids fluttered like butterfly wings, his eyes opened, and he sat up. His wandering soul, waylaid by the white cat, had returned.

A STORY FROM OAXACA, MEXICO[6]

ALARMING THE SOUL

It is important to our health not only that our spirit returns to our body, but also that it returns safely and gently. If the return is anything but gentle, illness and death can result. In the last several hundred years, we in the West have shocked ourselves into waking consciousness, awakened by the frightening ring or beep of an alarm built into our clocks. Of course, it's all because the marketplace calls—we must get to work on time. From the time that we enter school, we govern our lives by the clock. Buzzers, clangs, bells, whistles, radio voices—all bring us into wakefulness, move us to the next place. It is almost as if we are trying to overpower the spirits of the night instead of allowing ourselves to leave them slowly and emerge gently into wakefulness.

For thousands of years, many peoples have paid great attention to how we are awakened and have affirmed the importance of the gentle return of the spirit to the body of the sleeper. As the spirit or shadow wanders far abroad, it requires time to return to the body. For the Xingu people of central Brazil, there is a danger in waking a person too quickly, for the spirit, which was traveling in distant regions, might not have time to return and the sleeper might die. Rosie Plummer, a Paiute Indian, stated a strong sentiment of her people when she declared that when someone is sleeping, it is a danger to awaken him suddenly: "His soul may be away doing something. It may be far away. If the person is suddenly awakened, his soul does not get back. He will lose his mind. He will get sick and if a shaman does not doctor very soon, he will die."[7] So the belief was for many American Indian peoples. The Havasupai, for instance, also felt that there is a delicate thread between the nighttime traveling soul and the body of the dreamer and that any sudden awakening might not allow the soul time enough to return to the body.

For the Maori people of New Zealand, their understanding of the spirit and body in sleep also affects their social customs. They consider it a breach of manners to awaken a guest from sleep. If some necessity demands that they do, however, then it will be done gradually. The host first calls in a soft, low tone, gradually increasing in volume until the visitor is awake. Once again, the spirit must have time to return to its physical base.

Thousands of miles away from New Zealand, in central India, the Kol follow the same etiquette of waking guests, and for the same reasons. In Australia, the Murngin people don't awaken someone except as a last resort, and then it is done slowly and with great care and gentleness so that the soul will have time to return to the body. Heeding this principle of the gentle awakening are the new "Zen" alarm clocks that start with low soft sounds that slowly increase in intensity.

In Africa, the Azande and Masai peoples both caution against waking a person suddenly, for much the same reason we have learned—an aggressive awakening may lead to death. In Japan, too, the Ainu call for waking people slowly to allow the soul and body to reunite, as do the Bororo Indians of Brazil, the Toradja of the central Celebes, and the Andaman Islanders of the Pacific.

Among the vast numbers of people who believe in gentle awakening, there is a deep consideration for the sleeper and his welfare. Among the Balinese, this is merely a part of a gentleness inherent in the culture itself. Many Balinese, for example, who find it an offense to wake a person suddenly also consider patting a small child to be a form of violence.

Of course, we know clearly that people awaken suddenly every day and do not die, and that while you need a license to purchase a handgun, you do not need one to purchase an alarm clock. But to dismiss the experiences of innumerable other civilizations out of hand would be to miss the point.

If we look broadly at the fact that in the industrialized world millions of people awaken every day to the sound of alarm clocks every day, we may find truths that we can embrace. Perhaps something does die with sudden awakening. Perhaps the dream spirit dies. We violate our dreaming consciousness as we crash into waking life. Little wonder that so many people have difficulty remembering their dreams. It is as if we receive a morning shock treatment that pulls us violently into our daily lives.

Perhaps, ultimately, it is the delicate bridge between our waking and dreaming minds that is damaged a little bit more every morning.

ⓐ Dream Exploration ⓐ

Don't Be Alarmed

It's amazing how much the clock is part of our consciousness. Most people have the time inside their heads. For many, alarm clocks are not even necessary. This exploration allows you to see if this is true for you.

I. Check out your inner alarm clock.

Find out just what kind of clock you have inside your head. You might do this by guessing what time it is without looking at a clock or a watch. If you have a stopwatch, use it. Start the watch, close your eyes, and see if you can guess when sixty seconds have passed.

2. Try to wake up before the alarm sounds.

If you have a job that requires you to get up at a certain time and you use an alarm clock to make sure this happens, tell yourself that you will wake up before the alarm. You can have the clock set—just in case—but tell yourself that you will wake up before it goes off.

3. Try waking without an alarm at all.

Don't even set it as a backup. If you don't trust yourself during a workday, try it on the weekend or a day off. Once again, intention is important: Simply tell yourself that you are going to wake up at a specific time without any alarm at all.

4. Graduate to partial alarm.

When you feel comfortable waking without even setting the alarm, try using the alarm clock and your own inner alarm on alternate days.

5. The journal! The journal!

Keep a record of how you feel on both the alarm clock days and the days you rely on your internal clock. Do you notice any difference in how your day begins? Do you find any connection between the alarm clock days/internal clock days and those days you seem to get up on the wrong or right side of the bed?

6. What about dreams?

Finally, note how well you remember your dreams on both the days you use the alarm clock and the days you use your internal wake-up call. Then compare the two. What do you notice?

Regardless of our belief in the reality of our spirit's nightly journey, learning to awaken quietly, gently, and slowly, rather than shocking ourselves from our dream consciousness every morning, can be in our own best interest. And regardless of our belief in the soul, it may be the best way to honor that part of ourselves that flies to new times and places each night, bringing back wondrous visions and experiences.

Notes

1. Verrier Elwin, *Muria Murder and Suicide* (Bombay: Oxford University Press, 1943). I have taken the liberty of combining three stories related by the author.
2. Quoted in Phyllis Kemp, *Healing Ritual: Studies in the Technique and Tradition of the Southern Slavs* (London: Faber and Faber, 1935).
3. Verrier Elwin, *The Muria and Their Ghotul* (Bombay: Oxford University Press, 1947). Retold by Sarvananda Bluestone.
4. Monica Hunter Wilson, *Rituals of Kinship Among the Nyakyusa* (London: Oxford University Press, 1957).
5. Frederica de Laguna, *Under Mount Saint Elias: The History and Culture of the Yakutat Tlingit,* Smithsonian Contributions to Anthropology, vol. 7 (Washington, D.C.: Smithsonian, 1972).
6. Elsie Worthington Clews Parsons, *Mitla, Town of the Souls, and Other Zapoteco-Speaking Pueblos of Oaxaca, Mexico* (Chicago: University of Chicago Press, 1970). Retold by Sarvananda Bluestone.
7. Willard Z. Park, *Shamanism in Western North America: A Sudy in Cultural Relationships, Northwestern University Studies in the Social Sciences,* vol. 2 (Chicago: Northwestern University, 1938).

DREAMING WHOLENESS:
SHAMANS, HEALERS, AND DREAMERS

Sto, ovaj, upamtim, ja upamtim.
Sto ne upamtim ja sasnim no i
Well, what I recollect, I recollect.
What I don't recollect, I dream [up] in the night.

SERBIAN HEALING CHANT

Some people scorn dreams, omens and portents. But I know that
I have often made a diagnosis from dreams and, guided by two very
clear dreams, I once made an incision into the artery between the thumb
and the index finger of the right hand, and allowed the blood to
flow until it ceased flowing on its own, as the dream had instructed.
I have saved many people by applying a cure prescribed in a dream.

GALEN, GREEK PHYSICIAN AND PHILOSOPHER

All Crows agree that even the use of certain herbs for treating various diseases was
originally revealed to them in their dreams.

MAGPIE-ON-EARTH, CROW HEALER

Anyone can get to be a shaman by dreaming. In the dreams,
spirits such as those from the eagles, bear, owl, and antelope, deer, mountain sheep,
mole or falling star appear. The spirit that comes in
the dreams is the shaman's power.

PAIUTE INDIAN

We humans are divided beings, creatures of a number of unique dualities. Within the animal kingdom we are likely the only species that can feel one thing and simultaneously think another. Our mind may be in one place and our hearts—our emotions—in another. We can *believe* things strongly, but feel something entirely different. Our head—that is, mind—can be in one place and our body in another.

Many cultures have long accepted the duality of ourselves and world as an aspect of life itself. The Hopi and Shoshone, for example, see the entire universe as dual. As we learned in chapter 4, they believe that life energy, or Buha, is the energy that causes the earth to produce plants, birds to sing, and animals to know how to be. Buha is thus creative energy. At the same time, they feel the presence of Diji Bo, which is the negative force that destroys life, stunts creativity, and disrupts the connection between people and other life-forms. Each force has its own spirits: Positive life force spirits are called Buhagant and negative forces are called Tsoavite. A person can experience an imbalance of these life forces and become possessed by Tsoavite, which are often manifested as evil spirits in bad dreams.

One of the biggest questions to ask—and a focus of this chapter—is how we can be healed of such imbalances and divisions. With so many ways in which we can be divided or split, the dictionary definition of the verb *heal*— "to make sound or whole"—takes on real significance.

Wholistic medicine—treatment of the whole individual, mind, body, and sometimes even soul—is not new. For thousands of years humans have recognized that wholeness is health and that if the body and soul are not connected, if there is imbalance or division, illness results. Imbalance is the source of illness in the understanding of the Garifuna people of the Caribbean. In their view, every adult has five distinct elements: the physical body, the vital force or soul, the spirit double or guardian spirit and protector, the shadow or reflector, and the personality. Any imbalance in the interaction of these elements leads to illness.

Interestingly, for a vast number of the world's cultures, dreams are seen as a powerful means for overcoming such imbalances. While some dreams, such as those nightmares of the Hopi, have often been seen to reflect or indicate illness, dream consciousness, with its inherent surrender of control, has been looked to overall as a means to wholeness and health. For the Garifuna, for instance, it is through the *iuani*, or vital source—which travels in dreams—that directions for healing may come.

 Dream Story

Killing the Pain in a Dream

The pain in his shoulder was exquisite—sharp, like the point of an arrow. It had become familiar, but as an associate, not a friend. He had tried everything to get rid of it but nothing worked.

Then one evening he drifted off to sleep and dreamed that he'd been shot—an arrow, a bullet, or a spear had pierced his shoulder. The pain was real.

When he awoke, the pain in his shoulder had gone and did not return.[1]

For many of us here in the West, the split between our mind and our body or between our mind and our heart is enormous. We place great emphasis on teaching and learning what is taught. We are taught, at school and at home, everything from the multiplication table to what is right and what is wrong—but rarely are we taught to trust our own perceptions, our own truths. What do we think? What do we feel? These are questions we often ask and attempt to answer in the offices of our modern shamans—psychiatrists, psychologists, and counselors. These professionals take care of the mind and sometimes the soul, while physicians, our healers, take care of the body. Such a division of labor is often the reality.

Division—even in the roles of those who heal us—simply follows a model that is as old as the beginning of the development of machines and the modern industrial age three hundred years ago. But this mechanical model—especially as it translates to medicine—is not the only one in the world. Many other forms of healing are coming to the fore, such as acupuncture, homeopathy and other vibrational medicines (see chapter 5), and herbal medicine. Western ethnobotanists, for example, are "discovering" curative plants that have been known and used in other cultures for millennia.

There is a great deal to be healed today—and there is a great deal of wisdom about healing that exists outside of our experience. As they were for many Native Americans, dreams were the very basis of life for the Mohave Indians. Mohave healers relied on dream guidance for specific remedies, but even more, the Mohave felt that in dreams we return to the very source of creation, where the origin of all things is revealed.

In a recent study of a traditional Puerto Rican community, it was found that healers often associate a physical illness with a spiritual cause. The role of wives and mothers is to seek advice on healing from those spirits in their dreams. The author of the study discovered that in this way, clear cases of asthma, fever, and menstrual cramps have been cured by dream consciousness.

Dreams are powerful, indeed.

⊙ Dream Explorations ⊙
Health = Wholeness

Making the Connection
The reality is that we all have times when we feel divided or split, but in our highly specialized societies of the industrialized West, most pronounced is the split between the mind and soul on one side and the body on the other. Just as waking consciousness must gently make the acquaintance of dream consciousness, so the mind must gently get in touch with the body. In this exploration, we give it a try.

1. Create for yourself a place and time where you will not be disturbed.
This does not have to be at bedtime, but if that's the place and time that works for you, go for it. Wherever and whenever, it's most important that you're able to focus.

2. Turn your attention to an area of your body where there is some tension, close your eyes, and focus there.
This tension need not be severe enough to be causing physical pain. A small amount of tension is more than adequate for this exercise. If you have no tension anywhere in your body, you may be eligible for the "loose as a goose" award. You might find tension where you carry your stress (for instance, in the neck and shoulders), or you may find it where you've had an injury or wherever you commonly feel aches and pains.

3. What color is this tense area?
That's right—what color is it? Imagine a color for this place of tension. Allow it to sink in, and remain aware of how this color feels.

4. What is the shape of this tense area?
For example, is it circular or rectangular? Does it have a shape all its own?

5. What is the texture of this area?
From steel wool to cotton candy, from plate glass to steam, from water to rocks to melting candles, the world is filled with objects that have textures. Some are bumpy, some rough, some gritty, some

smooth like glass, some soft and doughy, some sharp-edged. What texture does this area have?

6. Of what substance is this spot made?
Is it metal, glass, wood, fire, earth, something else? Be as specific as you can.

7. Does this tense spot move around at all?
If it does, focus on how it moves and where it moves.

8. Go to this area.
Be in it. Note how you feel when you're in it.

9. Move this tense spot.
You're in it; it's yours. You can move it any way you wish, anywhere you wish.

10. With eyes still closed, take in all that you've noted.
And allow yourself to return to your usual state. Compare how you feel now with how you felt before the exploration.

This exercise can be explored with two people, which makes its impact even greater. Another person's presence and participation can help to make deeper realizations. One person acts as the reader, asking questions 3–7, while the other, after locating an area of tension in his body, takes the role of the respondent, noting the answer to each question and saying it out loud. In each instance, the reader repeats the respondent's answer before proceeding with the next question. After the respondent has completed steps 8–10, he and the reader switch places.

Mending a Split
Health is wholeness. Split is illness. When we are divided against ourselves, we are in stress. Of course, mending the division between our waking consciousness and our dream consciousness is the substance of this book, but each of us has a number of other divisions that we can identify—and once we have, we are on the way to healing them. Here is a healing that came in a dream.

1. List on a piece of paper a few splits that you recognize in yourself.
List each split using the following language. For a division between thinking and feeling: "What I think and what I feel." For a split between wanting and actually getting: "What I want and what I get."

2. Think of specific circumstances or situations in which these splits present themselves.
Write a brief description of each. Remember, it's always helpful to be as concrete as possible. And remember not to judge yourself in

this exploration. Such divisions are part of the human condition. Everyone experiences them.

3. Rewrite each split so that it's "mended."
For example, in the split between "What I think and what I feel" I might write, "I am aware of what I feel." Similarly, a split between "What I want and what I get" might become "I want what I get." And a split between "What I show and what I feel" would become "I show what I feel."

4. Bring these to bed.
Read them aloud before you go to sleep. You might even put them under the pillow.

DREAM HEALING IN THE WEST

In the dream state, where we are bound neither to our bodies nor to the physical plane, our dualities can disappear. We can then experience realities unseen in waking consciousness. By allowing us to transcend the waking universe, dream consciousness allows us to transcend our bodies, creating a potent force for healing that people have used for ages.

Beyond freeing us to transcend the body, dream consciousness also liberates us to transcend time and space—which means that any healing guidance received in the dream state also transcends time and space. An incident involving just this type of transcendence serves to illustrate the healing power waiting in dream consciousness. Decades ago people were astonished at the work of Edgar Cayce. Known as the Sleeping Prophet, Cayce would enter a form of sleep and, in that state, learn healing modalities. These he would use from his altered state to heal people thousands of miles away.

In the West, dream healing both began and reached its apex in ancient Greece, with the recognition of Asklepios, the god of healing. So strong was the cult of Asklepios that all over the country the Greeks built healing sanctuaries dedicated to him. As we discovered in chapter 2, the method of healing in these sanctuaries was dream incubation. Seekers underwent purification through diet and meditation until they received a dream that called them into the sleeping chamber. There they waited in a narrow, womblike room for a healing dream in which Asklepios, in any of his forms, would appear. It was this dream visitation of the god that healed.

The practice of dream healing eventually spread from Greece to Rome, where Asklepios became Aesculapius. Soldiers and slaves, emperors and patricians all visited the temple of the healing god to receive guidance in their dreams.

With the fall of Rome, however, ancient dream healing practices also declined. The new Christian church cast all of the pre-Christian gods into the flames of hell and, in time, the entire notion of illness and disease changed. Hippocrates had viewed disease as the result of imbalances, and the famous Roman physicians Galen and Rufus added to this conception. To the early Christian church, the devil was the cause of all illness and disease. In fact, this belief held sway through the medieval period. As for dreams, the church in medieval times held that only saints could distinguish between dreams sent by God and dreams sent by the devil—but it made clear that most dreams were sent by demons. As a result of this outlook, dream healing suffered a serious decline in the West. We have yet to return in numbers to this form of healing that we once deemed so powerful.

A MULTITUDE OF VIEWS ON THE CAUSES OF ILLNESS

Among the peoples of the world there exists a variety of notions as to the causes of illness and disease. Recently, an American acupuncturist and healer wrote a book provocatively entitled *All Sickness Is Homesickness*. Home is our center, the source of nurturing, the basis of life itself. In the author's understanding, if all sickness is really homesickness, caused by being dissociated from our home, then healing comes from finding our way.

For many cultures, this loss of home is reflected in the soul being lost, which is itself the basis of illness. And the time when the soul may most easily go astray is during sleep.* Among the Tarahumara people, for example, it is in the land of dreams that illness is found, for if the soul, which wanders during sleep, cannot return to reenter the body because it has been frightened, lost, or eaten, the sleeper will sicken. Not all of the soul wanders at once—if it did, death would result—but the little that is left is insufficient and the person is thus open to illness. The Iban people of Malaysia also feel that the soul, wandering abroad in dreams, can become lost or captured by an ill-meaning spirit. In fact, in their understanding, the most common cause of illness is that the soul, wandering in a dream, is unable to return home. Similarly, the Hmong of Southeast Asia believe that disease is caused by the soul wandering too far

* See chapter 5.

afield, and if it does not return, the body will die. The Ashanti people of Africa likewise attribute a person's illness to a lost dream soul that left when that person was sleeping. The role of the healer, according to the Ashanti, the Iban of Malaysia, the Algonquin of North America, and others, is to bring the soul back home, often by finding a substitute for it in it's new place. This is a task that can be met only in a dream state.

From its very pervasiveness, it's easy to see that the lost soul is a powerful human metaphor. After all, the split between our home and ourselves is one of the most profound there can be. When our soul is lost—when we are separated from our very source of life—only illness can result.

But a lost soul is not the only cause of illness. While some dream spirits are benevolent and aid in healing (as we shall soon learn), there are also those that work mischief and cause disease. For this reason, the Navajo are among those cultures who see dreams as a source of either health or disease, based on how they affect the people who have dreamed them. Ultimately, they feel that the gods, dreams, and sickness are causally connected.

Sometimes ancestors can be a cause of illness. The Garifuna people are extremely watchful of the various aspects of ancestors, believing that if they appear in a dream, they must be respected. Dream visitations signify that the ancestors are asking for something. If they are ignored, they may start to punish their descendants by afflicting them with sickness. If it is not clear what the ancestors want, the dreamer might call a *buye,* or healer, who would read the indications and determine the correct ritual.

Even the healing power of dreams might itself be a source of illness. For some cultures, rejection of a healing spirit's visitation could bring illness. Among the Southern Paiute people, for example, because healing power came through dreams, whoever received a visitation was to accept it honorably and responsibly. Rejection of the spirit power brought illness. The way to cure such an illness was to accept the calling of healer proposed by the dream spirit.

SPIRIT HELP IN HEALING ILLNESS

On all continents and through time, people have gone to dream space to find the keys to healing, for there healing spirits—like Asklepios—could appear and guide.

The mountain Lapp people speak of a companion or follower who hovers around every person and offers protection from disaster. Far from perfectly helpful, however, this spirit can also bring destruction. Each family has its own companion spirit inherited by the son and daughter from the father and mother, respectively, and it can take the form of any animal. It is only in dreams that people can see these guardian spirits.

In many cultures the past lives in the present and the lessons of those long gone find their way into the dreams of those still living. In this way, the spirits of ancestors have been involved in dream healing. The Bhil people of Rajpipla and West Kandesh in India experience their deceased relatives in dreams, though these relatives cannot instruct and foretell. But among the Senoi people it is common for the spirit of a recently deceased healer or adept to appear in a dream in order to instruct the dreamer, who then himself becomes a healer. Similarly, among the Garifuna people, an ancestor may appear in a dream to instruct a healer as to the cause of an illness. In North America, too, among the Sinkaietk and Okanagon people of the Pacific Northwest, a deceased relative might present healing powers in a dream.

Many Native American peoples, such as the Mundurucu, have consulted ancestors in their dreams to receive guidance from those long gone. A Plateau Indian aspiring to be a healer might have slept in or near a cremation place so that he could come into contact with the very forces of life and death. There he might have received the help and teaching of deceased healers, who became his dream guides and mentors. (For more on the role of ancestors in healing, see the section "The Shaman's Dream Guidance," on page 153.)

⊚ Dream Exploration ⊚

Honoring the Ancestors

Most of us, at one time or another, in one way or another, feel compelled to honor our ancestors. It is part of being whole and healthy, and even if we haven't received instruction from any forebear, in either dream consciousness or waking consciousness, it instructs us by giving us a sense of home, of where we come from. Honoring our ancestors is, then, a form of healing.

Hanging pictures on the wall or placing them in scrapbooks is one way to honor your ancestors. Visits to a cemetery are another. Wearing or carrying with you an object that has been passed down through the family and even making a recipe that's been handed down are ways of paying respects. This exploration provides one more way of honoring those who have come before.

1. Find a picture of a relative who preceded you by at least two generations.
This means anyone in a grandparent's generation or before. It can be a photograph or a painting.

2. Take some time to study the picture.

Look at the person as if you are seeing him or her for the first time. Study the features. Look into the eyes. Note the shape of the mouth or nose. Note what the person is wearing. Note his or her expression, the way the person holds him- or herself.

3. Thank the ancestor for giving you life.

Say this out loud and, while you do, note how you feel. At first you might be self-conscious, but after you've let that go, see what feelings are stirred.

4. Create a small shrine dedicated to your ancestors and keep it in place for a while.

The shrine might be on a table or small shelf, or part of a larger dresser or shelf. Include in it more than one photo or other likeness, if you wish. Find other objects that will remind you of one or more of your ancestors—notes or letters in their handwriting, a piece of jewelry, an article of clothing that's been handed down to you.

Include whatever feels right to you—flowers or candles, which seem to be a universal symbol of light, life, and remembrance. Use your own creativity to develop a place that stirs your memory.

5. Spend a moment each day at this shrine.

No need to do anything special. Simply take the time to notice and remember. So often the pictures that we place around the house become invisible the more we see them. Perhaps you might spend some time at your shrine right before going to bed. Of course, note the dreams you have after doing this.

The Iroquois of North America had their own particular healing spirits, called False Faces, that appeared in dreams. The name derived in part from these spirits' distorted features. After a dream visitation, the dreamer would awake and render the spirit's face as a mask.* Of course, not every Iroquois dreamed of a False Face. These spirits presented themselves only to those who would be worthy of being a healer and willing to take on this role. If a person dreamed of a False Face while ill, it was an indication that the spirit would cure him. Anyone who received a dream visitation from a False Face was qualified to become a member of a False Face band.

---

*A large number of False Face masks are in the collection of the American Museum of Natural History in New York City.

☼ Dream Story

The False Faces Heal Drags-a-Canoe

Her people called her Drags-a-Canoe. To the white people she was Lydia Sugar. She was a Mohawk woman in generally good health, until one day her face began to swell. She had no idea of the cause of the swelling and tried various remedies, but nothing seemed to work. It remained and seemed to have become a permanent part of her life.

Then one night, while Drags-a-Canoe was sleeping, she dreamed she saw two men entering her door. At first she was alarmed because they were wearing False Faces.

The two men looked at her and said, "We come to cure you." And then they blew at her through their hands and left.

The next morning she was better. The swelling had gone down.

That evening she dreamed again of the False Faces. The two from her first dream returned with a leader and others. They burned Indian tobacco, rubbed her with ashes, and ate mush.

Drags-a-Canoe had good health from the time of that visit, and in her dreams, as thanks, she periodically invited the False Faces into her home.

There are other specific spirits besides False Faces that enter dreams to aid the dreamer in some way. Among the !Kung Bushmen of Africa, one such spirit is Gaolna, who is generally benevolent and appears in dreams to give direction to hunters and aid to healers, telling the dreamer, for instance, where to find a tree with honey or where an anthill is located. One medicine woman described how the spirit had come to her in a dream and taught her a healing song. He then stood beside her, instructing her to sing the song over and over until she had learned it.

The Bella Coola people of the Pacific Northwest also have a leading spirit, Álquntäma, a beneficent and healing spirit that appears in dreams to aid people in a variety of ways. The Sac and Fox Indians have a benevolent spirit, Meshaum, that makes its presence known in dreams, and likewise the Iban have guardian spirits that instruct them in their dreams.

Echoing the dream healing incubation temples of the Greeks, the Iban people of Malaysia have their own dream houses in which a healer's dream helper appears, usually in the form of an animal. Similarly, in a number of North America cultures the spirits of birds and animals appeared to people in dreams in order to impart their instructions. Thus, the Chippewa (Ojibwa) received healing dream power from animal spirits, and a Blackfoot accepted guidance when it was brought by an animal spirit who agreed to be his helper. A Yokut Indian of what is now California might also have received his power from a bird or an animal. For the Yokuts, dreams featuring animals— visions that were both sought and not sought—were considered a source of supernatural powers.

Among the Temiar people of Malaysia, the spirit of either a familiar plant or a known animal may appear to the dreamer, be released in the dream, and subsequently bestow upon the dreamer a song that imparts the ability to heal. In North America, the Mescalero Apache healer similarly received power and guidance in a dream from the spirits of plants or animals. Such a spirit would assume animal or plant form before assuming human form. This particular belief is telling in that the native peoples of North America, perhaps more than any other peoples, saw the spirits of animals, plants, and birds as the holders and benefactors of healing power, which they shared through dreams. The Jicarilla Apache of the desert, the Sinkaietk of the Pacific Northwest, the Maricopa and Paviotso of the West—all experienced healing spirits as animals that appeared in dreams. (For more on animals as the bearers of healing powers, see the section "The Shaman's Dream Guidance," on page 153.)

Dream Story: Two Mothers, Two Animal Spirits

The Dog

When I was ten months old, my mother died. She was a physician and had diagnosed the leukemia herself. Her parents, sisters, and brother were across the ocean in Great Britain, but my father's family moved in full force to take care of the widower and his young son.

With them they brought a dog, a shepherd named Brutus, who was so old that he was missing most of his teeth. Immediately, Brutus became my guardian. No matter where I went, he was with me. I could stick my fingers in Brutus's ears and even eyes, and the old dog endured with a patience that was almost maternal. But if anyone approached me with even the slightest hint of anger, Brutus would bite, albeit mostly with gums. He was a fierce protector.

A half-century later I had gone through many changes in my life's path. This particular one found me as a psychic reader. I sat in a hotel in the legendary Borscht Belt of the Catskills.

A client sat next to me, looked at me before I began the reading, and asked, "Do you have a dog?"

It was a strange question and not one that people normally ask before receiving a psychic reading. Actually, about twenty years earlier I'd had two dogs—two extremely stupid basset hounds. While I've always been a cat person, throughout my life I've been able to relate to dogs. It had to be a vicious dog, indeed, to in any way ruffle me, even when I was a child.

"No," I answered. "Why do you ask?"

She replied quickly. "Because I see an old shepherd dog curled around your feet, glaring at me."

I swallowed and told her about Brutus.

Three days later, my daughter, Hira, and I went into in a laundromat. A good friend of Hira was sitting on one of the dryers with a dog, one of those one-of-a-kind mutts so smart and sweet that people wish they could create a breed like it.

As I walked past the dryer where my daughter's friend sat, the dog leaped off and ran behind me, growling. I looked behind, surprised—I'd never received such behavior from a dog. But the dog wasn't looking at me directly. It was looking around me, behind me, and in front of me.

He was looking at Brutus.

The Spider

Hariet, my movie partner, and I were rushing to catch a show. As we drove off down Sawkill road, a lovely country way, I noticed a spider hanging from the window visor. It was tiny and dangled helplessly as we swayed around the curves of the winding road. I didn't like it at all. Even an arachnid that small bothered me.

Hariet took the spider by the single strand of thread it clung to and placed it outside the window. We both joked at what the little being must have thought, suddenly propelled at fifty miles an hour.

"Why are you afraid of spiders?" Hariet asked

"I don't know. They just scare the hell out of me. Always have."

"But the spider is the Mother," Hariet answered.

I had known that in many cultures, spiders were the old wise women of the animal kingdom, that for many people the spider was the Great Mother. But there in the car, this information at this time resonated inside of me in a way it hadn't before.

We all have fears, many of which date back to our childhood. But rarely can we pinpoint the actual event that first triggered a fear. My fear of spiders was an exception to this, however—I knew exactly when it was that I became frightened of spiders.

It was a year and a half after my mother had died, and my father had remarried. She was a young schoolteacher, full of life and patience. She would become my second mother.

I was two. My father, my new mother, and I went for a kind of honeymoon together. It would be very shortly thereafter that my father would leave for the war and not return for four years. To me, at age two, the world was meant to be explored. In this case, the world consisted of a cottage that my parents had rented on the shore in New Hampshire.

My father and new mother sat on the bed. I was on the floor. Even though I walked quite well, for someone my size there were still advantages to crawling, and so I began crawling across the floor, heading toward the fascinating electrical outlet on the wall. The world was my oyster and the way to explore it was through my fingers. Those tiny holes looked so inviting—and my fingers were probably just small enough to fit.

Even if my parents on the bed had seen me crossing toward that outlet, chances are I wouldn't have listened to any noise they might have made to stop me. In fact, there wasn't very much that anyone could have done at that point to prevent me from reaching my goal.

But when I was no more than an arm's reach from that electrical outlet, out of nowhere a spider raced across my path. It was large and hairy and it ran right between me and my goal in the wall.

To this day I remember how terrifying that spider was. I remember how I screamed in fear and leaped back from the outlet. I can see now that only that spider at that time could have prevented me from reaching the wall. I can see now that it was a wise spider, indeed—a mother spider, perhaps my mother.

⊚ Dream Exploration ⊚

Calling Your Animal

Wherever we may live—in big cities, small towns, or in forest or countryside—animals are all around us. Humans have never lost their connection to the animal world, and animals have not lost their connection to humans. This is especially evident in the intimate connection between people and their pets. But even creatures that aren't pets interact with humans, even in the most congested city—everyone has had contact with squirrels and pigeons, starlings and spiders, and, perhaps, cockroaches.

In the Native American worldview, there are no bad animals. All animals and birds and plants are simply part of the whole. We are part of the animal species and the animal species are part of us.

This exploration can better attune you to those creatures of the world that bring dream healing to many.

1. Close your eyes.
There are fewer distractions when your eyes are closed, which makes it much easier to focus.

2. Think of your favorite animal.
It can be a bird, an insect, a fish, or a mammal. It's fine to choose an animal you've never seen in the flesh. My father, a physician, was away in the war when I was six. He used to write me letters in which he created the continuing saga of a friendly amoeba. Years later, when I visited India, where amoebic dysentery ravaged non-Indians, the notion of the amoeba did not conjure up the same things for other people that it did for me.

3. Visualize this animal.
In your mind's eye, focus on the animal's features: its colors, its shape and size, its movement and mannerisms, and so forth.

4. What do you like about this creature?
Think of as many different things as you can.

5. Where have you encountered this creature?
Do you have one around home? Did you see it in a zoo? In a field? In a book or magazine?

6. Give the animal a human voice.
Would it be deep and resonant? Would it be high pitched? Would it be loud or soft? Would it be musical? There are many different kinds of voices in this world.

7. If you were going to speak to this creature, what would you say?
Don't worry—nobody will hear you. Simply use your imagination.

8. If the creature could speak to you, what do you think it would say?
What would it have to say about life? About the world? About humans?

9. What advice might this creature give you?
Again, this is about using your imagination. You have to know what you want addressed and you must pretend that you're this creature in order to be able to offer any wisdom.

Try this exploration a few times—before going to bed or, perhaps, with another person so that each of your creatures can speak to the other.

SHAMANS AS HEALERS

Striding the world of both dreams and waking consciousness as healer is the shaman. The word *shaman* itself comes from the Tungus language of Siberia, where it derives from the verb *scha,* which means "to know." A shaman, then, is one who knows, but this knowledge is not a static thing. Instead, it is a process—the process of knowing that comes from a consciousness beyond the ordinary waking consciousness. It is not, as ordinary knowledge is, something that is part of other people's experience. It is one's own experience.

Across cultures the name changes. In Turkish the shaman is *kam.* In Yacuto in central Asia the female shaman was *udujan* and the male was *ojan.* For the Samoans it is *tadibe.* For the Lapps the shaman is *moita,* and for the Hungarians it is *táltos.* Western observers have used the term *medicine man* in referring to shamans among the native peoples of America, but this can be misleading if we think of medicine as a practice made up of prescribing tablets or injections. Among Native American peoples the term *medicine* encompasses much more than it does in our Western allopathic, physician-oriented tradition. Medicine, for the indigenous peoples of North America, refers to a kind of spiritual power. Naturally, a healer's medicine is power imparted.

The *Cambridge Encyclopedia* defines a shaman as "a person to whom special powers are attributed for communicating with the spirits" and for influencing them "by *dissociating* his soul from his body. The spirits help him do his chores, which include discovering the cause of sickness, hunger and any disgrace, and prescribing an appropriate cure." Steven Larsen, a leading scholar of shamanism, has called the shaman the "archetypical technician of the sacred." Jamie Sams, a Native American scholar of indigenous American peoples, says that a shaman is "a healer who has experienced the world of darkness and who has fearlessly confronted his own shadow as much as the diabolic of others, and who can successfully work with the powers of darkness and light."

Generally speaking, there are three key abilities that define shamans: First, they can, often at will, enter an altered state of consciousness; second, they can in this state feel themselves travel; and finally, they use these journeys to acquire knowledge or power most often to help and heal the people of their community. Shamans derive their power from their unique position between the everyday world and the world of spirits and from their unique ability to travel from one world into another. Having entered the unknown and experienced the greatest fears, shamans are both the masters and the students of dream consciousness who can aid in healing.

Dreams and shamans are, in fact, inseparable, for the dream is the avenue the shaman healer must travel to obtain the power of curing. The medicine men and women of the Meskwaki Indians of the American Midwest received diagnosis for illness in dreams. They also received, in the dream state, visions of what herbs to use and in what combinations. After administering the remedy to the patient, the shaman often returned to the dream state further to dream over the case.

This illustrates one of the most fundamental abilities of a shaman healer: that of being consciously able to reach the dream state, to make his waking consciousness meet his dream consciousness. The result is neither a state of full dream consciousness nor a state of waking consciousness, but rather a blending of the two. To the observer it appears the shaman is neither awake nor asleep, but both.

The *loima-yamus* or shamans of the Water Nomads of Cape Horn were able to fuse waking consciousness with dream consciousness at will in order to deal with specific questions and cures as they arose. The Caraja healers of Brazil also have the ability to put themselves into the dream state at will, and in the arctic, the Chukchi shaman beats his drum as a way of transporting himself into a different consciousness, where his soul can see whatever he wishes.

The visions received in the shaman's unique state of both dream consciousness and waking consciousness represent the meeting of the two worlds. The shaman's attempt to reach this union, however, does not constitute an attempt to control the dream state, as in lucid dreaming. It is an attempt to join the two states, rather than control them.

The shaman's means to this dream guidance, to this place between the worlds, can take various forms. The shamans of the Southern Paiute have, for over a century, sought power in the Sun Dance. The power dreams of the Mohave, Yuma, Akwa'ala, and Desert Cahville shamans often use jimsonweed as a means to this alternate state. The Papago neophyte shaman was kept in seclusion until the dream visions came, and the Arapaho shamans received their dream power through periods of prolonged fasting and isolation.

Not all cultures, however, have supported a conscious searching for dreams. Even among the native peoples of North America there are differences in this practice. Among the Iroquois and many of the nations west of the Rockies, shamans receive their power primarily through unsought or spontaneous dreams.

In the Temiar culture, the dreamer does not enter the dream in order to ask the spirits for help and the patient does not request a healing. It simply comes.

Whether sought or unsought, whether spontaneous or "captured," the dreams make the healer. The power and effectiveness of the shaman healers is directly connected to the volume and quality of the dreams they receive.

⑨ Dream Exploration ⑨

On the Wings of the Breath

Many techniques have been used to alter consciousness. Drumming and dancing are two of the most common, but in Japan a variation of Buddhism arose in which, in fact, doing nothing was emphasized. Zen Buddhism has no goal—its practice is simply sitting, which is the meaning of *za-ze*. The ancient Japanese poem says it perfectly: "Sitting silently, doing nothing, Spring comes and the grass grows by itself."

We are such doers in the West that if we can drop doing—even for a second—our consciousness changes. Here's a simple adaptation of a simple Zen technique.

1. Find a comfortable spot.
You don't have to be on a mountaintop in Tibet to practice this exercise. Just make sure you're comfortable. It also helps if you can count on being undisturbed for a while.

2. Close your eyes and take a few deep breaths.
Breathe in through your nose and out through your mouth. Make sure that the breaths are deep and slow. There is no rush. Do it a few times.

3. Then let yourself breathe normally.
No need to keep up the deep breaths.

4. Simply count your breaths.
Each inhalation and each exhalation is a full breath. Just count. There's nothing else to do. If you find your mind wandering, simply bring it back to the breath.

5. Do this for about ten minutes.
You can set a timer ahead of time, if you wish.

Try this exploration at various times of the day—in the morning or afternoon, or right before going to bed. And remember, there are no goals.

Often dreams are the avenue by which a shaman first receives his calling. The Kpelle people of Liberia distinguish between two kinds of people who become healers. The first are those who spend time in the bush studying with another healer. The second are called *ngung ma nuu, or* "two-headed people," who learn healing by entering into an association with a dream spirit. Similarly, among the Shona people of Africa, a healing spirit makes its presence known in the dreams of a particular person who will then dream of practicing as a healer and will be shown what to do. Similarly, the traditional *curanderos,* or healers, of the Southwest receive their gift in a dream. Among the Tapirape of Brazil, the *pance,* or shaman, is the one who dreams frequently and thereby gains firsthand knowledge of the supernatural world. Among the Mohave, the calling of all chiefs, war leaders, and shamans comes through dreams.

The Shoshone people classified into one of three groups those who received supernatural powers in dreams: the general practitioners or shamans of general curing ability; specialists, or those shamans able to cure only specific ailments; and those whose powers were solely for their own use and benefit.

Often healers are called by their dreams to a specific field of healing. Inca healers received specific instructions on what they could heal. Midwives in a number of cultures were visited in a dream by the person who gave them power, instruments, and specific training. In many cultures it was common to have a very clear definition of precisely what a healer was called to heal in his dream. Some were called to cure gunshot wounds, some to make babies grow straight; one healer might have been called to tend rattlesnake bites, while another was called to fix broken bones. In Zimbabwe, healing men and women are called *nganga.* A Western writer interviewed a large number of these healers and discovered that most of them received quite specific information in their dreams. One healer had a dream that showed him how to cure a swollen abdomen, and a second that showed him how to cure pneumonia by making incisions in the wall of the chest. Other dreams followed that showed him which herbs to use to treat headaches, how to cure diarrhea with blood, and how to handle scabies. Jaromeka, a woman healer, also dreamed her herbal recipes.[2]

Like Jaromeka, the Kpelle of Liberia receive specific dream instructions on herbs and how to employ them, as do healers in rural Thailand. In Borneo, as well, specific medicinal charms are revealed by spirits in dreams. Among the Blackfoot the designs of the medicine bundles as well as the constituents of these bundles came from dreams.

In many cultures, the shaman's dreams begin in childhood, a period of life that has often been seen as a time of power. As Pablo Picasso said, "I used to draw like Raphael, but it has taken me a whole lifetime to learn to draw like a child." It is natural, then, that the innocence of childhood is a place where power dreams reside, even if they are forgotten. The Mohave people, who felt that all great success in life depended on having the right dreams, believed that the unborn soul, still in its mother's womb, journeyed to Avikwame, their sacred mountain, to receive special powers. After a child was born, she would forget the prenatal journey but would dream it again, usually in adolescence.

Children around the world have received dreams imparting healing power, and the adults in many groups have both accepted and encouraged such dreams. In Zimbabwe, adults encourage children as young as ten to find the correct remedies to cure a sick person. If a child is successful in doing this, adults will encourage her to continue with the next dream. In Liberia, among the Kpelle people, some children are said to receive their medicines from heaven. They are born with them but may consult dreams for answers to particular problems. Shoshone healers begin in childhood, receiving dreams in which spirit helpers convey healing power. A Southern Ute child may begin as early as the age of seven or eight to begin to dream of strange and wonderful things—a precursor to healing power. Among the Maricopa people, power dreams come first in childhood. In the northeastern part of what is now Washington state, the Salishan people encouraged girls as well as boys to search for guardian spirits. Starting at sunset the child would head for a destination several hours away. Arriving there, she would stay awake all night until a vision came. Out of this dream vision came shamanistic healing power.

Sometimes the shamanistic dream experience was part of the rites of adolescence. Among the Yokut people, a person wanting to become a shaman would seek dreams beginning in adolescence. Similarly, among the Kaska people of the southeast Yukon, a girl often received healing spirit guidance during menstrual seclusion and a boy began his search for a power dream around the age of sixteen. Those adolescents who received dream visits continued on to teach themselves. No formal instruction in shamanism occurred.

 Dream Story

The Voice in the West Wind

Grandfather had told it. He was in the valley and the West Wind was blowing. It sounded different; the West Wind made a new sound that day. It was like this: *ziii . . . ziii.*

He left the valley that day and thought about the sound of the wind. In the middle of the night the sound entered his head and spoke to him—just a whisper. He could barely hear it. He wanted to be a healer and so could tell no one about this experience.

A few nights later the West Wind's voice again came to him from the place where he first heard the whistling. He woke up then, put on his clothes, and ran back to the place where first he heard its voice. There the voice spoke again in a whisper: "Now be a good man, doctor your own people, and save them always as long as you live. Go back to where you were sleeping. Wake up before sunrise. Drop yourself into the water, bathe. Do this on four mornings.

Then begin to doctor some man, but do not charge any fee the first time. See what you can do for him." Thus did the voice in the West Wind speak. And thus did Grandfather become a healer.

A STORY FROM THE WASHO NATION[3]

THE SHAMAN'S DREAM GUIDANCE

The shaman's dream was a means for some force to visit the potential healer to bestow its power and to share its wisdom. Among the Blackfoot people it was *natoji,* or sun power itself, often disguised as a person, that visited the dreamer.

Most common, especially among North American peoples, the spirit that appeared in the dream took the form of an animal. While it might also take the form of a man, woman, or child, it usually appeared as a bear, coyote, wildcat, lion, eagle, mountain sheep, badger, owl, or other wild creature. The Paiute novice dreamed repeatedly of an animal that he would struggle with until he overcame it. Once overcome, the animal gave the novice his power not simply as a gift but as something that had been earned by the dreamer. In this way the potential shaman was actively involved in transforming the power of the spirit and making it his own.

> Joe Green, a Paiute, summed up the experience of animal dream helpers in this way: "Indians were put here on this earth with trees, plants, animals, and water, and the shaman gets his power from them. One shaman might get his power from the hawk that lives in the mountains. Another may get his power from the eagle, the otter, or the bear. A long time ago, all animals were Indians (they could talk). I think that's why the animals help the people to be shamans."[4]

 Dream Story

The Gift of the Eagles

Once when I was on the Teton River, I came to a large cottonwood tree in the top of which some bald eagles had their nest. They had killed a very large rabbit and carried it up to the nest. I said to myself, "These birds seem to have some power. I will sleep here." So I made a shelter of brush to sleep in. In my sleep I heard the two eagles disputing with each other as to their respective powers. The male turned himself into a person, took up some yellow paint, rubbed it on his arm, then took a knife and cut the veins. Then the female bird turned herself into a woman and called to me, "Now, watch me, I shall cure this man." She took some white paint, spat upon it, and rubbed it upon her forehead. At once the man was cured. Then she addressed me again, "Now, my son, when you doctor a person whose veins have been cut, you should do as you saw me do." Since that time I have had the power to stop bleeding.

A STORY FROM A BLACKFOOT MEDICINE MAN[5]

Other peoples also experienced dream helpers as animals. For instance, the guardian dream spirit of the Temiar shaman usually took the form of a tiger. A Yuman child might receive a bird or animal in a dream, and though he would dream of the creature repeatedly, he would not speak of the dream until he was a man, when, in his late twenties or even much older, the creature would tell him to begin curing.

But the dream spirit could take a number of other forms besides animals. A power dream for a Southern Ute child might have been one in which the sun or moon or stars appeared, whereas thunder might have appeared to both the Shoshone and Apache shaman. The River Yuman people received the healing dream spirit in the form of a mountain.

Sometimes the spirits in dreams were not those of creatures or forces in the natural world, but were instead those of people, often of departed shamans who taught novices. Among the ancient Scandinavians, those who aspired to be *noidi,* or shamans, received dream instruction from departed noidis. Similarly, for the Andaman Islanders it is the spirits of the dead who communicate with the shaman, or *oko-jumu,* enabling him to cure illness.

Interestingly, the process of mourning has long been one path to connection with healing dream spirits. One of the most famous healers of the Crow people gave testament to this fact. Magpie-on-Earth had lost her first husband. Deep in mourning, she was traveling near the Big Horn when one evening, while camped in that area, she received a vision of spirits. They surrounded her, showing her a variety of herbs along with how to prepare them and which to use for a number of diseases. She took the lessons of the spirits and went on to become a famous healer, noted for her successful treatment of many serious illnesses.

The Western writer who interviewed the healing men and women in Zimbabwe discovered that a number of them received specific dreams of healing following the death of a relative. One, Makubaba, the son of an herbalist, began to dream about herbal cures after the death of his father. Tambadzai, a woman who specialized in sucking out illnesses and treating barren women, began to dream of her cures after her aunt, an herbalist, died. Perhaps mourning brings us closer to spirits because it brings us closer to our hearts. Another Crow woman, Muskrat, lost her husband and her brother and was pregnant while grieving the death of her husband. A spirit came to her in her sleep, showed her a weed, and told her that if she chewed on it, she would give birth without suffering. And so she did.

SHAMANS IN THE LAND OF DREAMS

The careful balance between the waking consciousness and the world of dreams is the working territory of the shaman. The challenge of the shaman is to obtain, in this state, information that is relevant to the particular case at hand.

One way in which healers have attempted to bridge the gap between the waking question of how to treat an illness and the answer of the dream spirit has been to go to sleep with a significant object, such as an article of clothing belonging to the sick person. In the Libyan desert women healers use this technique; they are aided in learning the cause of a person's illness by sleeping with the patient's garment. Similarly, an Iroquois healer wrapped an ear of corn with an item of clothing belonging to the sick person and then placed this bundle under his pillow so that he might more easily dream of the person's healing.

But physical objects are not the only means to bridging the ill person and his cure. The healers of the Northern Yaka people of Zaire use both smell and touch to access dream guidance. A healer will smell something that has been in contact with the afflicted person in the area of the heart. Then, the night before a consultation, the patient will rub a coin on his chest, near his heart. The healer will then put the coin in his ear and keep it there while sleeping in order to learn the message.

In some cultures, dream songs and rituals are part of the healing modality. For the Temiar and Senoi, spirit guides reveal healing songs to the dreamer. Regarding rituals, the Mayawyaw of the Philippines have several ways of determining which might be used for a particular illness. Sometimes the nature of the disease presents the right cure. And while some of these might be familiar rituals and techniques that have been shared, new healing rituals come through dreams.

⊚ Dream Exploration ⊚

Work It Out in Your Sleep

"I'll sleep on it." We've all heard this expression, which today means, "I'll give this particular problem some thought and rest," but we probably haven't thought about its origins and real meaning. The fact of the matter is that people have been sleeping on things for a long, long time—it's been the shaman's and healer's means to finding a cure, and has been the best method of problem solving in many areas of human endeavor, when, after days or even years of wakeful thought, it seemed no answer would come. Answers can miraculously come in dreams.

A classic example of this was the breakthrough of Professor Herman V. Hilprecht, one of the leading scholars of the ancient Middle East, who struggled with two Babylonian inscriptions that had not been recognized as complementary. He worked at it until he could think about it no longer—but that evening, as he slept, an old Babylonian priest appeared in his dream and gave him the key to solving the puzzle. The professor had slept on it and had been rewarded.

1. Wait until you have a problem that just will not be solved in the waking state.
This is the kind of problem you've been wracking your brains to solve.

2. Right before going to bed, state the problem as clearly as possible.
Make it as clear as you can to yourself—spell out exactly what it is that you are trying to solve. It's always best, of course, to say it out loud *and* to write it down in the journal.

3. Tell yourself that you're going to let your dreams help solve the problem.
See what happens. If it doesn't work the first time, don't give up. Keep it in the back of your mind as a method to try whenever you have a problem that just won't be solved in waking consciousness.

◈ Dream Stories:
Two Healing Stories from the West

Dream Dates and a Cure
Christopher Wren was a man of many talents and interests—all of them in the realm of science. A Fellow of All Souls at Oxford, he made drawings of the human brain for a textbook on anatomy; he devised a method of blood transfusion, which was later used to successfully transfuse the blood from one dog to another; he invented a surveying instrument to measure angles, an instrument to find direction at sea, and military devices for defending cities and fortifying ports. In 1657 he became professor of astronomy at Gresham College in London. Mathematician, optician, and astronomer, Christopher Wren was a prime example of the scientific flowering that began in the seventeenth century, but it is as the architect of St. Paul's Cathedral that he is best known.

While in Paris in 1671, Wren became ill and feverish, was unable to urinate, and suffered from pains. He sent for a physician, who, according to the practices of the day, advised him to be bled, thinking that he had pleurisy. Wren put off this treatment for one day.

That night he dreamed that he was in a place where palm trees grew—he supposed it was Egypt—and there a woman offered him dates. The next day he sent for dates, which cured him of his illness.[6]

The Shamans and the Doctors

The conference was held in Council Grove, Kansas, in 1971. There, ninety medical doctors, psychiatrists, psychologists, and psychoanalysts were gathered for the annual conference on voluntary control of internal states. A medicine man of the Western Shoshone was there at the invitation of the conference to both participate and give the keynote address.

During the conference, one of the participants badly injured his leg and had to use crutches to walk. The Shoshone shaman, after his address, agreed to perform a healing on the injured man. The doctors examined the man before the healing, certifying that indeed he was in pain; had a large swollen, discolored bruise on his shin; and could not put his weight on the leg.

The Shoshone's healing ceremony for the man lasted an hour and a half, after which the bruise had completely disappeared, and along with it the pain. The swelling had gone down as well and the man was able to put his full weight on the leg. Indeed, he was able to walk normally without the aid of crutches.

The doctors thoroughly examined the man again and certified the absence of any indication of a bruise or injury. They could offer no explanation of the quick recovery in the context of Western medicinal knowledge.[7]

A DEMOCRACY OF HEALING

There is something quite democratic about the healing quest. Each person can find her own dream power—her healing spirit. Among the Klamath people, for example, everyone may seek supernatural aid—men and women, boys and girls, and everyone, at least once in his life seeks such aid. Similarly, among the Pukapuka people of the Cook Islands there was no hereditary shamanic power. Each healer began anew through his own dream experience.

In fact, there is even the notion that shamans, in their calling, receive healing. For the Paiute and many other peoples, the very notion that the healer doesn't pick his calling—that the calling picks him—implies the basic belief that healing heals the healer.

To think that all knowing comes solely from dream consciousness would be as myopic as thinking that all understanding comes from the waking mind.

People, over time and space, have discovered that dream inspiration and waking consciousness must work in harmony. Among the Apache of the nineteenth century, dreaming was one of many criteria that determined a healer. But practice in the waking world was essential and, of course, nothing succeeded like success. The Havasupai felt that dreaming came before practice, that a potential shaman needed the dream experience, but that practice in waking consciousness determined the ability of the healer.

The Chemong people of Malaysia establish a clear balance between waking practice and dream instruction. A shaman, or *putao,* can be anyone, man or woman, who must study hard in waking life with an existing *putao.* It is only after this study that he or she may meet spirit guides in dreams.

Healing is about wholeness, integration, mending divisions such as the fundamental split between our waking consciousness and our dream consciousness; between the conventional medicine of the West and the traditional medicine of many cultures of the world; between the heart and the mind that can justify to some owning vehicles that cost more than it would to feed a family of six for a number of years.

The ancient Chinese believed that every human being is a microcosm of the universe. If this be the case, we are all microcosms of the vast splits that rend our world. Our dreams, then, can help both us individually and the entire world to become whole, to heal.

Notes

1. This was told to me by Juhi Bendahan, who treated the person in the story.
2. Recounted in Michael Gelfand, *Witch Doctor: Traditional Medicine Man of Rhodesia* (London: Harvill Press, 1964).
3. A Washo relates this tale as told by his grandfather in Robert H. Lowie, *Ethnographic Notes on the Washo* (Berkeley: University of California Press, 1939). Retold by Sarvananda Bluestone.
4. Joe Green, quoted in Willard Z. Park, *Shamanism in Western North America,* in *Northwestern University Studies in the Social Sciences,* vol. 2 (Chicago: Northwestern University Press, 1938).
5. Clark Wissler, "Ceremonial Bundles of the Blackfoot Indians," in *American Museum of Natural History Anthropological Papers* 7, part 2 (1912). Retold by Sarvananda Bluestone.
6. Brian, Hill, *Gates of Ivory* (New York: Taplinger, 1968).
7. Richard Ora Clemmer, "A Comparative Study of the Effects of Non-Indian Jurisdiction on Hopi and Western Shoshone Communities," Ph.D. dissertation, University of Illinois, 1972.

REMEMBERING THE FUTURE:
DREAMS, DIVINATION, AND DÉJÀ VU

*And it shall come to pass afterward, that I will pour out my Spirit upon all flesh; and
your sons and your daughters shall prophesy, your old men shall dream dreams,
your young men shall see visions.*

JOEL 2:28

*The people know everything by dreams, how they are going
to die and other things.*

WOMAN OF THE HARE INDIAN NATION

*The Dyak revelation is communicated by means of dreams
or visions, they therefore consider dreams as oracles from the gods; they
read their dreams and pretend to understand them as we do
the Holy Writ. In all their pursuits they are guided by their dreams.*

WILLIAM HOWELLS,
MISSIONARY AMONG THE DYAK PEOPLE OF BORNEO, 1908

*If there be a prophet among you, I the LORD will make myself known unto him in
a vision, and will speak unto him in a dream.*

NUMBERS 12:6

SPEAKING OF THE DEVIL:
THE BACKGROUND OF FEAR

What does the word *clairvoyant* call to mind? We may think of fortune-tellers, mediums, supernatural sensitives, perhaps an old aunt who knew when something (usually painful) was going to happen. Maybe it calls to mind somebody who gave you a reading on the boardwalk in Atlantic City—and she was on the money. Maybe you think of someone a little bit scary, or someone who has a gift.

Clairvoyance, a French word, literally means "clear seeing." But we understand it to mean clear seeing beyond ordinary sight. In the tongue of the Klamath people of the American Northwest, the word for clairvoyance is *dode'uka*. In their language this word also means "to dream." Clairvoyance, then, is the vision of dreams. Echoing this, the Trumai Indians of central Brazil speak of dreams as a way of seeing while sleeping.

Second sight is another term for clairvoyance. Here, too, the language conveys meaning. Our first sight is the ordinary visual perception of the eyes in waking consciousness. Without it, we are blind to the world around us. The prejudice of our culture holds that most things that cannot be perceived with first sight are nonexistent or, at best, irrelevant. But millions of people have ascribed both relevance and reality to all things perceived with second sight. For the intuitive among us, imagination and creativity guide us to see ourselves and the world with new eyes—with second sight. There is more to reality than the optic nerve alone determines.

Sixth sense, ESP, clairvoyance, psychic ability, intuition—there are so many terms that attempt to describe this consciousness. Of course, part of the reason for this abundance of labels is that it is difficult to define. The word *divination* seems to best express the power that yields second sight. For most of our history, countless different cultures have expressed the transcendence of routine consciousness as contact with the divine. Divination is not fortune-telling, which is little more than a fraudulent perversion of our legacy of divination, a vulgarization of something very precious. Fortune-tellers, throughout history, have played upon human fear of the unknown and have provided an illusory security for countless clients who want to know what is going to happen in the future.

Divination, by contrast, transcends the boundaries of waking space and time and enters the unknown. From the beginning, it has been linked to dream consciousness, that state in which we go beyond our waking routines. In dreams, we enter the unknown.

While knowledge deals with that which has already been discovered, imagination steps beyond knowledge to the unexplored frontier. It is the dream of the wheel, the dream of taming fire.

In this way, imagination and divination are sisters. Each of them deals with the unknown and each goes beyond knowledge to step into territory that is unexplained. As we've seen before, without imagination there would be no vision of what could be. Similarly, divination also involves stepping into unknown territory.*

Our Western culture has, unfortunately, made divination into many things it is not. The cinema is replete with those who have "special powers"—the Wicked Witch of the West with her crystal ball, magical men who need only look at you to know your thoughts, fairy tales, horror movies, cold science fiction—the message is that divination and its step into the unknown is both scary and unreal.

In truth, the ability to see beyond routine consciousness is something that belongs to all of us. Divination is part of our heritage as human beings. Yet we in the West have lost our connection to the roots of divination, and the agent of this loss has been a fear of divination that has been part of Western history for a millennium. For a thousand years Europe lay in darkness, ruled by an absolute theocracy. Those who openly swayed from official dogma faced death as heretics. In the late medieval period the Inquisition of the Catholic Church burned millions of people, mostly women. During the Reformation, as the power of the Church began to disintegrate, the new Protestant powers enforced their own form of theology and the fires continued. In England, Protestants accused and burned Catholics and vice versa—and to the clergy of both, the penalty for divination, an abomination in their eyes, was death.

Divination contradicts all organized theology and any attempt to place it in any one worldview. Like imagination and creativity, divination is profoundly individual and cannot be taught or tested—and like imagination and creativity, it cannot be controlled. It is no wonder that all organized religions in the West have portrayed it as an evil. As compared to the one truth of each organized religion, in divination there are infinite truths, each of which emanates from an individual. In many organized religions a priest, minister, rabbi, or imam interprets the divine truth for the rest of the flock—if each individual determined his own spiritual reality, there would be no need for any form of gospel. But with divination each person can, on her own, transcend her routine waking consciousness to contact the divine.

---

* For more on this, see Sarvananda Bluestone, *How to Read Signs and Omens in Everyday Life* (Rochester, Vt.: Destiny Books, 2001).

The irony, of course, is that every organized religion began with divination. The Bible, for instance, is filled with visions, prophecies, and, yes, dreams. By the early Middle Ages, however, theologians began to determine that only special people could pay attention to their visions or dreams. From Judaism through Christianity, the pagan gods were agents of Satan and dreams were often their vehicle.

The Judaic-Christian religious tradition in the West divided the divine itself into good and evil, and both angels and devils fought for souls. In the early Middle Ages dreams were perceived as a bridge to the supernatural, as they had been for thousands of years, but they could be sent by angels or demons. Dreamers were not to trust their dreams, which became one of the main battlegrounds in the struggle between God and Satan.

By the time Europeans reached the New World, the Inquisition had effectively stamped out heresy and any trust in dreams and divination. Little wonder that the emissaries of the Inquisition had no use for the dream practices of the indigenous peoples they encountered in the Americas. Speaking of the Incas, a Spanish official of the mid-sixteenth century wrote of sorcerers who "sleep and in their sleep speak with the devils and they tell them all that is happening and [all] they wish and ask for. They are sleep sorcerers."[1]

❄ Dream Story

"They Are Not Good Christians That Regard Dreams"

King William II, son of the Conqueror, was called Rufus, due to his red hair or perhaps his fiery temper—but in either case, he was no one to be tangled with. He always quarreled with his brothers and he was most unpopular with the clergy, for he loved to extract large sums of money from them.

On the night of August 1, 1100, however, King William was thinking of none of this and instead dwelled on his hunting trip, which he would begin the next day. He went to bed with visions of stags and arrows.

But his slumber was troubled. Throughout the night he dreamed that an extremely cold wind passed through his sides. Strange, he thought the next morning, for it was, after all, summertime. When he told the hunting group of his dream, some tried to dissuade him from going, but William refused to call off his sport. "They are not good Christians that regard dreams," he answered.

King William II went hunting that day. And that day an arrow flew wildly during the hunt and killed him.

The prejudice against and fear of divination and dreams is part of the Western unconscious. Unlike most cultures throughout the world, we have lost much of our individual connection with our own skills of divination and have replaced them instead with superstition.

Superstition is belief in a body of knowledge that does not come from experience. Few people have actually experienced misfortune after a black cat has crossed their path, but millions believe it, even if only a little. How many people have actually known seven years of bad luck after breaking a mirror? Yet how many believe the superstition, or at least feel a nagging little dread after throwing away the pieces of glass?

To be sure, the West has no monopoly on superstition. We are all superstitious in one way or another, if only to try to achieve some degree of security and control in a world where there is very little of either. Superstition creates the illusion of certainty in an uncertain existence and is a fixed way of looking at reality. In this sense it is similar to religion.

Superstition and fear are brothers. Black cats, broken mirrors, umbrellas opened indoors, the number 13—all are fearful signs. At the same time that superstition provides a false sense of security—after all, we can avoid walking under ladders—it also reinforces fear, which in turn reinforces superstition in a cycle that can keep us from accessing our own inner wisdom.

⊚ Dream Exploration ⊚

Superseding Superstition

We all have our certain superstitions that we believe, even if our conscious mind tells us that they're silly. Originally the number 13 was sacred, referring to the number of lunar months in a year. Each lunar month is roughly equivalent to a menstrual cycle. Thus, in the days when people revered the Goddess instead of the God, when folk worshiped the moon instead of the sun, 13 was magical and important.

With the advent of Judaism and Christianity, the Goddess was no longer in charge. It was the light of the sun and not the pale glow of the moon that lit the theology of the West. Males ruled and with the new religion, 13 became a number of evil and bad luck—a superstition that was all about politics.

Knowing all that, however, doesn't stop me from breathing a sigh of relief when I pass my thirteenth lap while swimming. To some extent, we all believe some superstitions. So if we can't beat them, let's join them.

1. Make a short list of your own superstitions.
Come on, now, *everybody* believes a few of them! They can be superstitions that are yours alone—you know, the lucky shirt that you have

to wear on every first date. One person I know who acted in a number of plays in college had to listen to Aaron Copland's "Appalachian Spring" before call on the opening night of every show in order to ensure a successful performance.

2. What do these superstitions have in common?
Try to determine what all your superstitions share. If you really can come up with only one, describe its features.

3. Choose one superstition and violate it.
For example, I might rejoice when I hit that thirteenth lap. Or, and this one is really big, I might actually adjust my watch to a new time zone *before* the plane lands. Take a superstition and turn it upside down.

4. Do this for a few days.
Note how it feels. Are you surprised you've survived? After you've upended one superstition, try it with another.

DIVINATION NOW AND ITS PLACE AMONG DREAMS

While Einstein showed us that time does not follow a straight line, he wasn't the first to note this. It seems as if most cultures have seen time as far more complex than we in the West have seen it. Our notion of past, present, and future is very linear, a two-dimensional world that is the province of the fortune-teller.

Prophecy and divination, however, are not two dimensional. In dream consciousness they transcend time and space. Divination, very much rooted in the here and now, focuses on seeing clearly into the moment so that one can see beyond it. Jesus said to the Pharisees, "O ye hypocrites, ye can discern the face of the sky; but can ye not discern the signs of the times?" The signs of the times are here and now.

Vision is the last of our senses to develop and the one that is most conditioned by our upbringing. We learn how to see. For example, those who have spent much of their lives reading or performing work that is close may, perhaps, lack a developed sense of visual depth, or may be less likely to perceive certain things that are at some distance from themselves. Because our sense of sight develops and is conditioned, and eventually deteriorates, what we visually discern is not always representative of what is.

Divination does not rely on our sense of sight. In fact, with divination, we see better with our eyes shut, which explains its long association with dreams. In dreams, too, we go beyond our eyes.

Of course, as we are learning, not all dreams are divine or prophetic. In the fourth century a student of dreams named Macrobius divided dreams into five types. Some of these, he felt, were useless, like the *visium*—hypnagogic delusion occurring when we are half awake and half asleep, which he believed to be worthless because he considered only dreams we have while sleeping to be important. Macrobius was interested only in the three types of dreams that revealed truth: the *oraculum*, in which an authority such as a parent, priest, or god appeared to give the dreamer a picture of what was going to happen and to advise the dreamer on what to do; the *visio*, which was a vision of a future event; and the *somnium*, a figurative vision of the future.

Like Macrobius, the Mohave people made a clear distinction between ordinary dreams and great dreams. However, for the Mohave all dreams had meaning so that even ordinary dreams presented signs that could be helpful to the dreamer. The Crow, too, made the distinction between ordinary dreams without spiritual significance and dreams that were filled with visions.

The word *mnyam* means "omen" to the Tiv people of Nigeria. For them there are two types of omens, the mnyam of the day, which are portents, and the mnyam of the night, which are dreams. For the Tiv, some dreams are lies and some are true.

The Iban people of Malaysia attach a greater importance to dreams than to omens, believing that all dreams can tell us a great deal, even if they are not prophetic. Omens are perceived in the waking consciousness, but for the Iban the lessons of dreams are much longer and are more lasting. When a dream foretells something and conflicts with an omen, the Iban will definitely listen to the dream.

The Dogon people of the Sudan have six main forms of divination, one of which is the dream. Similarly, the Azande people of the Sudan and Congo speak of oracular dreams—the dreams in which the soul journeys and allows the dreamer to see what is in store.

For many cultures the messages in dreams were merely a guide, not a map. After all, divination is not an exact science. Our dream consciousness can provide us only different insights into our waking world. While there are many kinds of dreams, it lies with the dreamer to determine the nature of the dream and it remains for each person to determine his dream's lessons.

◈ Dream Story

A History of What Was Yet to Be

He was of the Bear Clan of the totem of the Makwa of the Ojibwa people. His was an ancient tribe on the banks of what would later be called Lake Superior, and his role in the tribe was *jossakid*—a seer, one who pays attention to his visions.

He fasted, took vapor baths, and shut himself off from the rest in the prophet lodge, and then he dreamed. He could not ignore his dream, for to do so would be an affront to the spirits who brought it to him.

After he received his dream, he gathered his people and revealed what he had seen. It was both wondrous and frightening to those who heard:

Men of a strange race, with skin as white as snow and long hair covering their faces, came across the great water to the land of his people. Strange were their wondrously large canoes, and stranger still were the poles in these canoes that stuck up straight and were hung with large cloths that billowed in the wind.

The snow-faced men carried long knives and wore iron shirts, but most terrifying were the long sticks these men carried. Fire and thunder and smoke came from them and filled him with terror, even in his sleep.

For a day and a half the people listened to the jossakid, and then they agreed to send an expedition along the lakes and the great river toward the rising sun to search for the dream. For weeks—for months—they traveled, passing through the lands of friendly tribes who knew nothing of the dream or of its meaning.

Finally, the delegation of the Ojibwa reached the mouth of the great river, and there they found an amazing sight. In the forest was a great clearing—even the largest trees had been cut down as if by the teeth of a giant beaver. The jossakid told them they had reached the place of the men in his dream. They were frightened as they saw the power in the clearing and more fearful as they thought of meeting the men who had made it.

A few days later they reached an encampment. The men there were white-skinned, their faces covered with hair, like beasts. They carried long knives and some held the thunder sticks. Later, the Ojibwa would see the large canoes.

And so it had been foretold in a dream. The Ojibwa of the Makwa had met the French.[2]

DREAM INTO ACTION

For many peoples intuition has been a tool. The revelations of dream consciousness can inform the actions of waking consciousness. Intuitive dreaming, for many, was considered creative. Rather than encouraging people to be passive observers, the understanding and clairvoyance that dreams imparted allowed people to change their world. Thus, the connection between dream consciousness and the waking mind is interactive. Nowhere is this clearer than in the stories of the Australian Aborigines.

For 150,000 years, the native people of Australia have told their stories of Dreamtime, the epoch when the world was created. As the Ancestors moved across a barren and featureless land, each day they acted from their dreams of the night before. In this way they created the ants, emus, hills, valleys, fowl, plants—everything.

In a similar way, in the *Yogarasistha,* an ancient sacred Hindu text, the visions of dreams were opportunities for humans to create their world by dreaming it as the gods created by dreaming.

The intuitive knowledge of the dream world is the basis of all in Mohave life. Shamanistic power, myths, songs, good fortune in war, success with women or in gambling—every special ability was dreamed and then passed into the waking world. A dream, for the Mohave, might give foresight of some obstacle to a goal or might provide the solution to a problem. In Mohave life, knowledge came only partly through experience. In each person, knowledge was enhanced by dreams.

In the southern Philippines, isolated from central Luzon, is the province of Nueva Vizcaya. A river valley surrounded on three sides by mountains and home to the Mayawyaw people, Nueva Vizcaya has long been an area little influenced by outsiders. The Mayawyaw, mostly farmers and hunters and fishermen, consider dreams not merely auguries of good or bad luck, but the causes of fortunate events or misfortune as well. For these people, the dream and waking life exist cooperatively; what is true in dream reality becomes true in waking reality.

Other cultures believe that intuitive awareness in the dream state can be experience unto itself. Many Native American cultures feel that the wisdom of dreams comes first. The Maricopa people see dream experience as the basis of all success—dreaming precedes learning in the waking state, and, while each individual acquires skills through practice, the Maricopa believe this is neither successful nor significant unless the individual has dreamed.

The intuitive dream can be a guide, allowing us to take home with us the wisdom that we receive in our dream consciousness. The Naskapi of Labrador go first to their dreams for guidance and then take to their waking life whatever knowledge they receive. A Naskapi hunter might have a dream about hunting, but it might be vague, without focus on a specific locality. It might not tell him exactly what route to follow or what landmarks he will find, but instead gives a more general indication. The hunter then must bring back the dream divination to his waking consciousness. He might then use divination tools in his waking state in order to focus his question. In this way his dream divination leads his waking divination.

Many cultures believe, like the Naskapi, that there is an interaction between waking reality and the reality of dream consciousness. In Malaysia, for instance, the Iban people believe that no one can achieve success unless it is foretold in dreams. On the other hand, they feel that such dreams come only to those who are worthy, diligent, and capable. Having a fortuitous dream is not like winning the lottery, but instead is the result of preparation. In this the Iban recognize a working partnership between waking consciousness and dreaming consciousness.

🌀 Dream Exploration 🌀

Bringing It Back Home

As I started to organize this chapter I realized that I had an abundance of material. First, I had a tremendous amount of research material. It seems as if every culture includes divination as part of its dream experience. Second, divination is a subject close to my heart. It was the focus of my first book, *How to Read Signs and Omens in Everyday Life,* and I continue to be a practicing psychic reader. I soon realized the meaning of the phrase "an embarrassment of riches." There was so much material that I didn't know where to begin or end.

That night I had a simple dream in which I was looking for something. Particularly I was searching for something that would pull my life together. Just what parts of my life I was pulling together were unclear in the dream, but the object of my search was quite apparent because I found it. It was something that looked very much like an elastic band that girls use to keep their ponytail together. It both pulls the hair together and allows it to hang loose.

I awoke and realized that I needed something to pull this chapter together. Even the word *ponytail* seemed to be guiding me—if I didn't want the chapter to sound like a phony tale, I'd better find something to keep it together.

The dream didn't tell me exactly what to do. It simply pointed me in the right direction, just as the dream pointed the Naskapi hunter in the right direction without giving him the precise location. For my chapter, I knew I had to clearly define divination and then pull the many threads together. My intuitive dream had helped inform my waking action.

In this exploration, you give your dreams a chance to do the same.

1. Choose one of your recent dreams.
Try to recall how you felt both during and after the dream. Also try to write what was going on in your life at the time of the dream.

2. Look for a window in the dream.
That is, see if there is something in the dream that can help you in waking life. Remember, you won't necessarily find what you think you'll find, but keep looking, nonetheless.

3. Apply the dream to your waking life.
That's right—take an aspect of the dream and bring it into your waking consciousness. Do something with it, or simply allow it to help you adopt a different way of looking at a situation. At first this might seem difficult and, certainly, elusive. However, if you make the attempt, something can happen.

POWER SPIRITS AND DREAM MESSENGERS OF THE DIVINE

Where do intuitive dreams come from? Many humans have believed that such dreams represent visits from spirits of superior wisdom and intelligence to the dreamer in her waking consciousness. These special dreams that give the dreamer both insight and foresight are thus literally bequeathed to the dreamer. The Dyak people of central Borneo see dreams as the way that gods and spirits convey their commands or warnings to humans. People might desert their homeland or even separate from their spouses on the basis of such divinatory dreams.

The Mohave experienced two kinds of dreams that enabled the dreamer to transcend waking time. The simpler of these could shed light on the immediate future through the appearance of symbols. Anyone could have these dreams often. But in another kind of power dream, more potent and more rare, the dreamer went back in time into the presence of Mastamxho, the founder of the Mohave nation. This powerful ancestral spirit then foreshadowed what would occur and transmitted this to the dreamer.

Sometimes divinatory ancestors came in dreams to the Nyakyusa of Tanzania. They were not always agents of goodwill, however. Sometimes they brought illusory food and other times they brought truths of what would be.

From Kenya to Utah, many peoples tell of the appearance of divinatory spirits and guides in dreams, and some have believed it is a deity himself who has given the gift of foresight. The Lapps reported on spirits of divination appearing to them in sleep. The Gros Ventres of Montana have two kinds of dreams: One is a visitation by a dream spirit, a power dream whose message is clear. The other is the kind of dream that requires interpretation. Near the roof of the sky, in the Himalayas, the Mun people feel that dreams are sent by supernaturals. The Mun also divide dreams into two classes: those that foretell a future natural event and those that foretell the supernatural. In Kenya, the seers and healers are called *waganga*. A significant group of these gifted people claim their skill came either as a gift from God or the spirits or in a dream. Even members of organized religions tell of such dream encounters. In a Mormon tract an author sees God appearing and declares, "[T]he Lord frequently communicated through dreams and visions, often-times revealing to prophets the events of the future even to the latest generations."[3]

All kinds of dream spirits were included in the Greeks' assemblage of gods. The leader of the group was Hypnos, the god of sleep. (It is interesting that our word *hypnosis* is a state that is in between sleeping and waking.) Hypnos is the twin of Thanatos, the god of death. In this relationship, the Greeks linked sleep and death in much the same way as the Yakutat Tlingit people, who say, "Sleep lives face to face with death." Other siblings of these twins were Moros, god of doom; Nemesis, goddess of divine retribution; and the Fates, who were female spirits that punished offenders against blood kin. With deities like this, sleep was probably not an unbridled joy for Greeks.

Both Hypnos and Thanatos inhabited the Underworld. The offspring of the god of sleep were the Oneroi, the gods of specific kinds of dreams. The most important of these was Morpheus, who appeared to humans in the shape of a man and, at the same time, gave shape to the beings that inhabited dreams. Together with his brothers, Phantasos, Icelos, and Phobetor, Morpheus visited mortals in their dreams. In rural areas of modern Greece, people still consider dreams to be messages from God. The ancient Iroquois supreme god was Tha-ro"-hya-wa'-ko", who was always concerned for the welfare of human beings and worked through A-ï-ko", the dream god. For the Iroquois a dream was a message from Tha-ro"-hya-wa'-ko". The Iroquois believed the commands and requests of such divine dreams were the responsibility of the dreamer and the tribe. To ignore the lessons of the dream would be a sacrilege, much like ignoring God himself.

Throughout the world people have explained dreams as messages from the divine, and for many societies certain dreams are, by definition, divination. In the Western Judaic-Christian tradition, God speaks through dreams and foretells events. Within the Bible, Daniel and Joseph in the Old Testament and Joseph, the husband of Mary, in the New Testament stand out as the beneficiaries of divine instruction through dreams. The dream is a vehicle throughout the world for bringing deities into the consciousness of the dreamer. There people have felt the divine presence and have learned lessons they could bring to their waking lives.

Divination gives instruction to the dreamer and in this way forges a link between the dreamer and a higher consciousness. The divine consciousness then becomes the higher consciousness of the dreamer.

 Dream Story

The Messenger of the Gods

The Dream had received its message from Jove, the Supreme God. It went out and soon reached the ships of the Achaeans, where it searched for Agamemnon, son of Atreus, for it was to him that the message was to be delivered.

The Dream found Agamemnon in his tent, wrapped in a deep slumber. Shifting its shape, Dream took the form of Nestor, whom Agamemnon honored first among his counselors, and spoke thus to the sleeping Agamemnon:

"You are sleeping, son of Atreus. You are one who has much care upon his shoulders. Hear me, Agamemnon, for I come as a messenger from Jove. And, though Jove be not near, he thinks of you and pities you."

The Dream continued to the sleeping king:

"Jove bids you get the Achaeans instantly under arms. You are to take Troy. The gods are united in this. Woe unto the Trojans at the hands of Jove. Remember this, and when you wake, see that it does not escape you."

The Dream then left the slumbering king, for Agamemnon had not known what was in the mind of Jove.

When King Agamemnon awoke, the divine message still rang in his ears. He sat upright and put on his new, soft shirt and, over this, his heavy cloak. He bound his sandals and slung his silver-studded sword over his shoulder. Then, with the staff of his father, he sallied forth to the ships of the Achaeans.

HOMER, *THE ILIAD*[4]

◉ Dream Exploration ◉

Inviting the Guests

We can allow ourselves to be open to those spirits that may come. One way to do this is to invite people into your dream. Here's how.

1. Decide whom you would like to see in your dreams.

It's best to pick someone you really want to see, maybe someone you haven't seen for a while.

2. As you are going to sleep, think about this person.

Try to be as visually specific as possible. What did this person look like the last time you saw him or her? Focus in your mind's eye on this person's specific features and on what you most associate with this person.

3. Invite this person into your dream.

It's always best to say such things out loud. And remember intention—tell yourself as you are going to sleep that you will meet this person, and repeat it a few times.

4. Try this for a few nights.

Again, all explorations are best approached with few expectations. Simply see what happens. You may not actually dream of the person you're inviting, but you might receive something in the dream that the person might well have given you.

HUNTING THE DREAM

The Tiv people of Nigeria see dreams as things that come unbidden. They call them "omens of the night." In truth, dreams of divination come both unbidden and bidden—and both kinds are important. Most people can have unbidden divinatory dreams. But those dreams that are sought by the dreamer in order to find answers to specific questions have long been the province of only shamans and healers.

Among the Iroquois and the Mohave people, medicine men do receive spiritual guidance through spontaneous dreams. And among the Klamath, divinatory dreams can come unsought to men or to old women. The Yuman tribes of the West Coast of America experienced dreams entirely spontaneously. Among these people, the power dream came first in childhood, showing the path for both the individual and the tribe.

The Kaska Indians of northern British Columbia and the southern Yukon experience many of their dreams as glimpses into that which is becoming. But while for the Kaska dreams come on their own and are outside the will of the dreamer, there are those who have a history of powerful prophetic dreams.

We humans are both an inquisitive and an acquisitive species. If dreams can bring new insights about the waking world, why should we have to rely on chance encounters with the dream spirits? Why shouldn't we go to them? The Creek Indians felt this impulse and said, as they went to bed, *"Posálkán hoboyälankäs"*—"I am going to hunt a dream."

⊚ Dream Exploration ⊚

Dream Catching

Before opportunity knocks, we must consciously open ourselves to opportunity. Or, to put it another way, if the door is locked and the tenants are wearing their earplugs, it doesn't matter how many times opportunity bangs on the door.

While we can't force dreams (that's one of the beautiful things about them), we can use our waking consciousness to pave the way for them. When a Creek Indian said that he was going to hunt a dream, he knew, as any good hunter knows, that patience and watchfulness are important parts of successful hunting.

There is no conflict between dreams that are requested and dreams that are not. Reality resides with both. Here we both hunt a dream and let the dream hunt us.

1. What are you hunting?
If you want to find a buffalo, you don't go searching for rabbits. The first thing to do is to decide what it is you want to learn. Remember, you're not seeking prediction; you're seeking guidance. Focus on a question facing you for which you'd like some direction.

2. Phrase the question as clearly as you can.
The more general the question, the less useful the answer. For example, the question "How can I be happy?" will not yield an answer as meaningful as an answer to the question "How am I creating obstacles to my own happiness?" The more specific, the better.

3. Repeat the question before you go to bed.
Out loud is best. And write the question in your dream journal as well—writing and speaking together carry more force than thinking alone.

4. Let the dream come.

You may not get a direct response to your question. Remember that dream consciousness does not follow the logical path of our waking consciousness. Simply allow what happens to happen. It will be a gift no matter what.

5. Try to perceive how the dream connects with your question.

Stretch it. After you've stretched it and looked at it a bit, things might emerge that make sense.

6. Repeat this for a few days.

You might get different perspectives on the same thing. That's exciting. Don't throw away the gifts because you don't seem to be getting what you want. Maybe the answer you think you want isn't the answer at all—if you knew the answer in your waking consciousness, you wouldn't be asking your dreams, right?

For many, hunting a dream meant seeking out the dream spirits. This could involve a wide variety of practices to induce dreams.* For many people this has meant bringing waking consciousness into the dream state, a practice that has been reflected by the lucid dreaming movement in the West. However, for many societies the goal of hunting the dream was not to capture the dream spirits or control them, but instead to place the dreamer where he could encounter the spirits who would give him foreknowledge. Sometimes this meant going to special places where dreams could be incubated or simply preparing in some way to be receptive.

Although all of us dream spontaneous dreams, there are those who can walk among the spirits and dream at will. While all of us can see with our eyes shut—in our mind's eye—there are those who can dream with their eyes open. The waking dream is a vision, the place where dream consciousness and waking consciousness meet and embrace. Dreaming at will and inducing visions has long been the province of the shaman. For the Plateau Indians, a person had to be able to dream at will in order to call upon supernatural power. For these people, the shaman was one who could program his dream.

In many cultures there were those who were called upon to focus their dream consciousness on certain problems. To learn the fate of overdue war parties, the Comanches would call upon a seer and the intuitive might dream upon the question. The Cherokee, too, used directed dreams as a form of divination.

* See chapter 2.

In many societies, the line between visionary dreaming and wakeful dreaming is blurred. Among the Gros Ventres of Montana, divinatory power came invariably from supernatural beings, but it might have come either during a dream or while the person was awake.

◎ Dream Explorations ◎
Visions

The Shape of a Vision

Dreaming with your eyes open? Sounds a little crazy. Just remember this: One person's crazy is another person's sane. After all, imagination is nothing less than seeing things that don't exist in the optically visual world—and optics is not necessarily the main criterion for reality.

Many cultures encourage their people to seek waking dreams or visions. The Utes, for instance, emphasize the importance of the individual in seeking visions, and any Ute who claims to have received one is respected and accepted.

We cannot, need not, and must not control our dreams. However, we can attempt to emulate dream consciousness in our waking consciousness and in this way bring the two closer together. Here we start with shapes.

1. Look around your immediate environment.
This can be inside your living space or outside. It's important only that you can relax and observe. And it's always a good idea to have your journal ready.

2. Find some object on which to focus.
It can be anything—a tree, table, lamp, clock—anything that strikes your fancy. First hits are the best; don't spend a lot of time thinking about it.

3. Note the shape of the object.
The world is filled with infinite forms, but there are a finite number of general shapes. There are circles, ovals, rectangles, squares, cylinders, spirals, and so forth. What shape is the object you're observing?

4. Close your eyes and think only of its shape.
Hard as it is, it's important to concentrate on only the shape of the object.

5. Think of other objects that have this same shape.
If, for example, you're looking at the face of a wall clock, the shape might be circular. Coins are also round, as are the sun and moon, some people's faces, doorknobs, and so on.

6. Choose one of these other objects.
I was once giving a talk at Mohonk Mountain House in New Paltz, New York. The youngest person there was a seven-year-old named Rebecca and the oldest was eighty. I asked everyone to look at the round wall clock, think of its shape, and then call out other objects that have the same shape. The adults took too long, but Rebecca said, "A plate," and then, "A Frisbee." These were her other objects for the wall clock, and the ones she'd choose from for this step.

7. Close your eyes and imagine the two objects side by side.
In Rebecca's example we might have the clock face and a Frisbee side by side.

8. Merge the two objects so that they become one, yet retain their individual characteristics.
Rebecca and I had the round clock flying through the air like a Frisbee.

9. Let the image sink in.
Voilà! You've created a vision.

Play with this for a while—during the course of the day, take shapes and change them, embellish them. If you wish, draw these newly created visions, or describe them in your journal.

The Sound of a Vision

Moses heard the voice of the divine in a burning bush that crackled, sizzled, and whispered. But it was the fire that first drew his attention. It was a beautiful fire that seemed like it would go on forever burning and glowing brightly. The beauty of that fire began to hypnotize him, but the divine voice wanted to be heard rather than seen and called out, "Moses, Moses!"

Can you imagine it? It's not hard to imagine the crackling, whispering voice calling out "Moses, Moses . . ." People have been hearing the voice of the divine for ages in the call of birds, in the rushing of the streams, in the howl of a wolf. Let's try to hear it too.

1. During the day, find a sound that is repetitive.
There are lots of sounds in this world that are repetitive. Inside houses there is the humming of an oil furnace or the whir of a dryer or washer. Outside, in the city or country, there are the songs of insects or birds, the burbling of a brook, or the rush of passing traffic.

2. Focus on the sound.
Listen to it—to all the sounds within the sound. Remember that one reason it's repetitive is that it has a beginning and an end, with perhaps a bit of variation in the middle. There are probably a thousand different sounds that a cat could hear in the burble of a stream. Surely we can pick up a few.

3. What do these sounds sound like?
It can be anything that rings true to you—cries, whispers, a lonesome train whistle, violins—anything.

4. Mix the two sounds in your imagination's ear.
If the brook sounds like a train, hear both of them together. Really listen. You've been doing this since you were a child without being aware that you were hearing this way.

5. It might be fun to explore this as you are going to sleep.
Use any repetitive sounds in your bedroom. And pay attention to any seasonal sounds. In the spring, for instance, there are raindrops, peepers, and crickets in the country. In the city there are repetitive sounds twenty-four hours a day. Focus on one of them as you are falling asleep.

6. As always, write any discoveries in your journal.
Though it sounds repetitive—write, write!

 Dream Stories:
Two Tales of the American Civil War

Harriet Tubman and John Brown

Harriet Tubman had been born a slave and she had the mark in her forehead to prove it. There, years before, an overseer had hit her with a hammer as a punishment for insubordination. She nearly died, but instead she lived to escape from the slave South and become one of the most outspoken foes of slavery. Many times she returned to the South to help bring other slaves to the North and freedom. Her base of operations was in Auburn, New York, close enough to the Canadian border to help folks slip from a country where the institution of slavery was protected to a country where it was not.

John Brown brought Old Testament fire to his fight against slavery. In Kansas, he led the settlers from the North, the Free State immigrants, in an armed struggle against the settlers from slave Missouri. He was fierce in his struggle, his sword reddened with the blood of pro-slavery settlers—for slavery must fall, Brown believed, and if at the sword, so be it.

John Brown and Harriet Tubman met as he was trying to raise money for an expedition into the deep South—into the very heartland of slavery. He proposed to create an armed antislavery base within the slave South and from there declare the slave states to be forever free. It was a bold plan and, among the abolitionists of the Northeast, it had few supporters.

The moment that Harriet Tubman met John Brown, she felt a chill. There was a memory—or was it a vision? She saw him wounded, with snakes writhing around his legs and around his sons, who were dying at his side.

Several years later she remembered this vision when, in an attempt to take over the federal arsenal at Harpers Ferry, Virginia, John Brown was wounded and his sons were killed.

April 1865

The weariness and stress of the war weighed heavily upon him. He had been up late waiting for dispatches from the front, and as soon as he got to bed that night he fell immediately into a troubled sleep in which he soon began to dream.

In his dream there was a deathly stillness around him, and then he could hear subdued sobs, as if a large number of people were weeping.

He rose from his dream bed and went downstairs. The deathlike silence was broken by loud sobbing, but no mourners were visible. He went from room to room and could find no living persons in sight, but still there was the same sound of distress. There was light in all the rooms—he saw all the familiar objects, but he knew not where all the grieving people were.

It was both puzzling and alarming. He wandered on until he arrived at the East Room. When he entered it, he was sickened to find a catafalque on which was a corpse wrapped in funeral garments. Around it there were soldiers acting as guards and a group of people gazing sadly upon the corpse. The face of the corpse was covered.

"Who is dead in the White House?" he demanded of one of the soldiers.

"The president," the soldier answered. "He was killed by an assassin."

Then there was a loud burst of grieving from the crowd and President Abraham Lincoln awoke from his dream.*

*Reported by Ward Hill Lamon, who was present with the president, Mrs. Lincoln, and some friends when Lincoln recounted his dream, which he had less than two weeks before he was assassinated. From Ward Hill Lamon, *Recollections of Abraham Lincoln, 1847–1865* (Lincoln: University of Nebraska Press, 1994). Retold by Sarvananda Bluestone.

PROPHECY AS DIVINE GUIDANCE

The Yokut people of the American Southwest knew that the supernatural could be conveyed through dream experience. For the Yokuts, anybody could establish contact with this extra-normal world, though some people had greater ability to do this than others. However, people could improve their ability—the more people practiced, the easier it became. Prophecy has always come from the extra-normal world. But what is prophecy? *Merriam-Webster's Collegiate Dictionary* defines it first as "an inspired utterance by a prophet" (sometimes dictionary definitions can be frustrating); then it goes on to define it as "the inspired declaration of divine will or purpose." Only in the third definition is it "a prediction of something to come."

Though human history is filled with prophetic people and the Bible is replete with prophets, we in the West have unfortunately associated prophecy with either perfect saints or unscrupulous fortune-tellers.

There is not, as yet, a scientific explanation for the phenomenon of prophecy, yet it has always existed, continues to exist, and will no doubt always be a part of the human experience. Perhaps Einstein's guidepost is as close as we can come to an explanation: Time is not linear. For him the notion that time consists of past, present, and future was both mechanical and unreal. Time, for Einstein, was folded and twisted. He showed us that the linear construct of time is just that—a construct, a created concept.

Dream time is very different from waking time, for it is in dream time that the altered nature of dream consciousness allows us to travel through the time boundaries of waking consciousness. Little wonder, then, that there has been so much prophecy associated with dreams, and that such prophecy is seen as the expression of divine or higher consciousness. Dream prophecy as divine guidance is actually another form of divination, one of the multitude of ways that humans have touched higher consciousness through dream consciousness.

The Bella Coola people of the American Pacific Northwest feel that a person may contact his supernatural representatives in dreams and from them learn what is in store for him during the coming year and every phase of existence. This is not simple prediction but extra-natural guidance.

Iran has had a long history of dream prophecy. At the beginning of the third century, Persia was in disarray. The ancient land of Cyrus the Great was divided and chaotic when Papak, a nobleman, sought to unite the country under the rule of his family, the Sassanids. It was a daunting effort, but he had a dream indicating the success of the dynasty—and his dream was accurate. The Sassanids ruled Persia for almost four centuries. In traditional Persian society, *t'abir,* or the interpretation of dreams, was one of the five main kinds of divination.

The Aymara people live in Bolivia, Peru, and Chile around Lake Titicaca, the world's highest lake and, like the Iranians, they use the interpretation of dreams as one of the main elements of prophecy. In traditional Japan as well, the oracular dream, or *reimu,* was one of the main forms of divination.

 Dream Story

The Mountains of Kilimanjaro

In the time of the great Chief Horombo, there was in the district of Mwika an old man name Mosi. He was a wise man and his dreams were truly wondrous.

One night after Mosi had a dream, he awoke at dawn and immediately summoned his sons and grandsons and took them to the top of a hill. There he pointed to the rising sun.

"My sons and grandsons," he said, as the rays of the rising sun grew brighter, "see how that sun rises so rapidly and beautifully. You will rejoice in it. This shall be your symbol." Mosi's sons and grandsons listened as the old man continued. "When you are old men there will come from the East men with white skin and hair that shades their heads."

The sons and grandsons listened quietly. Never had such men been seen. Their land had been in peace ever since the great Chief Horombo had driven away the Masai from the plains east of Kilimanjaro.

The old man continued: "These people shall destroy the power of Horombo and will bring back the Masai. They will make a broad way from the rising to the setting sun and they will pass through our country. They will not delay coming. The lion and the leopard they will take by their hands and their color shall be white and their speech like that of children."

The old man had finished. In a few years, Englishmen had penetrated the district of Mwika. In one generation his prophetic dream had come to pass.[5]

Dream Exploration

Déjà Who? Remembering the Future

It's funny how things sound so much more exotic when we say them in a foreign language, especially French. *Mousse au chocolate,* for instance, is "foamy chocolate," and *champignons au poivre* is mushrooms with pepper.

Déjà vu sounds particularly mysterious. It literally means "already seen" and refers to the feeling that what we are experiencing at a given time is something we've experienced before. Most of our déjà vu experiences occur when we are doing simple, everyday activities: As we're walking down the street, a boy rides past on a bicycle, and suddenly we have the weird sense that we've experienced this very scene before—this boy on this street at just this time of day. What is intriguing about déjà vu is that the sense that something has occurred before being introduced to our waking consciousness.

Sometimes déjà vu is experiencing something before it occurs, albeit something very ordinary. A friend of mine was in a restaurant with her daughter when all of a sudden she had a vision of the waitress walking through the swinging doors, coming over to their table, and delivering their glasses of water. A moment later it happened exactly the way she envisioned it.

There are undoubtedly a variety of sources for déjà vu. There are likely times when our mind registers things before our consciousness. That incredibly small gap between perception and awareness can feel like memory. Dreams probably account for a large number of déjà vu experiences: We have experiences in our dreams, then later have similar experiences in our waking life. Often we've forgotten the dream, but a memory remains. We are remembering the "future" as we had experienced it in our dreams. In this exploration we try to identify a personal déjà vu experience.

1. Review your dream journals.
Look through the dreams that you've noted there. Read through the details.

2. Pay as much attention to the feelings associated with the dreams as to the dreams themselves.
Remember, how you feel is at least as important as what causes you to feel it. The effect is as important as the cause.

3. Choose one or two dreams that stand out.
Review them in your memory. How did you feel during and after them? What was the situation that you faced in these dreams?

4. Check out any experiences in your waking consciousness that have echoed the dreams.
Here you can be as broad as you wish. The waking experience doesn't have to be an exact duplication of what happened in the dream. Look to find repeated feelings and repeated themes.

5. Add these experiences of waking consciousness to your journal.
And continue to note any waking experiences that seem to have been prefigured in some way in your dreams.

WHAT IS ASKED AND WHAT DREAMS TELL

There are a number of questions, big and small, that people have looked to dreams to answer—When will a child be conceived? What should this new child's name be? Where is the best place to hunt this year and how shall we fight our next battle? Where shall we build our new home? There is also much divinatory information that dreams have offered unbidden—information that has informed many a decision around the world.

Children are considered by a number of cultures to have a unique connection to the world of dreams and vision. Many cultures have believed that the spirit of a child exists inside the womb. Among the Mohave, future shamans, while they were still in their mother's womb, dreamed of the powers they would use after they were born. They even dreamed of their particular skills. A child forgot this prenatal dream, but when he was older, usually in adolescence, he had the same dream again—a kind of déjà vu.

Children, in their different stages of life, with so much of their life in the future, have long seemed connected to aspects of divination. The naming of children, for instance, has been associated with dreams and divination. In many cultures the spirit of the child is considered divine and thus the naming of this divine being can best be done by consulting divine spirits. And what better place to do this but in dreams?

It was a common practice, especially among Native Americans, to receive names for children in dreams. The Gros Ventres of Montana relied frequently, although not exclusively, on dreams to name their children—and it need not be the child's parents who dreamed the name. Similarly, the Blackfoot people felt that the naming of children came from the Dream People, but also believed that receiving names in this way was not limited to infancy. An adult could dream another name for himself. One Blackfoot, named Running Wolf, dreamed the sun god came down to him and told him, "I take you for my friend, and I bestow upon you my supernatural powers." After Running Wolf told his people about this dream, they changed his name to Natosin Nepe-e or "Brings-Down-the-Sun."[6] Each Chippewa (Ojibwa) had two dream names. The name the parents gave the child would very often have been received in a dream. This name, however, had no power. At puberty, the child went into isolation and fasted in order to receive her ceremonial name—her animal dream name—from the spirits in a dream.

Among the Delaware, all names came from dreams. Without a dream, a child would have no name and it was not unheard of for a Delaware child to go for several days without a name, until a parent or grandparent, going to bed with this on his mind, would awake with a name from a dream.

On the other side of the world, in Kenya, people also sought guidance from dreams in the naming of a child. If no such guidance came, the parents consulted a waganga, or diviner, who consulted his dreams or visions to find the right name.

Dream Story: Two Naming Tales

Gray Wolf

Wahee was the war chief of the Eastern Cherokee Nation. Although he was only in his late twenties, his hair was steely gray, which was appropriate given that his name, Wahee, meant "gray wolf."

Yet he did not have this name right away. After his birth, as was the custom of his people, his name could come only through a dream. And so it did. All four of his grandparents went into a tepee to dream a name for their infant grandson, and there they remained until all four had dreamed the same name.

He was to be Wahee—gray wolf. And so he was.[7]

White Skunk

Coming Daylight was proud of her infant grandson. Yet he had no name. One night she dreamed that there was a big gathering where she was looking for her infant grandson, though in the dream the child was three or four years old.

As she searched for the boy, a very old man dressed all in white came up to her, pointed, and said, "Why, there goes White Skunk—up that way." She looked where the old man was pointing and saw her grandson running in the distance. Only now he seemed not four years old, but a tall young man.

Upon awakening, Coming Daylight told her daughter of her dream. Her daughter then told her husband, and all agreed that the infant would be named White Skunk.

A STORY FROM THE GROS VENTRES[8]

Like children, women too have a unique bond with the dream world. As the bearers of children, women have links with the source of life itself, and as the primary nurturers of children even today, mothers continue this bond. Little wonder that in so many cultures, including our own, women and intuition have long been connected.

It has historically been a powerful connection, one that many revered and which was represented in the worship of the Goddess. While several thousand years of male rule, both socially and spiritually, have reduced recognition for the power of women, the link between women and divination is still strong.

Women still bear life and the connection between mother and child, both in and outside of the womb, is itself the basis of divination.

Dream divination as it relates to children has most often been the province of women. In Burma the dreams of a pregnant woman are extremely important, for it is in such dreams that the mother may discover what her child will be like, including what deceased person the child will incarnate. Among the Siriono of eastern Bolivia and the Yuman people of Colorado, a woman might learn of her pregnancy in a dream. If such a dream occurred before intercourse, she could determine whether she would conceive.

In Silwa, a Muslim village in the Egyptian province of Aswan, women are known to be more capable of dreaming and to be better interpreters of dreams than men. Similarly, in Muslim India, the *dainyals,* or diviners, are most frequently women who are supposed to have received the psychic gift from the shadow of a fairy falling on them in their sleep.

After their children are born, women often continue to be guided by dreams. In fact, Crow mothers often sang lullabies that were originally revealed to them in a dream.

But the divinatory powers of women were not related solely to children. Among the Celts, women dream diviners played an important role. If a ship was missing, the specific ritual to find it required that a virgin be selected to sleep so that her spirit might leave her body and search for the ship. The woman had to be of strong mind, for if the wind changed while her spirit was absent from her body, she stood a good chance of going insane. When her spirit returned to her body, the young woman awoke and reported the findings of the dream spirit—where the ship or its wreckage could be found and what the fate of the people aboard had been. There must have been a certain degree of accuracy in this procedure because it was used for hundreds of years.

 Dream Story

Mother Reads Dreams

Hank was a good boy—he loved his mother, did his chores, and cared for his kid brother when he was told to. But he was also a normal boy growing up in Brooklyn in the 1930s and, like any other boy, he got into his share of mischief. He didn't particularly like school, he hitched rides on the back of a bus, he stole an occasional smoke, and once in a while he would snitch something from a delicatessen.

Of all these infractions, Hank's mother most often told him never to hitch a ride on a bus. But he had to yield to temptation from time to time. You waited for the bus to start leaving the bus stop and then you jumped on the back fender as it drove off. The excitement was double: You'd get a free ride and a deliciously dangerous trip, swinging from the back as the bus swayed through the crowded streets. He couldn't give it up—but he was smart enough to do it miles away from his house, in parts of Brooklyn that his mother never visited.

That's where the surprise came in. Every day after Hank had hitched a bus ride, his mother approached him at breakfast and said, "So you hitched a ride on a bus yesterday . . ." Hank, shocked by his mother's information, would confess and then wonder, every time, who had ratted on him. Whether he rode on the bus alone or with friends, his mother always knew what he'd been doing.

And the bus wasn't the only thing she knew about. The occasional cigarettes, the once-in-a-while snitching from the deli or fruit stand—Hank's mother knew about all of it. The next morning after Hank had done his mischief, his mother approached him with her information, and it always left Hank wondering at either the miraculous powers of his mother or the treachery of the mysterious companion who always ratted on him.

Then one night, as he tried to fall asleep and thought about counting sheep, he heard a gentle knocking at his door.

"Hank?" It was his mother. As he lay there with his eyes closed, she pulled up a chair next to the bed and sat down. He felt her hand on his forehead as she said, "Now tell me what you did today, Hank."

After that, Hank no longer worried about who had ratted on him—he realized that he ratted on himself every night, divulging his secrets in his sleep.

Throughout time the personal, larger decisions and broader concerns have been based upon dream information. Dream divination has long played a role with leaders throughout the world. Among the Crow people, the person who held the office of The One Who Owns the Camp (the chief) acted upon his dreams and visions to guide his people to places where there was an abundance of meat and game and safety from enemies. Such a chief, deriving his instructions from dreams, had absolute authority in the camp. In fact, the true government of the Crow was based upon dreams and when a Crow camp was about to relocate, the chief and other leaders would meet to discuss their dreams.

Divinatory dreams determined the authority of the headsman among the Sinkaietk people of the Pacific. The headman was not appointed by the chief but instead held office solely because of his ability to dream where to direct his people for successful hunting and fishing in the summer and camping in the winter.

The Iban people of Sarawak, Malaysia, have three ritual offices: *manang,* or the office of shaman or healer; *lemambang,* or the office of bard; and *tuai burong,* or the office of augur. All of these positions are gained through dream experiences in which a person is told of his calling. Similarly, the Maricopa chief dreamed his position. In fact, among the Maricopa, all special abilities, from shamanic power to the ability to lead in war or to serve as chief, came from dreaming.

To those of us brought up on the maxims of Benjamin Franklin, promising that hard work brings its own reward, all of may sound strange. Where could the merit possibly be in choosing a leader based on the nature of his or her dreams? It would be easy to dismiss such a practice as superstitious. But the fact is that it was the success of the dreams in determining good hunting, a safe camp, or forage that lent authority to the dreamers. For many people, the leader was the one who was able to join waking and dream consciousness. And nothing succeeded like success.

The same held true in the arena of war, in which many cultures reserved a role for dream divination. A white traveler through America's Northwest of 1827 was amazed to find dreams as a determinant for war within the Sauk and Fox Nations. Any member of the tribe, he remarked, could put forth a divinatory war dream, and those whose dreams bore successful results came to be respected as war leaders. "Those Indians who prepare for war by dreams," he wrote, "may be any common Indian in the nation. . . ."[9]

Dreams could also provide warnings. The Sauk and Fox would immediately return from a war expedition if there was an unfavorable dream. The Blackfoot, fierce warriors who considered desertion by a member of a raiding party to be a cowardly act, also heeded dreams when beginning their war expeditions. If a member of a Blackfoot raiding party had a dream warning of disaster, he was allowed to return home with no disgrace. Such was their respect for dream warnings that any warrior who accused another of cowardice because he heeded his dream would himself be killed on the expedition. Similarly, the Jibaro people, fierce fighters of the Andes, excused anyone from a military expedition if he had an inauspicious dream.

Crow military expeditions originated in dreams and the Crow sought dreams or visions before undertaking all movements against hostile tribes. The Maricopa warriors not only dreamed their strength in battle, but also dreamed the nature of the confrontation and the warriors' formations, which they followed. In fact, every Maricopa war party included a clairvoyant dreamer.

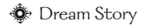 Dream Story

The Dream of Bin Sa'ud, King Abdul 'Aziz al Sa'ud

So it is told that in the year of the Battle of Jaráb, when Bin Sa'ud (may his memory glow as brightly as a star in the evening firmament) was king of Sa'udi Arabia, His Majesty had a dream.

It was, as the king told his friend, a startling dream. He saw himself at a well drawing water with a leather bucket such as the Bedouin use. He filled his bucket to the brim with water and was bringing it up to the top, hand over hand.

The water filled the bucket to overflow as the king (he, ruler of all Sa'udi Arabia) pulled it higher and higher. But just when the bucket was within arm's length and close to the top of the well, the rope suddenly broke. Bucket and water crashed to the bottom of the well.

Bin Sa'ud awoke from his dream, sorely perplexed. He related it to his friend and countryman Shaikh Abdul 'Aziz al Nimr and asked him for interpretation.

The Shaikh was saddened by the dream of the king, his friend. It was, said the Shaikh, quite clear that the king, Bin Sa'ud, would go on conquering his enemies. That was the meaning of the image of the king bringing the water hand over hand up to the surface. And well did the Shaikh wish that the dream had ended there. But it had not.

In the dream the cord with the water broke. Within a short year, said the Shaikh, his friend and countryman, King Abdul 'Aziz al Sa'ud, would suffer a great defeat and setback.

Within the year the armies of Bin Sa'ud met the forces of Ibn' Rashid at the Battle of Jaráb. The king lost the battle and half of the tribes (may their deception live in infamy) deserted him.

Such was the dream of King Abdul 'Aziz al Sa'ud, ruler of Sa'udi Arabia.

A STORY FROM THE BEDOUIN OF SAUDI ARABIA[10]

Not only did chiefs and warriors derive their power in dreams and visions. Shamanistic leadership and power also came from divinatory dreams. Among the Hare Indians, old and wise medicine men were said to be able to see more clearly because they dreamed true. Likewise, Mohave shamans and shamans of the Tapirape in Brazil received their power through dreams. (See chapter 6 for more information on shamanism and dreams.)

☀ Dream Story

A Dream of Hives

Charles O. Card was a respected member of the Church of Jesus Christ of Latter-day Saints. It was 1887 and the Mormon Church gave funds to Charles Card and a small group to found a colony in the Idaho Territory. The group set forth in the spring of that year and on April 17, 1887, they reached a place near Standoff, Idaho, where they planned to stay for ten days.

On the night of April 27, ten days later, Card dreamed of bees arriving at a hive. This vision was enough for Card, who felt they had reached the right spot, the place where they were to establish a "hive" to attract others. He and his small group planted their gardens and, on May 3, left for Utah to get their families.

The settlement of Cardston, Idaho, had begun in a dream.[11]

Dream divination has determined the location of towns, the foundation of shrines, and the building of dwellings. Across the globe people like those in Card's group have relied upon dreams to locate themselves.

A group of Maori in New Zealand decided to settle in a new district and prepared the logs for the building of their village. Just as they were about to begin construction, the son of the chief dreamed that the timber drifted off to sea. Then he saw it cast upon an island on which were some of his friends. After hearing the dream of the chief's son, the Maori abandoned the proposed settlement immediately.

The Mantia of Malaysia feel similarly—a man would not choose a locality for a plantation unless he had a favorable dream about it—as do the Seminoles: A young Seminole couple, planning to build a house, might sleep at the chosen place. If either spouse suffered bad dreams, they selected another spot.

If dreams could indicate an auspicious place or a safe place, they could also indicate a sacred place. In Malaysia, many a sacred place—*karamat*—was revealed to people in dreams. And in northern India dreams reestablished the location of buried shrines and obscured sacred places.

◉ Dream Exploration ◉

Ask a Dream

The Aymara people live high in the mountains of Peru. When a person wants an answer to a question, he asks a dream. Anyone may seek answers of his dreams. Anyone means you too.

1. Think of a question that's important to you.
Of course, the catch here is that you need to define what's impor-
tant to you—not a simple task for some. It can be as general as
"What's going on?" Simple yes or no questions are boring.

2. At night, right before you go to sleep, write down the question.
If you want to change your question a little, change it a little. But
write it down. And say it out loud at least once, slowly.

3. Go to sleep and agree to meet your dream halfway.
This means that you will ask your question and think about it, but
then you'll let your dream consciousness take over. Otherwise, you'll
be staying awake all night.

4. Record your dream as you wake up.
If you don't remember your dream, make up a dream. In doing so
you'll be using something that's there just beyond your waking consciousness.

5. What did you feel in your dream?
What you feel is important. Perhaps, in some sense, how you felt in
your dream constitutes a kind of answer to your question.

6. What did you see in the dream?
What happened? What images did you see? How do they connect
with the question?

**7. How did your dream answer your question—and what was the
answer?**
You probably didn't hear a voice whispering in your ear, but it's
divinely possible that you've received an answer. There are so many
truths—one of yours is bound to be there.

8. In this there is no one answer.
Repeat: In this there is no one answer. In this there is no one answer.
In this there is no one answer. Try it again and see if you can be even
clearer about what you ask. And if you don't receive any answer that
you can find, it's no big deal. But remember, like so much else in
life, this exploration gets much better with practice.

Divination and imagination have been part of the human experience for as
long as we have been human, and the vehicles people have used to facilitate
connection with the divine are innumerable: tea leaves, the fingernails of young
boys, scapulas, clouds, llama dung, the sound of the wind in the leaves, clear

pools of water—all have been instruments for altered perception, for divination.

Amid all these divinatory tools, however, a dream is the one that seems common to all cultures. In dream consciousness we are all in contact with an altered, even higher, consciousness. Rather than something we consciously do, divination comes naturally—even unbidden—to us all. We just need to sleep on it.

Notes

1. Juan Polo de Ondegardo, "Informaciones acerca de la Religión y Gobierno de los Incas" [Information Concerning the Religion and Government of the Incas], *Colección de Libros y Documentos Referentes a la Historia del Peru,* vol. 3 (1916).
2. From G. Kohl, *Kitchi-Gami* (London: Chapman and Hall, 1860).
3. James E. Talmadge, *A Study of the Articles of Faith, Being a Consideration of the Principal Doctrines of the Church of Jesus Christ of Latter-day Saints* (Salt Lake City: The Church of Jesus Christ of Latter-day Saints, 1976).
4. Translated by Samuel Butler and retold by Sarvananda Bluestone.
5. Charles Dundas, *Kilimanjaro and Its People* (London: H. F. and G. Witherby, 1924). Retold by Sarvananda Bluestone.
6. Regina Flannery, "The Gros Ventres of Montana," in *Catholic University Social Life Anthropological Series,* part 1, no. 15 (1953).
7. From a discussion c. 1975.
8. Regina Flannery, "The Gros Ventres of Montana," in *Catholic University Social Life Anthropological Series,* part 1, no. 15 (1953).
9. Thomas Forsyth, "An Account of the Manners and Customs of the Sauk and Fox Nations of Indiana Tradition," in Emma Helen Blair, ed., *The Indian Tribes of the Upper Mississippi Valley and Region of the Great Lakes,* vol. 2 (Cleveland: Arthur H. Clark, 1912).
10. From H. R. P. Dickson, *The Arab of the Desert: A Glimpse into Badawin Life in Kuwait and Sau'di Arabia* (London: George Allen and Unwin, 1951). Retold by Sarvananda Bluestone.
11. Lowry Nelson, *The Mormon Village: A Pattern and Technique of Land Settlement* (Salt Lake City: University of Utah Press, 1952).

MAKING LOVE TO YOUR PSYCHE:
UNDERSTANDING DREAMS

*I have no theory about dreams, I do not know how dreams arise.
And I am not at all sure that my way of handling dreams even
deserves the name of a "method." I share all your prejudices against
dream-interpretation as the quintessence of uncertainty and
arbitrariness. On the other hand, I know that if we meditate on
a dream sufficiently long and thoroughly, if we carry it around with
us and turn it over and over, something almost always comes of it.*

CARL JUNG

*Don't you know that all of this is a dream? I am a man in your dream, and you are
a man in someone else's dream.*

THE *YOGAVISITHA*

The way we think by dreams, white men don't understand.

HARE INDIAN WOMAN

THOUSANDS OF REALITIES: GOOD-BYE TO AUNT SALLY

It was a dream unlike any that I had ever had. For one thing, I saw absolutely nothing. There were no visuals, no pictures—nothing that registered with my dream eyes. For another thing, the whole dream lasted as long as one sentence, and a five-word sentence at that. That was the dream—one sentence, and a voice.

However, it was no ordinary voice. And I did not hear it in my ears alone. The voice was outside of me, inside me, it was around me and through me. All it said was, "There are thousands of realities."

There are thousands of realities. At the sound of those five words, I felt a wave of joy. No, it was beyond joy—the feeling was as close to ecstasy as I have ever experienced, involving every part of my being. It was emotional, physical, intellectual. So powerful was this voice that I awoke.

Of course, there are infinite realities. But the mind is finite and has a difficult time comprehending the notion of infinity. That takes imagination—like that of Albert Einstein, who said: "Knowledge is limited. Imagination encircles the globe."

A year before my dream, I discovered the writing of a fourth-century Babylonian rabbi named Hisda. This wise man told of a dream that he had brought to twenty-five different dream interpreters, from whom he received twenty-five different interpretations—and all, he said, were right. I realized then that there was no *one* truth.

It was such a relief. I had uncovered the story of Rabbi Hisda just as I finished my research and directly before I began to write this book. A year later, as I began the last chapter, my dream consciousness reminded me that there are thousands of realities. Or perhaps it was a divine message or a dream visit from Rabbi Hisda. Maybe it was my own higher consciousness—or perhaps it was all of the above. So many truths and realities. The timing was perfect. Before I wrote the last chapter, it was important for me to realize, once again, that what we already know is only one truth. In the realm of dreams and their meaning, the realities are limitless.

This means, of course, that there is no one way of understanding dreams, and there are no common universal symbols. We all experience our own reality through our dream consciousness. At the same time, each culture has certain generally accepted symbols. But because there are thousands of cultures, each with its own identity, there can be no common universal symbols.

When we seek guidance or understanding from our dream consciousness, we are exploring. Just as the dreams themselves constitute an adventure into unknown territory, so too does our sense of our dreams become a trip into the unknown. There is no right or wrong answer to the question of a dream. It is the rich and multilayered texture of dreams that allows us to explore them in a variety of ways. As long as we remain open to the realities of our dream consciousness, we can truly appreciate the kaleidoscope of its wisdom.

Once we accept that there can be two truths, we can accept limitless realities. Sounds simple, but sometimes we forget how much we are conditioned to think in terms of right and wrong or in terms of one truth alone—ours. It requires a conscious shift on our part to get away from the old habit of judgment.

This wisdom of our dream consciousness is transmitted through the language of dreams, which is different from the language of everyday life. The language of dreams is closer to the language of poetry than it is to that of prose. It illuminates rather than describes and is not logical. If we are determined to place logic as the main criterion for understanding our dreams, we will start out with two strikes against us.

The language of dreams is made up of symbols, which stand for things beyond themselves. What, for instance, might a chair symbolize? A few things come to mind: It might stand for taking a break, or a seat of power (like a throne), or paying attention (like we did in chairs in school). Come up with your own meaning. Symbols allow us to see with new eyes, though sometimes they become too familiar. That's when we can begin to use metaphors. Like symbols, they stand for something beyond themselves, but tend to encompass a little more. We began chapter 1 talking about metaphors—they can carry us from our waking consciousness to our dream consciousness and back again.

Metaphors and symbols are magic mirrors that reflect more than we would see in a regular mirror. My friend Prartho Sereno states it well:

> Some say that metaphor is the glue of the universe, how everything is held together. I say that everything is already together and metaphor is just everything mirroring everything else. I have heard metaphor defined as "comparing two dissimilar things," and it always makes me wince because it seems to me that "dissimilarity" is our blind spot, and metaphor opens our eyes.

How do we learn this language of symbol and metaphor? Actually, we already speak it. We merely need to pay attention—and to remember to those thousands of realities. If we think there is only one way to look at a symbol or one way to read a metaphor or one way to understand a dream, we will find ourselves excluding a lot of richness. When we look at the world through our own cultural lenses, it can be easy to forget that we're wearing them and impossible to imagine seeing any differently.

When I started writing this chapter, my reality included the belief that all traditional interpretations of dreams were nonsense—ridiculous superstitions that sounded pretty funny, too. In my reality I had to convince people that they should forget all they have been told about the symbolism and meaning in their dreams, and instead find out these things for themselves.

But as I looked at various dream symbols from around the world, I realized that people everywhere use the symbols provided by their own culture, and that it is these symbols that are used by dream consciousness to communicates its wisdom. I began to see standard dream interpretations in a new way—as another reality.

In truth, there are no right symbols and no wrong symbols. But because they do resonate with nonrational parts of ourselves, symbols can be very powerful. This is, in part, why they have been so often used to manipulate people. The swastika, for instance, became one of the most powerful symbols of the twentieth century. Well skilled in the use of manipulating symbols, the Nazi leadership consciously created a repertoire of visual symbols that resonated with millions of Germans. Beyond the swastika, they employed the lightning bolt insignia of the Luftwaffe, echoing back to the legends of the Norse gods; the death's-head insignia of the SS, and the thousands of torches at nighttime rallies. Symbols resonate with us. The more we are aware of them, the less we can be manipulated by them and the more we can enjoy them for what they tell us about ourselves.

Now, of course, there is a tidal wave of literature that can tell us the meanings of all the symbols in our dreams. When I was nine my babysitter had a thick book called *Aunt Sally's Dream Book*. Being of curious disposition, I took a look at this listing of thousands of images that might come up in a dream. Each image was accompanied by a brief description of its meaning. Aunt Sally was clearly taken with fortune-telling, for all of the symbols related to things that were going to happen.

I remember thinking at the time that there was something silly about Aunt Sally. How could one symbol—any symbol—mean the same thing to everybody? Could a person living in a penthouse in New York City and a Bedouin camped out in the Libyan desert see the same symbol in the same way? A scholar of the Nupe people of Africa suggested that even among the people he studied, there were diverse principles of interpretation—so diverse and so different as to defy any universality at all.

What I didn't know when I was nine was that Aunt Sally was part of a long tradition—thousands of years—of dream books.

The first dream book probably appeared in the ancient Middle East, in the Fertile Crescent. It was here also that the first book of omens was printed. Long referred to as the cradle of Western civilization, it was here that humans were first able to create large-scale, settled agriculture that could produce, for the first time, an agricultural surplus. No longer did people have to live or die by the vagaries of nature.

With the growth of such farming, there grew a class to administer it. These were the administrators, and even the priests and kings, who saw to the vast workings of their societies, including putting forth official views on subjects—unified views of right and wrong—that had previously been more local and individual. It was from this leading group that the first book of dreams came.

No longer was the interpretation of dreams a personal or even a social concern. It became part of an organized belief system. And, of course, it reflected the point of view of the men who wrote the dream books. The focus of interpretation shifted from personal revelation to a social belief system.

Egyptians wrote a dream book dating back over four thousand years that gave specific meanings to dreams and their symbols. In India, from 1500 to 1000 B.C.E., the Atharva Veda also gave specific meanings to dreams, and in China, around 1020 B.C.E., a dream book appeared entitled *Chou Kung's Book of Auspicious and Inauspicious Dreams.* It was a highly systematized text, with sixty-eight entries for dragons, snakes, and wild animals and fifty-six entries for mountains, rocks, plants, and trees.

Later, in the West the Greeks contributed a dream book. Early Islamic culture saw the art of dream interpretation as a science—*ilm ul tâbír,* or the science of dream interpretation. This gave rise to various *tâbír naneh,* or dream books, which flourished in Islam. In the eighth century a Persian dream book appeared, and in the fifteenth century the Turks created a book of dreams, the *Book of Dede Qorqut.*

Within Arab countries dream interpretation was a part of everyday life. Scholars worked to systematize and categorize dreams. Perhaps the most ambitious of the books produced was the *Taatire El-Ana mbitabir El-Manam (To Make the World Happier by the Intepretation of Dreams).*

Dream books generally arose in those societies where a managerial and priestly class determined and directed affairs. With this process of making dream interpretation a matter of public policy rather than private understanding, the dynamic, living, and spontaneous interpretation of dreams became instead fossilized bits and pieces of knowledge that were passed on from generation to generation.

Dream books codified the interpretation of dreams for this process—and they still do. But from ancient Assyria to Aunt Sally, such books have distanced the dreamer from her own dreams. They provide an acceptable method of interpretation that is external to the immediate experience of the dreamer. To this extent, dream books have always represented an attempt to homogenize the dream experience of a culture.

The fact, however, is that we dream alone. Each dream is our own reality. The waking mind can be molded and shaped, but it's hard to control a dream. While socially acceptable notions of dream meaning can control interpretation, the dream is still unchained.

Similar attempts at cultural and individual constriction occurred in the West in the first centuries of the first millennium C.E., when the fathers of the early Christian church were concerned about the power of dreams and concerned that people were more apt to pay heed to their own dreams than to the ministers of the church.

The inherent paradox here is that on the one hand, church hierarchy discredited personal dreams, yet on the other hand the Bible, both Old and New Testaments, was filled with divine messages received through dreams. Was not the very birth of Jesus foretold in a dream? Clearly, the Church could not simply discredit all dreams—but if everyone thought that he could interpret his own dreams and use them as divine guidance, what kind of control would the Church have?

At the same time that the Christian church was struggling to ascend, rival sects did believe in the power and value of vision and dreams. Among these early rival Christian groups were those who saw their dreams as divine images. These were Christians who rejected the authority of Rome and believed, among other things, that the importance of a dream and its meaning were a matter between the dreamer and God. At this time the Church was establishing its own spiritual strength within the shell of the declining Roman Empire—but also within this shell there existed pagan tribes from Britain to northern Africa whose people were more inclined to listen to their dreams than to an emissary from the Church of Rome.

The Christian power in Rome could not abide sects. Nor could it countenance a position whereby individuals would take upon themselves their own salvation, whether through prayers or by dreams. And certainly the Church could not accept the beliefs of pagans. Because of this, dreams became a part of the battlefield on which the early Church fought pagans and heretics for the soul of man. Continuing a belief that emerged in Judaism, the Church divided all dreams in two. There were dreams that came from God and there were dreams that came from Satan. Tertullian, a Christian convert in the third century, echoed the beliefs of most Church fathers in seeing most dreams as coming from the devil. In fact, the Church saw sleep itself as a metaphor for sin and heresy, while the path from evil to good, from sin to grace, was symbolized as the journey from sleeping to waking.

Dreams from God? Dreams from Satan? How could you determine one from the other? The Church's answer, as it evolved, was simple: Only saints could distinguish between good and evil dreams. Therefore, the dreamer must either distrust and reject his dreams or bring them to a properly ordained and accredited minister of the Church, who would see to it that the true nature of the dreams was revealed. In the evolution of the Roman Catholic Church, the ministers of the Church replaced dream books in providing the correct interpretations of the divine will. The will of God as it permeates the consciousness of the dream is filtered through the medium of the priest.

This attitude has persisted. Where Christian missionaries contacted non-Christian cultures, the dream emerged as a threat once again. The missionaries often equated with idolatry the attitude of native populations toward dreams. Father Diego Durán, a Spanish Catholic priest in sixteenth-century Mexico, said it thus:

> Now that we are dealing with dreams, [the natives] should be examined [in confession] regarding what they dream; in all of this there may be reminiscences of pagan times. In dealing with these things, it would be good to ask them [in confession] "What did you dream?" and not try to skim over it like a cat walking on hot coals. Our preaching should be dedicated to condemning and abominating all this. [1]

Over time, many of the native peoples converted by the missionaries would no longer trust themselves when it came to dreams, preferring instead, like the Mayawyaw of the Philippines, to seek out a priest to interpret their dreams. But most native peoples continued to believe in the importance of dreams.

Three centuries after Diego Durán offered his observations in Mexico, another missionary expressed a similar view. William Howell, a missionary among the Dyak people of Borneo, wrote: "[T]he Dyak belief in both dreams and omens is most detrimental to the teaching of Christianity and . . . it is important to teach them to disregard both of these."[2]

But dreams are stubborn things. They don't disappear. Even if spiritual authorities tell people to reject their dreams, the dreams continue.

⊙ Dream Exploration ⊙

What Tribe Are You?

Many of us think of ourselves as cosmopolitan. In America, we have been taught that we are products of a melting pot that obliterates all previous ethnic distinctions. But we humans are tribal, and most of us in the United States are less than three generations removed from very specific ethnic identities in this country or another.

When we look at our tribe it is important that we do so without judgment. There are no "bad," inferior, or superior cultures.

1. What culture do you identify with?
If you can name several, choose one that you seem to identify with most. Clearly the culture that we grew up in is the one that is most formative in our lives, but this question is really directed more at our culture of origin.

2. What geographical location do you associate with this culture?
France? China? Puerto Rico? Name a specific place.

3. Is there someone in your family who is the "keeper" of this culture?
Often there is someone like a grandmother or an aunt who keeps alive the stories, foods, spiritual beliefs of the culture as they relate to the family. What stories have been passed down from one generation to another?

4. What are some of the specific things that you associate with this culture?
These can be objects, foods, customs, spiritual or geographical associations.

5. What are some attitudes and ideas that you associate with this culture?
These might be things that you learned when you were very young. Attitudes about work, play, love, death—you might focus on any of these, or others.

6. Which part of yourself can you see in your tribe? Which part of your tribe can you see in yourself?
While you might be able to spend a few years responding to this one, simple is best. And again, don't judge—you may be tempted to categorize these things as either positive or negative characteristics, traits, or elements, but resist. You might also look at the ways in which you are different or think differently from your tribe.

7. Which parts of your culture's stereotype do you see as accurate?
Every culture has stereotypes and in many of these there is a kernel of truth. Find the kernel. No judgment.

8. Keep a written response to these questions.
Maybe on the fridge—and read it from time to time, for fun.

CHECKING OUR LENSES

We humans are a social and tribal species. We live, eat, create, reproduce, and die in community. Though we are spread all over the globe, most of us live in distinct cultural groups, sharing common experiences, beliefs, and perceptions with our tribe—all of which make their way into our dreams. Of course, our dreams are filled with symbols that we know, as are the dreams of others in our tribe. This commonality in dreaming is the wisdom of dream consciousness using familiar symbols to communicate—symbols associated with both our culture and our place. Our individual cultures provide the lenses through which we see both our waking and dream worlds, though these no longer function when a culture breaks down.

In all dreams we use the raw material around us, which can sometimes lead to very direct symbolism that might be recognized by a number of cultures. For example, the Dinaric people of eastern Europe consider dreams of darkness, flight, and blood to be evil omens. But sometimes the raw materials around us produce those very specific symbols related to a culture's specific interpretations and understandings. For the Dinaric, hearing the wailing cry of the cuckoo in a dream, or seeing a church, cross, bier, or priests, signifies or foretells grief or death.

If you dream that you see a man naked, poverty will befall him. If you dream that you yourself are naked, then no harm will result.

FROM THE RIF PEOPLE OF AFRICA

We humans are forever straddling the known and unknown worlds. While it is the journey into the unknown that has propelled us forward, it has been the passing on of our knowledge and discoveries that has given us our cultural foundations.

In the past, when change occurred imperceptibly, it seemed things always remained the same—entire communities seemed to be unchanging. In Vermont, for example, at the beginning of the twentieth century, mountains had separated communities over generations. People largely remained in their valleys on either side of mountain ridges and were all related by common culture and often by blood.

Much of the history of the human race has occurred during times of slow change and closely knit communities. In such an environment, people share values, belief systems, and their interpretation of dreams as well. What have emerged from these cultures are commonly accepted symbols—oral dream books, if you will, in which certain dream objects have specific interpretations. Thus the Azande of Africa have a body of stock dream interpretations that they may draw upon to make sense of their dreams. And among the Kamchatka Siberian natives, there is a body of ritualized interpretations that people can refer to in order to understand their dreams.

Throughout the world, many cultures have also relied on people who specialize in the interpretation of dreams. From the women shamans of Kamchatka to the psychiatrists on Park Avenue, these are the bearers of the heritage and symbols of their culture as it applies to the interpretation of dreams.

If you dream that you are being kissed or called by deceased people,
it means death.

FROM THE KRAGUJEVIK REGION OF SERBIA

In our Judaic-Christian-Islamic culture, one model of the dream interpreter has been the Old Testament Joseph during his time in Egypt. Interestingly, women eventually became the major dream interpreters in Egypt. Among the Mundurucu of Brazil, certain people known as *cheseretaibitchanyen* (those who know how to explain dreams) were specially trained to interpret dreams beginning in childhood, when specific medication was administered to them.

Many if not most cultures have a set number of symbols that emerge in dream consciousness. Important to remember, however, is that dream consciousness uses these symbols to convey its wisdom, rather than the other way around. Among the Muria people in India, for instance, there is a creature, the Yer Kanyang, who lives in the river and feeds on the blood of washed menstrual cloths. The Yer Kanyang is a very lonely naiad who has no one to keep her company, so she visits young girls while they are sleeping. If a young girl dreams of the Yer Kanyang and sees the river, she knows she will have her period. If she dreams of fire or flying up to the sky, she will suffer irregular menses. And when she dreams of a dried-up pond, the end of the period is at hand. Here the dream consciousness uses the symbols of the people to communicate the wisdom of the body. Clearly, this interpretation must have some bearing in reality, and because a girl has usually twelve or thirteen menstrual cycles a year, there has likely been ample opportunity to test this interpretation.

In our own culture, Robert Van de Castle, a leading dream worker and scholar, found that pregnant women in the United States saw similar symbols in their dreams. Women seemed to translate the changes occurring in their bodies into dream symbols that reflected architectural images, such as tilting skyscrapers and new front porches. It was his conclusion that dreams could be clear indicators of physical changes that dream consciousness might reflect and translate into symbols.

⊚ Dream Explorations ⊚
It's All Very Symbol*

Symbols in Our Lives
Ben Franklin actually proposed that the turkey be the national bird of the fledgling United States of America. After all, the turkey had provided food to the colonists during their struggles to survive. Can you imagine how different our history would have been if the turkey had been our national bird instead of the eagle? What would our flagpole look like with a turkey sitting on top of it?

Symbols are all around us in our waking lives. While we respond to them all the time, most often we are not aware of how we respond. Here we try to identify symbols in our lives.

---

* For this Dream Exploration I am indebted to the work of Jane White-Lewis in "Dreams and Social Responsibility—Teaching a Dream Course in the Inner City" in Kathy Bulkeley, editor, *Among These Dreamers: Essays on Dreaming and Modern Society* (Albany: State University of New York Press, 1996).

1. Select images that resonate with you from magazines or newspapers.
These can be images in advertisements (which constantly play with symbols) or articles, drawings, or photographs. The only rule is that you have to respond in some way to the images.

2. Cut out these pictures.
Do this neatly so that only each image that you are concerned with is showing.

3. Identify a feeling for each of these images.
What feeling does each image bring to the fore? Are any of your memories or experiences conjured with any of these images?

4. Make a collage of these images.
Find a large piece of paper—you may have to get one at an art supply store, but it doesn't need to be fancy; a roll of smooth, brown kraft paper would do just fine. Then find some glue; rubber cement is best because if you don't saturate the paper, it can be pulled up and placed in a different position (though its fumes are toxic—open a window if you use it).

When you make a collage, the pictures can overlap—no need to have empty spaces on the paper! Think (but not too much) about how you want to place the pictures in relation to each other.

5. Which, if any, of these images have appeared in your dreams?
What would it mean to you if one, a few, or all of the images in the collage appeared in a dream?

What Are Your Symbols?

Symbols, like metaphors, stand for something beyond their immediate meaning. The torn flag that Francis Scott Key saw rippling in the wind during the War of 1812 was more than a piece of cloth. It was a star-spangled banner of hope in the midst of adversity. A bleached cow skull on the desert sand resonates differently in our minds and imaginations than a Big Mac, even though they've come from the same organism—they each symbolize something different to us.

In this exploration, we become aware of symbols that resonate with us individually—our own symbols.

1. *Without stopping*, spend ten minutes writing a list of nouns.
Remember our very basic definition: A noun is a person, place, or thing.

2. After you have written your list, read through it slowly.
Take your time. There is no rush.

3. Place a check after the items that stir a feeling inside you as you read and imagine them.
It doesn't matter what the feeling is. Any feeling earns a check.

4. Choose ten items from the list—the ones that are most powerful for you—that is, the ones that resonate the most or stir the most feeling.
Remember, the feelings don't have to be positive.

5. Write next to each item the feeling that you associate with it.
Write the first thing that comes into your mind. Don't think about it.

6. Note one experience or association that you've had with each item on your list.
It can be something you actually experienced or it might be a vicarious experience from a movie or a book, for instance.

7. What does each item represent to you?
This is personal—think only of what each represents *to you*.

8. Pay attention to yourself as you come in contact with any of these things during the course of a day.
Note how you feel. Note what thoughts come to you.

9. Now that you've started a list of your symbols. . .
You might want to continue this exercise from time to time and keep the results in a notebook. As you grow and change, your symbols may too.

Metaphors and symbols are the language of dreams, presenting their messages. To understand the messages, to translate the language, we all must come to our own understanding of these symbols, based on our current culture, our cultural heritage, and our own personal resonance. Finally, it's important to remember that dream messages merely point us in a direction. From there, it's up to us to move.

Sometimes a Snake is Just a Schlong*

As you might have guessed by now, there are no universal meanings for symbols. Snakes, for instance, have been slithering around for quite some time, through many cultures and many parts of the world. In the Judaic-Christian tradition, a snake is Satan in disguise. It is the snake that cajoles Eve to take the

---

* *Schlong* is the German word for "snake." In Yiddish, which derives many words from German, it became the word for "penis." Did Sigmund Freud speak Yiddish?

apple; it is the snake that St. Patrick drives out of Ireland. In Judaism and Christianity, the snake has been a symbol of evil.

But once upon a time, for many of the pre-Christian peoples of Europe, the snake was sacred. In religions where people revered the Goddess, the snake, due to its habit of shedding its skin, became a symbol of change and rebirth. Thus St. Patrick, in driving the snakes from Ireland, was symbolically driving out the old religion.

Snakes figure symbolically in many cultures. In ancient Egypt the snake represented cosmic energy for good or for ill. In China, we see the snake biting its own tail in the formation of the yin/yang symbol. Two snakes twist around the Roman staff of Mercury to form the healing caduceus. The ancient Hindus saw the snake as representing the very life force—the *kundalini,* a serpentlike form that lay coiled at the base of the human spine. The release of this serpent energy could bring either enlightenment or madness.

In Arabic, the word for serpent is *el-hayyah.* The word for life is *el-hayat el-hay,* which translates as the "life giving" or "the one who bestows life." The snake is the giver of life. The Greek goddesses Artemis, Hecate, and Persephone are all depicted carrying snakes in their hands. While the snake, among the Greeks as well as the Egyptians, represented the female principle, for other cultures the creature symbolized both masculine and feminine. The Senoi of Malaysia also have a dual interpretation of snakes. In a dream a snake could represent either a thunder squall or incest, depending upon whether the serpent was inside or outside in the dream.

More often the appearance of a snake in a dream represented danger. In rural Bulgaria, when a soldier dreamed of a snake, he could practically be certain of death. High in the Himalayan villages of Sikkim, snakes represent a real danger, for there is an abundance of poisonous serpents in the valleys, forests, and cultivated lands. Thus, for the Lepcha people of this area, a dream of a snake represented a danger that reflected its danger in waking life. Interestingly, there are very few appearances of snakes in the mythology of the Lepcha, and there is no sexual meaning attached to snakes. A phallic dream symbol for the Lepchas is a corncob.

For the Ashanti people in rural Ghana, as for the Lepcha, the snake is no friend. In their reality, poisonous snakes can strike at any time. For the Ashanti, a snake in a dream symbolizes a very dangerous enemy.

The Badaga people in the Nilgiri hills of southern India treat dreams as diagnostic and view them as both predictive and descriptive. If a Badaga dreams about snakes, it means that there is something impure and threatening in his household. For the Pueblos of Oaxaca, Mexico, a snake is similarly seen as a negative symbol, indicative of a major quarrel or imprisonment, but it can also symbolize money.

For many of the native peoples of North America, the snake represents a source of power. If a snake appears in the dreams of a Paiute Indian, it can bestow shamanic power upon the dreamer. Similarly, the White Mountain Apache receive songs from snakes in their dreams as a gift and a sign to the dreamers that they conquered their fear.

In the repetoire of traditional dream interpretations for the Bhil people of India, a snake in a dream signifies merely a rope. Sometimes a snake is just a *schlong*.

The snake as a symbol has no universal meaning—in fact, in dreams and the world, it gets mixed reviews. Of course, the most famous recent interpretation of the snake is that of Sigmund Freud, who declared it to be the "most important symbol of the male organ."[3]

⊚ Dream Exploration ⊚

Snakes for You

It doesn't matter what we think. When it comes to symbols, the most important thing is not what we think, but what we feel. Snakes are no exception.

1. What's a snake to you?
First, identify what you feel about snakes, and make a list. Have you felt this way about them for a long time?

2. What has been your actual experience with snakes?
Have you ever actually come in contact with a snake outdoors? If so, what were the circumstances?

3. What is your experience with snakes in your imagination?
We hear stories, we read books, and we see movies. There are countless ways in which our feelings are shaped. Can you identify any times in your life when snakes affected your imagination? How was it affected?

4. Have you ever dreamed of snakes?
If so, what was the dream about and what role did the snake play? How did you feel about the snake in your dream?

5. Finally, write down what a snake symbolizes to you.
A list can be short (even one or two words) or longer. Again, there are no wrong answers. This exploration could also work very well with spiders. Or dogs. Or cats. Or just about any other creature that has some resonance in your life.

It's a Bird, It's a Plane

Birds have intrigued humans for ages—they can take off and soar through the sky . . . free as a bird. In the West, mythology is filled with references to birds, whether it be Icarus's fatal attempt to fly with his wax wings or Prometheus's death chained to a rock while birds peck at his intestines. Even further back in time than mythology, the ancient cave paintings in Altamira, Spain, portray a bird man flying in the sky. People have long seen birds as the link between heaven and earth.

A dream of many monkeys may mean that guests are coming.

SENOI DREAM INTERPRETATION

But what about the act of flying itself? Many of us have had dreams in which we have flown. For many, the most notable dreams have been those in which we actually felt that we were flying. What does this mean?

If one dreams of trees shooting up, an infant will be born who will have a long and a happy life.

JAMAICAN DREAM INTERPRETATION

Once again, the meaning of the symbol is not universal. For the Muria people of India, to dream of flying means certain death, which was also true for the Aztecs at the time of Spanish colonization.

For the Nyakyusa people of Africa, who felt that witches came to them in their dreams and could do them great harm, a dream of flying alone through the air meant that a witch had come to choke the dreamer. The Senoi interpretation is entirely different; they see birds as representing souls rather than people (or witches), a view that is shared by the Malays and Semang peoples.

For Sigmund Freud, dreams of flying were open to a wide variety of interpretations. However, he felt that most typically they represented a return to the pleasure people had as children, when adults would twirl them around in the air.

Of the symbolism of flying, there are certainly thousands of realities. Once again, the culture provides the vehicle through which the dream wisdom speaks. But let's see how we might relate to some of these interpretations. How about the correlation between flying and death? A great many people could understand that association when the plane in which they're a passenger taxis down the runway. As for the association between flying and being flung about by adults when we were children—that seems to be a correlation that feels familiar to many of us. But, interestingly, those who are blind actually dream about flying much more than sighted people, experiencing it as a sensation of floating through the air. One blind man experienced this sensation in almost three quarters of his dreams! So it would appear that flying in dreams has many meanings and is not the province only of those tho can see the earth and sky in waking life.

And then there are the Lepcha of Sikkim in the Himalayas, who live, it seems, nearly touching the ceiling of heaven. Surely their dreams of flying must take them even higher. In reality their interpretation of dream flying is quite down to earth. For the Lepcha, a dream of flying merely means you have inadvertently eaten bird droppings.

To dream of catching fish means the coming of wealth.

FROM THE GARO PEOPLE OF ASSAM, INDIA

⊚ Dream Explorations ⊚
See How This Flies

Fly, Fly, Fly—It's All About Resonance

"What does it mean to me?" When trying to determine the meaning of a symbol, this is the first and most important question to ask. Symbols belong to us or else they are irrelevant.

The night before I wrote this, I had a dream in which someone was going on and on about what dreams mean. After this person was finished, another person asked me whether I agreed. In the dream I answered, "It's all about resonance."

It *is* all about resonance. If we don't resonate with a symbol, then it has no meaning for us. A symbol that evokes no feeling is no symbol at all.

1. Think about flying.
Think about all the different kinds of flying with which you are familiar, including everything from airplanes to birds.

2. Make a list of different kinds of flying.
After you've thought, it always helps to write things down. It's like thinking about something twice, in two different ways.

3. What feelings do you associate with flying?
These can be different, even contradictory, feelings. For example, the feelings you associate with flying in a plane might be different from the feelings you associate with birds in flight.

4. What is your own unique feeling about flying?
Determine this and write it down. You now have a basis to look at flying in a dream.

Dream Flying

Many if not most of us have had dreams in which we fly. Often they're memorable enough to linger with us for a long time. This exploration helps you to connect such a dream with your waking life.

1. Recall a dream in which you were flying.
If you can, remember when you had the dream.

2. Recall what was happening in your life at the time of the dream.
If you weren't keeping a journal at the time, this might be difficult, but try anyway.

3. Remember the details of the dream.
What were you doing? Where were you flying? Try to remember what happened and what you saw.

4. How did you feel in the dream?
It's worth repeating: Our feelings in a dream are every bit as important as what we see in a dream. Sometimes, in fact, they are more important. So even though this is the last question of this exploration, it can be the first question you ask yourself every time you're waking up from a dream. Once you're used to asking it, it's also the question that's easiest to answer.

Do-It-Yourself Flying

This is for those who have never had a flying dream. It's also for those who have.

1. Find a quiet place, get comfortable, and close your eyes.
You can do this in the middle of the day or at bedtime just before you go to sleep. The results will be quite different from each other.

2. Imagine you have the ability to fly.
With wings or without (it's up to you), you're capable of taking off and flying at will.

3. In your mind's eye, take off.
Be as thorough and realistic as you can be—don't just fly through the ceiling; open a window in your imagination. It's easier that way.

4. Pay particular attention to the sights along the way.
You can go as high as you want. Or you can skim the ground. It's your choice. You can fly wherever you wish, as swiftly as you wish. Look around—what do you see in the air? How do things appear from high above? What do you see that you can't see from the ground?

5. Come back to earth.
How did it feel?

It Doesn't Mean What You Think It Means

If you dream that you're sick, you'd better worry, right? If you dream about losing all your money, you'd better run to the bank, right? Wrong! If dreams were that simple, we probably wouldn't bother dreaming at all.

The language of dreams is stranger than English. Things are not what they seem to be. In fact, sometimes they are exactly the opposite of what they seem to be—and of what they seem to mean.

If you dream about red tomatoes, a baby will die.

FROM THE MAYAN INDIANS OF YUCATÁN

Throughout the world people have noted the strangeness of dream language. Many peoples interpret dream images by focusing on their opposites. In rural Iran, for example, if you dream of seeing someone as a corpse, it means you will see the person full of strength and health. If you dream of bloodshed, you will have a pleasant experience.

Likewise, among the Zulu, if someone dreams that a sick person is dead, it means instead that he will get well, while if one dreams of a wedding or a man dancing, it is a sign of death or sadness.

The Ashanti people of Africa also interpret most dreams in contrasts or opposites. If you dream you are falling into a latrine, it means you are going to get money, but if you dream you have found money, you will always be poor.

Dreams about merchants, strangers, and the like are always dangerous and foretell illness or death.

FROM THE MAYAWYAW PEOPLE OF THE PHILIPPINES

The Kol people of central India interpret a dream in which there is weeping as a sign that happiness is on its way, and a dream of death means that someone who is ill will soon get well. On the other side of the globe, the Mayan people of Chan Kom also felt that to dream of weeping people was a sign of good fortune ahead, whereas the dream of happy, laughing people was a portent of sadness. The Nupe believe the same: If, in your dream, you weep, you will be successful; if you laugh, you will die.

The Chamar people of the Himalayas enjoy dreams in which they see themselves dead, for a person who dreams himself dead will live a long and healthy life. However, a person who dreams that he is well dressed or going out will die soon. The Fanti of Africa also interpret a dream that someone is dead as a portent of long life. Following this trend of opposites in interpretation, if you dream that you are picking up money, you will be in debt, but if you dream that someone is taking money from you, a great deal of money will come your way.

To dream of losing a tooth means that you will lose a relative.

FROM NINETEENTH-CENTURY VIETNAM

The Apache likewise felt that the meaning of dreams about ourselves were the opposite of what we dream. An Apache who dreamed he was going to be sick understood that he was going to be well. Conversely, if he dreamed himself well, he knew he would be sick. Other Apache dream meanings that are opposite what we assume they would be include that it's good to dream that a snake bites you, and that if you die in your dream, you will actually live a long life.

"It is highly probable that all complicated machinery and apparatus occurring in dreams stand for the genitals (and as a rule male ones) . . . Nor is there any doubt that all weapons and tools are used as symbols for the male organ: e.g., ploughs, hammers, rifles, revolvers, daggers, sabres, etc. . . . In the

same way many landscapes in dreams, especially any containing bridges or
wooded hills, may clearly be recognized as descriptions of the genitals."

SIGMUND FREUD

In matters of love, this method of interpreting the opposite of what a
dream may seem to be saying could lead to sadness, for it means a positive
dream can have negative implications. Among the Zapotec people of Mexico,
if a man dreamed that he was having an agreeable talk with his sweetheart, it
foretold that he was about to be rejected.

Even excrement, unpleasant in waking life, has decidedly opposite symbolic meaning in dreams for many of the world's cultures. In Papua-Melanesia,
to dream of excrement on the veranda means that you will receive money; the
Ashanti who dreams of falling into a latrine is going to fall into money; in
Thailand to dream of feces means that there will be wealth and riches for the
dreamer; and in Tangiers, dreaming that your clothes are full of excrement
means that you will come into money.

Among the Lepcha of Sikkim there are various interpretations of dream
poop. A dream of solid excrement indicates a good buckwheat harvest, while
a dream of liquid feces means that the harvest will be destroyed by storms. And
a dream of being covered with filth means, of course, that wealth is on its way.

To dream of copulating with two women means that a hunter will bag two
animals the next day.

FROM THE SENOI PEOPLE OF MALAYSIA

At first glance it would be easy to dismiss as weird these symbols that
mean the opposite of what we think they might mean. But then we must
remember: There are thousands of realities.

The opposite interpretation of symbols in dreams does not come from
perversity, but rather from an understanding of the duality of the universe. You
can't have hot without cold or life without death. For many cultures, dreams
are part of this duality.

"In men's dreams, a necktie often appears as a symbol for the penis."

SIGMUND FREUD

The Zulu notion of dreams themselves expresses this duality. The hours of dark are the reverse of daylight. Thus the shades who are active at night behave in a way that is the reverse of their daytime behavior and their symbols are opposite what is usual as well. In this belief the Zulu articulate the duality of waking consciousness and dream consciousness.

If a hunter dreams of quarreling with a woman, it means he will bag a she-bear the next day.

FROM THE SOUTHERN APPALACHIANS

Among humans, perhaps the greatest duality is that of male and female, yin and yang, the animus and anima, which is part of our heritage. The Iranians of the past grafted this duality onto their dream interpretation. Thus they felt that the dreams of women should be interpreted in the opposite sense.

Of course the only thing that is consistent is inconsistency. It would be too simple to interpret everything in dreams as opposite what we anticipate. In fact, those cultures that see some dream symbols in terms of their opposites do not see *all* dream images in this way. For example, the Mayans who saw a dream of weeping as a sign of good fortune also saw dreams of darkness as ill omens. The Apache who saw a dream of death as a sign of life also saw dreams of overflowing water as indication of a flood. As one Westerner studying the Nupe people of Africa put it, some interpretations draw upon contrasts, some upon analogies. There is no consistent symbolism "nor yet any of the 'universal' symbols cited by psychoanalysts."[4]

As we explore our own dream consciousness, we can discover the language we ourselves have been speaking. Usually it is both refreshingly new and hauntingly familiar. This symbol language—this metaphor-speak—has layers upon layers and reveals wheels within wheels.

🌀 Dream Exploration 🌀

Being Contrary

The problem with prediction is that it takes time to play out. It's much easier dealing with the present moment. In this exploration we deal with the now.

Opposites are all around us. Our lives are made up of opposites. See how this can apply to our dreams.

1. Choose one of your dreams.
It can be any dream that you have recorded or remembered.

2. Make a list of some of the characteristics and particulars in the dream.
Choose those for which opposites can readily be found. For example, if your dream's setting was daytime, it would be easy to determine the opposite—night.

3. Next to each characteristic, write its opposite.
Be creative. There are quite a few opposites of everything in this world. If you are walking, one opposite is flying. If you are lost, you could be found.

4. Rewrite the dream using these opposites.
Instead of up, write down. Instead of happy, write sad. And so forth.

5. Read the new dream to yourself.
What does it feel like? Does it resonate at all?

✥ Dream Story

Never Be Too Sure: The Danger of Judgment

There was an old man who, though he was not old by today's standards, was old in his time. In his village, the neighbors took pity on him, but he never seemed to realize just how bad off he was—or, when things seemed right, how well off he was.

When he was a young man, his beloved wife gave up her own life as she gave life to his baby son, their only child. Suddenly he was left alone to care for the infant.

His neighbors came to him in sympathy. "You poor fellow," they said. "To lose a wife is a horrible thing. To raise a son alone is a great hardship."

But he replied only with, "Maybe yes. Maybe no. Who knows for certain?" And his neighbors went away mystified.

The man poured all his love into his young son, and the boy grew into a strapping young man whose devotion to his father was known throughout the region. The neighbors would come to the father and say, "What a blessing you have in a son so strong and devoted."

The man only shrugged his shoulders and replied, "Maybe yes. Maybe no. Who knows for certain?" And, as always, the neighbors went away perplexed, asking each other, "Doesn't this old fool know anything at all? Maybe the death of his wife has deranged him."

Now, while a devoted and loving son, the boy was a free spirit, and so was drawn to the band of wild horses that congregated near the village. One day, despite the warnings of the neighbors, the boy disappeared into the wilderness to capture the leader of the horses—a beautiful white stallion as free of spirit as the boy himself was.

When he did not return after a few weeks, many assumed that he was dead. The neighbors went to the old man and said, "Your son is gone. We fear he is dead and we grieve with you for your loss."

The man shrugged his shoulders and said, "Maybe yes. Maybe no. Who knows for certain?" And the neighbors walked away, shaking their heads. Perhaps the shock of losing his only child had been too much for the man.

Shortly thereafter the son reappeared in the village, astride the beautiful white stallion. He had captured and tamed the horse and people could see it was the finest horse in the entire province.

A neighbor patted the man on the back. "Surely God has favored you. Your son has returned, an event made twice joyous by the appearance of this magnificent steed."

The man only shrugged. "Maybe yes. Maybe no. Who knows for certain?" And the neighbor walked away, firm in his conviction that the old man had lost his senses.

While the white stallion obeyed the young man, it was not used to the crowds of people that gathered to see him, and often became nervous. One day, as the young man was riding his horse, a little child ran out to see the animal pass by. This startled the horse and he reared high, throwing the young man to the ground and causing him to break his left leg.

With his son unable to work, the man had to do all the work around the house and in the fields. He had grown used to the help of his strong son, and the neighbors came to offer their condolences. "Your son will not be of help to you for many months. Instead you must aid him. We are sorry for this unnatural state of affairs," they said.

The man's response had become familiar by now: "Maybe yes. Maybe no. Who knows for certain?"

A week later, a dragoon of the king's recruiters arrived in the village and all of the young men were forced to enlist in the army and go away to fight a war in a distant land. Those who refused would be executed. Naturally, they had no use for a man whose leg was broken and so the man's son was spared.

Grieving for their own sons, the neighbors went to see the man. "Oh, how

God has kissed you! We have lost our sons and will likely never see them again. You have your son, who will be able to work in a matter of weeks. How lucky you are!"

The old man answered as he always had: "Maybe yes. Maybe no. Who knows for certain?"

A STORY FROM THE SUFI[5]

SHARING DREAMS

We humans have been trying to understand our dreams for as long as we have been dreaming—and we have been trying together even more than we have been trying on our own. We are a social species. We live and are nurtured in community, and for many people around the world, the community has reinforced the importance of understanding dream consciousness.

The attempts to understand dreams often begin in childhood. Ojibwa adults encouraged children to both dream and remember their dreams. One Ojibwa father reflected the importance of dreams by, every morning, lying between his two sons, seven and nine years old, and asking them to describe the dreams they'd had the night before. The Ojibwa notion was that the earlier a child opened himself to dreams, the more receptive he would be when important visions came later on in in life.

The Jibaro people of eastern Ecuador and Peru also paid great attention to the dreams of young people. They felt that children's dreams could decide their entire future. While it was the job of the Jibaro youth to remember their dreams, it was the job of the adult men of the family to interpret them. In Malaysia a young Iban man takes an early active interest in the conversations of his elders in order to learn the interpretation of dreams used by his people.

"People who have frequent dreams of swimming and who feel great joy in cleaving their way through the waves, and so on, have as a rule been bed-wetters and are repeating in their dreams a leisure which they have long learnt to forgo."

SIGMUND FREUD

The cultures most famous for their communal work with dreams are the Senoi and Temiar of Malaysia.* In these cultures dreams are a path toward fulfillment of self and of community. These cultures encourage children to dream and then share their dreams. Discussion of dreams is, among these groups, a common morning experience during which children can listen to adults and learn.

Being gentle people, the Senoi and Temiar do not force interpretation upon children. In fact, they feel that imposing any authority on children can make them ill. For instance, trying to persuade a child to do something she does not want to do runs the risk of scaring away her soul, perhaps even killing the child in the process. However, all people, regardless of gender or age, may participate in the village councils. Thus, the children can share in discussions whose topics may range from serious disputes to dreams.

⊚ Dream Exploration ⊚

Dream Play for the Younger Set
Is there a kid in your life? For parents whose kids are still at home, the sharing of dreams is a great way to start the day. The idea is not to interpret dreams, but simply to share them.

1. Pick a time when everyone is together.
Breakfast is often a good time—people are, for a moment, out of the rush of routine. It's also a time when dreams are fresh in everyone's mind.

2. Offer to share your dream.
It's much better than starting by asking other people to share theirs. Of course, this presumes that you have a dream to share. So wait until you have a dream. Don't try to make sense out of your own dream. Just tell the story.

3. Ask others if they would like to share.
Usually kids, especially younger ones, will be more than happy to follow suit if a parent has already shared a dream.

4. Don't interpret.
If the kids want to try to offer some understanding of their own

---

* The work of Kilton Stewart, Richard Noone, and Dennis Holman popularized the Senoi. Later, G. William Domhoff revised the rather utopian view of the earlier authors. See Kilton Stewart, "Dream Theory in Malaya," in Charles T. Tart, editor, *Altered States of Consciousness: A Book of Readings* (New York: John Wiley and Sons, 1969); Richard Noone with Dennis Holman, *In Search of the Dream People* (New York: William Morrow, 1972); G. William Domhoff, *The Mystique of Dreams: A Search for Utopia through Senoi Dream Theory* (Berkeley: University of California Press, 1985).

dreams, fine. But you should avoid offering your interpretation in return. The object is for this to be a relaxed, enjoyable time—no agenda.

You might want to make this a daily experience. Dreams are forever new and interesting. Sometimes kids even start to make them up. No problem. That simply shows the merging of dream consciousness and waking consciousness—imagination. And there's nothing wrong with that.

The more dreams are part of everyday experience, the deeper will people go in examining them. In some cultures people share their dream experiences daily. The Yama of Cape Horn began every morning with one of the adults relating his dream. If someone had a particularly vivid dream, he might wake up his family in the middle of the night to tell them about it. Everyone among these people received dreams and everyone was concerned about them.

If a man dreams of a ladle for pouring out tea, his wife is adulterous.

FROM THE LEPCHA PEOPLE OF SIKKIM

Dream discussion among the Iroquois also involved everyone. They treated dreams both lightly and sincerely and, overall, regarded dreams as divine messages that should be followed.

To dream that a living person is lying dead merely means that the person dreamed of is lying sleeping with a full belly.

FROM THE LEPCHA PEOPLE OF SIKKIM

On certain festive days, the entire Iroquois community participated in dream guessing. A visitor with a sad and dejected appearance entered a house and announced that he had a dream. He then asked the residents to guess his dream and people would both guess and offer interpretations. The dreamer went from house to house until he found a dream that suited him, either an interpretation of an actual dream or a dream that someone adapted and offered as his own. The game would stop when the visitor stated that his dream had been correctly guessed. If the dream required action, he would follow it to the letter.

⊚ Dream Exploration ⊚

Dream Guessing

This is a variation of the Iroquois dream guessing game and is meant to be approached as a game rather than a serious or heavy analytical session. It works best with groups of more than three people who have some prior rapport.

1. Decide which person will be the dreamer and determine together ahead of time how long your dream guessing time will last.
The person who plays the dreamer can actually have a dream in mind or not.

2. The dreamer asks the others to guess her dream.
There should be a moment of silence after this.

3. The others begin guessing dreams while the dreamer listens.
Those of you who are guessing literally create dreams—the story, settings, feelings, and all the rest. Let the imagination move you. The dreamer takes in these various dreams, listening carefully to each.

4. After the dream guessing time has passed, the dreamer then begins to tell whether or not any of the dreams was really hers.
This can mean that someone has offered a dream that actually comes close to one of her actual dreams. More likely, one of the dreams can be adapted as her own.

5. The dreamer then offers a meaning for the dream.
Simple is best, but whatever feels right is fine. Remember to keep things light and playful. After the dreamer has finished her interpretation, another person volunteers to be the dreamer and the game continues until everyone who wishes to has played the role of the dreamer.

In Islam there is a long tradition of exploring dreams. Muhammad himself declared that dreams were part of the prophetic mission. Every morning he asked his disciples what they had dreamed during the previous night and then interpreted these dreams, either accepting or rejecting their communications according to their soundness. In these morning gatherings he also related his own dreams.

If someone sees a tiger in a dream, the next day a rich man will come to visit.

FROM THE MIAO OF WESTERN CHINA

Dream sharing has survived in many communities despite attempts to suppress it. In some Tzeltal Mexican villages, the only organized dogma is that of the local Catholic church. The sharing of dreams, long a custom of these people, is outside the pale of organized religion. Nevertheless, in the evenings, among relatives and friends, the villagers weave their dreams into myths and tales that are shared.

The impulse to share in this way is strong, and is one that is felt around the world. Far in the arctic area of Kamchatka and the Kirile Islands, the indigenous peoples, upon awakening, relate their dreams to each other. And for the Temiar, the sharing of dreams is so important a part of the culture that it has found its way into their very language. The standard Temiar greeting every morning is *"Ma-loo,"* or "Where have you been to?" after which the members of the household informally talk about their dream journeys of the night before.

◎ Dream Explorations ◎
Dream On

Communal Story
We can bridge the gap between our dreaming and waking consciousness by extending the dream into our waking life. This is a variation of a childhood game in which a story is composed by a group of people. It is best practiced in a group of three or more.

1. One person begins by relating part of an actual dream.
This can be either a recent dream or one from the more distant past. This initiator should say more than a few words, offering a small chunk of the dream and then stopping.

2. A second person picks up the dream where the first person left off.
Be creative, but try to stay within the framework of the dream. Again, it's best to say more than just a few words.

3. The next person jumps in when the second person stops . . . and people keep jumping in, following this pattern.
Remember to take off where the previous person left off. And remember to keep your "narrative" in dream mode—that is, remember that the story has to sound and feel like a dream.

4. Go around the group at least once.
Together you are all creating a waking dream. After you've finished, the group might decide to look at the dream as a whole and perhaps use other explorations to see what this "dream" might mean.

Continuing the Dream*

We continue a dream in this exploration as well, bringing our dream consciousness to bear upon our waking consciousness—only this one is a solo act.

1. Choose any dream.
The best dreams are those for which you feel there's something unresolved.

2. Write down the dream.
If you've already recorded it in your journal, rewrite it.

3. At the point where the actual dream ends, continue it.
That's right, keep the dream going—any way you wish, in any direction you wish—until it ends.

4. How does your new ending differ from the ending in the dream?
Is the feeling different? If so—how is it different? What has changed in the dream?

Perhaps no people in the world in times past relied upon dreams more than did the Mohave Indians. For the old Mohave, knowledge came only partly through experience. Dreams were the primary source of knowledge and dream sharing was a ritualized community experience. Great dreams were sung or told to the community at special gatherings, and each listener would find in them the symbols and meanings that were his alone.

If someone dreams of a house or something else on fire, the weather will be fair.

THE CHU'UN MIAO OF CHINA

For the old Mohave a dream could come at night. Or it might be a waking thought or flash of insight that opened the doors of understanding. Dreams could give awareness of obstacles as well as the means to overcome these stumbling blocks.

The community support of dream sharing makes the experience of dreaming richer for all of its members, which is why when the community disintegrates, so does the power of the dreamer. The Mohave culture gradually fell apart with the arrival and dominance of the white man and Christian culture, and as the culture crumbled, so too did the power of dreams diminish.

---

* Once again, my thanks to Jane White-Lewis for this idea.

More and more the Mohave dream symbols became those of the dominant culture: planes, trains, automobiles, church figures, and so forth. The richness of their unique dream culture faded away.

If someone dreams of himself or someone else as having long hair, it is a guarantee that he will enjoy a long life.

FROM THE EAST INDIES

⊚ Dream Explorations ⊚
Dreaming in Groups

Taking It Back*

In a group we can sometimes see things in our dreams that we never thought were there. This exploration must be approached with the notion that there are thousands of realities—even within our own dreams.

This exercise is best done with three or more people and the key is that the participants take on each dream as their own and respond to it in kind. The person relating the dream should write it down ahead of time, so advance planning is a plus. If possible, it is helpful for this same person to mention briefly what was occurring in his waking life during the period immediately preceding the dream. All discussions within the group should remain confidential.

1. One person reads his or her dream.
A recent dream is best—the fresher, the better.

2. As the person reads, the other participants write down the dream.
Verbatim—just as the person dictates it. No comments. No questions.

3. When the dreamer has finished dictating her dream, she becomes a listener while the other members of the group speak to the dream from their feelings, as if it were theirs.
There is no dialogue at this point. And the focus should not be on analysis. Those speaking in this part of the exercise should limit their responses to statements about feelings, and should phrase them in the first person ("I"), as if the dream were their own: "I feel lonely,"

---

* For this Dream Exploration I am grateful to the work of Montague Ullman and, particularly, Montague Ullman and Nan Zimmerman, *Working with Dreams* (Los Angeles: Jeremy Tarcher, 1979). The people who brought this to life for me were Claire Schmais and Ellen Foreman.

"I feel lost," "I feel jubilant," "I feel that things are confused"—these might be appropriate responses.

4. The dreamer listens and takes notes.
She silently transcribes all that the others are saying.

5. When the dreamer feels that she has all the responses she needs, she says, "I can take it back."
It's important not to say this too soon, however. The dreamer should give the respondents a chance to go though the range of feelings that are evoked by the dream.

6. The dreamer then tries to make sense of the dream based upon what the respondents have said combined with her own experience.
This is the time at which the dream and the life of the dreamer come together—the dreamer discusses what has been happening in her life and how it relates to the dream and the responses of the others.

7. Now there can be give and take.
People explore, as a group, various aspects of the dream.

8. When the discussion comes to a natural conclusion, another person becomes the dream reader and the process begins again.
This exploration can provide an incredibly fruitful way of growing with dreams. When it is done on a regular basis with a dream group, people become more familiar with their own themes and the process makes of the group a mini-community. It's helpful if the group meets regularly and can follow up on any discussion from the previous meeting.

Waking Dream in a Group*

This exploration follows the same format as "Taking It Back"—it's a group exercise and the dreamer reads her dream while others record it. But there's a significant difference—the dream is made up, composed, or constructed in the dreamer's waking life.

1. As the dreamer, you make up a dream and tell it to the group.
It can take the form of either a dream or a vision. Don't dwell on the fact that you're making it up.

2. The exercise then follows steps 3, 4, 5, and 6 in "Taking It Back."
Instead of making sense of the dream based on the respondents' comments and your waking life, let go of your imagination as you

* Thanks to Ellen Foreman, who tried this with us in the dream group.

create the vision. It's best if this vision is based on real experiences
and uses real building blocks as symbols.

While community sharing of dreams is considered invaluable in many cultures, it exists in delicate balance with individual exploration. It is the wisdom of many of the world's peoples that the dreamer himself is ultimately the best person to understand his dream. The Ojibwa, while supporting dream interpretation in community, also feel that a dream can truly be understood only by the person who dreams it.

The Naskapi of Labrador support the pursuit of dream consciousness as a community, for it is in dreams that the Great Man reveals himself. They believe at the same time, however, that each individual person must establish his own connection with the divine as it appears in his dreams. For the Naskapi the exploration of dream consciousness has great support in the community but is a very individual process, just as it is for the Micmac people of eastern Canada. The Micmac feel that dreams are not the same for each person. Some dreams have signs and meanings that can be known only to the individual who has dreamed them.

If you dream that stars are falling, people will be killed in a war.

FROM THE KRAGUJEVAC REGION OF SERBIA

The interpretation of dreams was an individual matter for the Ute people as well. In their belief every individual could seek visions and they embraced the claims of many vision recipients with great respect. However, the Utes never recognized any single dream or vision recipient as the sole possessor of all truth. For the Utes there were thousands of realities and many truths, which was one of the reasons why Christian missionaries had such a difficult time convincing them that there was but one truth.

If you dream of catching fish in clear water, you will get money.

FROM THE DELAWARE INDIANS

There are other cultures that have also believed that dreams are entirely a private matter. Among the southern Slavs, those who took dreams most seriously were those who would not share them, feeling that if they did, they might realize an evil or prevent a good. In Albania it was commonly believed that if an auspicious dream was shared, the good in it might turn to ill. The Seminole of Oklahoma felt that it was bad luck to share a bad dream with another. Any bad dream could simply be told it to a rotten tree stump. The Hare Indians, however, had the opposite view: A good dream should be kept to yourself; otherwise, it might not come to pass. Only after it had been realized could it be freely discussed. Bad dreams, on the other hand, could be freely discussed, for this prevented them from coming true.

Understanding dreams was the cornerstone of Shoshone spirituality. Among them there were no real shamans who stood between the individual and the divine. Instead, the dream was the doorway to the divine and it was the dreamer who held the key. For the Yuman people, the notion of a priest was also replaced by individual dreaming. Everyone dreamed and, while only a few had real power dreams, everyone could access his own dream consciousness. Similarly, among the ancient Celts, anyone could dream and gain entrance to the divine, and among the Mandan people almost everyone, men and women, had vision experiences. The power of the dream was shared by all.

REALITY CHECK: ARE YOU DREAMING?

If all can of us can equally access the world of dreams, how do we determine what is real and what is illusion? How do we know which dreams mislead us and which can guide us? Of course, there may be no dreams that mislead us— we may simply mislead ourselves. Nevertheless, people have always wondered which dreams to look to for true guidance.

To dream of muddy water is an omen of impending death.

FROM THE APPALACHIAN MOUNTAINS

The ancient Greeks spoke of the Gate of Horn and the Gate of Ivory as the means to telling true dreams from false. Living on Oceanus's western shores and appearing to mortals only in sleep, the Oniroi, the source of all dreams, who reside at both the Gate of Horn and the Gate of Ivory, sent forth true dreams through the Gate of Horn and false dreams through the Gate of Ivory. Ultimately, of course, it was up to the individual to determine which of his dreams was which.

The Tiv people also understood there to be two kinds of dreams: those sent by someone sleeping with or near the dreamer and those that came from the dreamer himself—and regardless of where they came from, some of these dreams were lies and some were true. For the Tikopia there are true dreams represented by the experience of the soul on its nightly journey and there are those dreams that are brought by malicious spirits who counterfeit familiar faces in order to deceive the dreamer. The Melanesians made their distinction between spontaneous and prophetic dreams. They believed that true dreams, which were prophetic, were the result of divine intervention and were not spontaneous, while spontaneous dreams came without reason or truth and were illusory.

Dream Exploration

What Time of Day? What Time of Night?
The Javanese classify dreams according to the time of night during which they appear. In the Islamic science of *tabir,* or dream interpretation, dreams occurring in the day are more reliable than those at night; thus, the truest dreams come at daybreak. The Maricopa people divided the evening into four parts. Significant dreams could occur at any time, but favorable dreams came in the middle hours of the evening. The Tzeltal of Mexico feel that if a dream occurs early in the night, it might take up to six months before the event portended in the dream takes place. However, if the dream occurs in the very early morning, the event might happen soon.

Western researchers into rapid eye movement (REM) have discovered that, while dreams apparently occur in cycles, there is more activity at certain times than at others. In this exploration, you can explore your busiest dream times.

1. Notice your dream time (or times) and record it (them) in your journal.
Remain aware of the times of night that you dream and the nature of the dreams you experience at these times. Keep a clock close to you so that you can see the time when you awaken without getting out of bed

2. After you've done this for several nights in a row, note any connection between the time of the dream and the kind of dream.
Be open to any connection that might exist.

Drinking liquors in a dream forebodes something bad, even death. To see dough, bread, or berries in a dream signifies good earnings or catches.

FROM THE FINNISH LAPPS

The Crows divided dreams into four grades. The lowest were the non-mystical dreams, which they called "no-account dreams." The next in order were the wish dreams, which had to do with property and the material well-being of the dreamer. Above these in importance were the medicine dreams—power dreams—and finally, the highest form of dream consciousness for the Crow was the dream that resulted from the vision quest. It was through this ritual that a youth prepared, sacrificed, and opened himself to the visitation of the divine.

Clearly, most people consider that not all dreams are the same. Some have greater impact than others. But what determines the importance of a dream varies from culture to culture. The Garifuna of Central America believe that all important dreams are connected with ancestors. These require action to mollify the ancestors, while all other dreams are mundane and require no action. The Lepcha of the Himalayas see many dreams as meaningless including dreams of flying, dreams in which a person lies dead, dreams of running, and dreams of naked people—all of which are often considered significant in other cultures. The Havasupai of the American Southwest believed that the truly important dreams were those in which the dead, ghosts, or spirits appeared.

So many realities. The Delaware Indians were able to embrace them all. For the Delaware, while some dreams indicated good fortune and long life and others led the hunters to special places where there was game, all dreams were significant. The Delaware understood what Rabbi Hisda understood—there are indeed thousands of realities.

If you dream of white horses fighting, it will rain the next day.

FROM THE MAYA INDIANS OF YUCATÁN

MAKING LOVE TO YOUR PSYCHE

It's time to put an end to the violence that we wreak upon ourselves. It's time to put an end to the rape of our dream consciousness. Strong words? Perhaps. But as the legendary politician Al Smith used to say, let's look at the record.

For the sake of argument, let's give our waking consciousness and our dream consciousness a persona—individuality. Imagine how two individuals might meet and become intimate. Think about how a love connection evolves. First, these two have to get to know each other—even when there is a kind of recognition or spark right from the start.

During this beginning time, each might approach the other—the ideal would be a gentle and mutual meeting at a time during which each could become more familiar with the other. There would be the sharing of points of view, the telling of stories. The coming together of lovers is a gentle, mutual process that is ideally characterized as the meeting of two souls who fully accept the individuality of the other.

But can Mr. Wake and Ms. Dream truly come together mutually?

In the West the common practice is to wake up and try to "make sense" of our dreams, to wrest meaning from them. We use our rational mind, our waking mind, and try to "figure out" what our dreams mean.

There is a certain violence in this. Ms. Dream is a rather shy individual who doesn't approach things in quite the same way as Mr. Wake. To her, there is no tenderness or gentle curiosity in Mr. Wake's ham-fisted approach.

To be quite honest, in our waking liaison with our dream consciousness, there is no foreplay.

It's time to make love to our dream consciousness—which requires mutual respect. Mr. Wake must recognize that, even though he does not understand Ms. Dream, real understanding can come only when he *allows* it. Only then can he can move tentatively toward her. Then he can encourage her to visit during the light of day and he can be her guest in the light of the moon.

The lines between dream and waking consciousness can be blurred—but only if we try not to control our dreams.

◉ Dream Explorations ◉ The Raw Material

Building Blocks

This exploration can help to erase some of the barrier that exists between our waking consciousness and our dream consciousness. If we pay attention, we can see how the experiences of our waking lives are translated into dream consciousness. The Bedouins of the western desert of Egypt believe that dreams reflect and are connected to what we see or do during the day. The Javanese even categorize some dreams according to certain symbols that are created or suggested directly from experience. Such symbols are termed here *building blocks*. For the Javanese, there is the dream called *cakra bawa,* which comes about because the dreamer has seen or experienced something that made an impression strong enough to affect his dream. Another kind of dream is the *sudarsana,* which is a dream affected by sound. If a woman goes to sleep hearing an owl, for instance, she might dream of an owl.

We in the West might dream of skyscrapers that turn into rubber after we've spent a day in a city with skyscrapers. We might talk to someone who has been in Australia and then dream about strange boomerangs or kangaroos. These building blocks are some of the symbols that we create from our daily lives.

Sometimes when we identify the sources of the substance of our dreams, we can learn about the dream itself. By isolating the "raw material" of the dream, we can understand what we are telling ourselves.

1. Prepare for your next dream by telling yourself that you will remember its details.
You've done this before.

2. Before going to sleep, be sure you have a pen and paper near the bed so that as you wake up you can immediately write down the dream before it disappears.
We are striving for freshness. This fish doesn't keep.

3. As you slowly awaken, write down the dream as clearly as possible.
You might want to wake up fully and write as much as you can before you forget.

4. Review your retelling of the dream and underline those aspects that relate to actual things that you experienced the previous day.
You'll surprise yourself with how many parts of the dream you can trace back to events of the previous day. A passing word, a conversation, an experience or occurrence, a sight—they all count.

5. How did your waking experience get translated into the dream?
We take the raw material of our daily lives and create a dream that contains it. We transform images and experiences.

6. Did your feelings about these things change from your waking experience to your dream experience?
For example, you might have had a lovely tuna sandwich for lunch, yet dreamed about being attacked by a giant tuna at night.

7. What feelings and thoughts do you normally associate with the things you built into your dream?
Do you like tuna? What associations do you have with it? Do you remember eating tuna at your grandma's every Saturday? You get the picture.

8. Play some more with these building blocks.
Do they tell you anything about how you are feeling or what you are thinking overall at this moment in your life?

Making a Road Map of Your Dreams

For me, my dream vortex is the Bronx. The funny thing is that I never lived there—my grandparents did. Yet I find myself lost in my dreams, time and time again, as I try to get out of the Bronx. As an adult I've created a dream Bronx—a super spaghetti of roads and highways that I find nearly impossible to navigate. Or else I find myself trying to get out of the Bronx on a subway more complicated than any train in the New York subway system.

We've all created places in our dreams, and most of us visit them again and again. Here we look at these places, and maybe learn a bit about where we really want to go.

1. Think of a place that you visit in your dreams.
It's best if it's a place you've visited more than once in dream consciousness.

2. Is it related to any place in your waking life?
Usually there is some correlation between a dream place and a place we've been to in waking life, though sometimes we do create brand-new places.

3. In your dream, what do you do when you visit this dream place?
Are you always doing the same thing? In my dream Bronx, for instance, I am always getting lost.

4. Where are you coming from and where are you going?
Try to determine where you've come from before reaching this dream place. Do you go somewhere else after your visit?

5. How do you feel when you visit this dream place?
Is there a certain feeling you get in your dream every time you visit this place? Does the feeling vary from visit to visit or change during your visit?

6. Make a road map that shows how to get to this dream place.
This, of course, is not a regular road map but instead a map that reflects the geography of your dream. Draw the steps or stops in your dream that get you to this place. You might even draw a picture of the place itself.

7. Check in with your waking life.
See what places in your waking life might be like this dream place.

☀ Dream Story

I Taught Myself with a Gun

The deadline for my manuscript for this book was approaching. The pressure was building. Many times I would feel like diverting myself and, of course, the Internet is a wonderful diversion . . . I forced myself to focus. It really was the only choice.

Then my dream consciousness kicked in. I was in the middle of writing the chapter on dream creativity when it seemed to me that I was trying to find the secret to something. What the "something" was I couldn't be sure—but I had a dream that I was looking for a secret password that would open the doors for me. I tried to think of it and as I did, the password kept popping up in my dream, as passwords sometimes do on my computer. It was my frequent flyer number to one of the airlines I travel. What was the message? I could unlock the "secrets" with what I already knew—and then I could fly.

After this, when I sat down in the morning once more to work on the chapter, I pushed myself. I forced myself and things began to flow. That evening I had a dream that I was teaching a class with a gun. As I proceeded with the class in this rather unorthodox manner, I knew that it was worth it.

The next day, as I wrote, I moved a little farther and a little more easily. After all, I was writing about imagination and creativity. I was writing about letting dream consciousness inform our waking consciousness.

That night I had a dream in which I'd invented a way of playing with words creatively. It was clear: Finally, I'd let my dream consciousness inspire me. Dreams are another truth, the continual reminder that we have two realities. They are teachers and if we let go of control, we can learn.

The idea is not to "make sense" of dreams but to "allow sense" out of dreams. When we ask "What does it mean? Is this right?" we pit ourselves against the universe instead of connecting with our source. Certainly there are times for the right answer, but in the world of dreams there is no right answer—there are thousands of them. That's the pleasure, the mystery, the fun.

It's important to remember that when we look into our dreams, we can never fail. Whatever we do, we can, without any formal dream training, see something there, because dreams are cornucopias filled with riches waiting to be consumed and enjoyed. They are treasure chests filled with bounty.

Carl Jung wrote, "If we meditate on a dream sufficiently long and thoroughly, if we carry it around with us and turn it over and over, something almost always comes of it." When we give space to dream consciousness, it will reward us. We can let our dreams sit and brew, and eventually what we discover is what we already knew.

In Thomas Mann's *Joseph in Egypt,* the Pharaoh complains that in interpreting his dream, Joseph has told him what he already knows. Joseph replies, "Pharaoh errs . . . if he thinks he does not know. His servant can do no more than to prophesy to him what he already knows." And there is nothing more powerful than the recognition of knowing.

⑨ Dream Exploration ⑨
Feeling and Learning—Together and Alone

Feel, Feel, Feel

The waking consciousness tells us to think, analyze, make sense. The dream consciousness tells us to feel. What we feel in a dream is central. Sometimes the only difference between a nightmare and an adventure is our feeling.

The first question that we need to ask ourselves when we awaken from a dream is not "What did it mean?" but "What did I feel?"

Whenever we're trying to learn from our dream consciousness, this exploration is central.

1. How did you feel?
That's all. No step 2 or 3 or 4. Just how did you feel? What did the dream feel like to you? What did you feel like when you woke up?

You Are All of It

We *are* the dream. That's one reality. One way of looking at a dream is to see every part of the dream as a part of ourselves. This idea was developed by Fritz Perls and is called Gestalt dream therapy.

This exploration is best practiced in a group, although each person can write down the answers rather than speaking them and then share them with all present.

1. Tell a dream.
And use the present tense. For example, "I am walking down the street" rather than "I was walking down the street."

2. Note which part of the dream stands out.
Is there a particular scene or person or event that seems more noticeable or prominent than others?

3. Become part of the dream.

Say your dream runs something like this: "I'm walking down the street when I run into my friend Harry. I go to say hello when a large eagle swoops down and carries Harry away." You could, of course, be yourself. Then you could become Harry. You could also be the eagle. You could even become the street.

4. Describe what it feels like being each part in the dream.

What does it feel like to be Harry? What does it feel like to be the eagle?

5. Give voice to each of the different parts of the dream.

Have a dialogue between them. The eagle, perhaps, speaks to the street, and then maybe Harry speaks to the eagle, and so forth. The point? We are all of the parts in our dreams and, therefore, we are whole.

 Dream Story

Lenore's Toilet Dream

It was Lenore's recurring dream, and she'd been having it from the time she was a child. It is a real classic.

In it she had to go to the bathroom quite urgently. In fact, she felt as if she was going to burst. Unfortunately, she was not at home; she was in some public place—usually the same place. She had to find a place to go, and she had to find it fast. We all know the feeling, don't we?

Fortunately, she found a public rest room, but in stall after stall the toilets were unusable—dirty, malfunctioning, foul, each one worse than the next, some full and some actually overflowing with urine and feces. Though she was in the rest room, there was no place to go. By the time she'd peeked in the third or fourth toilet stall, Lenore was almost in physical pain.

The dream persisted, as close to a nightmare as Lenore had ever experienced. Year after year the dream recurred. There seemed to be no end. And each time, just as she approached the last and most revolting stall, she woke up.

One night the dream played out as usual, and, as usual, she woke up as she approached the last stall. She shook the dream from her head as she got up and went to the bathroom.

And, then she realized something. This was the first time she'd ever climbed out of bed after the dream—and in this she found the key to what it was all about.

Her recurring dream was telling her, quite simply, to go to the bathroom. After that night, she never had the nightmare again.

⊚ Dream Explorations ⊚
Recognizing and *Not* Analyzing

A Sort of Sorting the Assorted

There are all kinds of dreams. Some seem deep and profound. Some seem rather ordinary. Some might seem unimportant in the moment but gain a certain importance as we look at them later. All dreams have some kind of significance. Without judging them as either good or bad, it would be helpful to try to recognize different kinds of dreams.

> **1. Review your dreams of the last month.**
> Page through your journal and keep an extra sheet of paper handy to write down any ideas that come to you.

> **2. Note which dreams resonate with you and have a certain power and which dreams seem more commonplace.**
> This doesn't mean that the ordinary dreams aren't important. You're simply distinguishing a degree of intensity. Which dreams seem to be the most powerful?

> **3. Look more closely at the powerful dreams.**
> What do you feel when you recall the dreams? Our feelings are the first road to our dreams. What is the difference between these and the "ordinary" dreams?

> **4. Did you bring anything from these powerful dreams into your waking consciousness?**
> Sometimes we change things in our lives as a result of dreams—even if we're not aware that we have. See if these dreams told you anything that you were able to use, consciously or unconsciously.

Meeting the Dreamer—Gently

Rushing to analysis is the easiest way to kill the power of a dream. When we instantly try to "make sense" of a dream experience we are ripping meaning out of the dream womb. How much better it is to be a gentle midwife to our own creative process.

In this exercise we let the two parts of our consciousness meet each other. And while no formal introductions are necessary, proper protocol is called for.

1. After you have dreamed, write it down.
Enter it, as descriptively as you can, in your journal.

2. Think about the details in the dream
Try to conjure as much as you can from the incidents, people, locale, colors, and so forth. Then recall the feelings you had during the dream. Try to remember how they connected to the things that were occurring. During this whole process, *do not* try to figure out what the dream means. Simply look at it very closely.

3. After you've recalled the dream and looked at it carefully, put it aside.
Actually, put it on the back burner. Put it away with the clear understanding that you will bring it forth from time to time to have a look at it.

4. During the course of the day, remind yourself of the dream.
Let it come back to you. Watch it. Look at it. See how it feels. See if there is any clear understanding that comes to you. But still do not try to "make sense"—no interpretations, no use of analysis, no attempt to extract meaning. After doing this for a day, you might want to jot down some ideas about the dream that have occurred to you. Slowly you'll see how meaning emerges differently from the standard forms of dream interpretation.

It's important to remember that amid all the learning made available in dreams, and with our growing comfort with merging our waking consciousness and dream consciousness, dreams are often just plain fun. Here are some explorations that allow you simply to enjoy them.

⊚ Dream Explorations ⊚
Playing Around

Having Pun with Dreams—Word Metaphors
A pun is a one-word metaphor. You use a word that means one thing, but the pun points to another meaning as well—there is the original meaning and the meaning beyond that. There is, for instance, a book entitled *Cancer: A Word Not a Sentence.* Here *sentence* has its grammatical meaning, but also means "prison time"—which cancer becomes for many people who have it.

Because they are metaphors, puns find their way into our dreams and are simply another reality of dream consciousness. This exploration is one way to find and experiment with the puns in your dreams.

1. Choose a dream from your journal.
Any dream will do, though it's best to have one in which there are lots of details.

2. Read through it and underline all the nouns.
Person, place, or thing.

3. Make a list of these words on a separate sheet of paper. Go through the list to find words that can be punned.
The puns don't have to be nouns. For example, the noun *eight* could be punned with the verb *ate*—or even with *hate*.

4. Do the same with the verbs.
Write could be punned with *right*.

5. Substitute some of these new words for the originals.
Then see how the meaning of the dream is changed. Substitute as many as you wish.

Dream Libs*

Poems, metaphors, dreams—they all allow us to see things with new eyes. In dreams our perspective shifts, enabling us to see things we've never seen before or to see familiar things in ways we've never seen them before. Maybe you see an elephant in a pair of high heels or a loved one in the body of someone else. Dream consciousness shifts our waking perception. Here we bring together the perspectives of dream consciousness and waking consciousness as a team. This is done best in a group.

1. Choose a dream.
The more detailed the better. It doesn't have to be recent, but usually fresh is best.

2. Write a list of details from the dream and number them.
For example: 1. an empty road; 2. a stranger with red hair; 3. an overcast sky. Be as specific as you can be. "An empty road" is better than simply "a road." Try to collect at least ten of them.

3. Make a separate list of big concepts or feelings with the word *is* after each one.
These need not come from the dream. For example, "Love is," "My life is," "Joy is," and so forth.

4. Assign each of these a letter, from A to whatever.
Again make a list of at least ten of these and then set the sheet aside.

---

* My thanks to Prartho Sereno for this Dream Exploration.

5. Take a third piece of paper and write a jumbled list of letters beginning with A and going as far in the alphabet as does your list in step 4.
Your list might begin: B, D, E, A, C, G, F. Write the list vertically, so that the letters are one under the other.

6. Next to the first letter on this list, place a 1, next to the second, a 2, and so on.
Your jumbled list in step 5 would read: B-1, D-2, E-3, A-4, C-5, G-6, and F-7.

7. Now take your list of dream details and your list of concepts and, referring to the list from step 6, read out loud the specified dream detail with the specified concept.
Let's say that B-1 turns out to be "My life is" plus "an empty road." The combination would read "My life is an empty road."

8. Match all of the letters with the numbers and read them out loud.
What do you notice? Don't get too serious! It's just another way of looking at your dreams.

Dream Libs, Version 2
Here we use just one piece of paper and only our dream.

1. Fold the paper lengthwise.
Lined paper is best for this. Keep it folded so that you only see one side at a time.

2. Choose a dream.
Again, one with a lot of detail is best.

3. On the left side of the paper, write a list of objects from the dream.
Write them from top to bottom, one under the other (you might list fountain pen, cashews, mirror . . .).

4. Write "of" next to each of the objects.
"Fountain pens of"; "cashews of"; "a mirror of" . . . then flip over the paper so that the right side is facing up.

5. List feelings or concepts from the dream on the right side of the folded paper.
Make sure you list them on the same lines as the objects on the left side of the paper, and make sure that you list the same number. (You might list shock, longing . . .)

6. Connect each of these with one of the feelings.

"Fountain pen of shock," "hotel room of longing," and so forth.

Of course it's all random. Or is it? The point here is that our waking consciousness is not in control when we do these two explorations. Instead it's working cooperatively with dream consciousness.

Memory into Dream

Memories and dreams have similarities. Memory is as elusive as a dream and, like a dream, it is never complete. Memory presents itself in fragments, and all dreams are fragments. Unlike stories, dreams have no beginning or end. There is only that piece that we remember. When we wake up and bring our rational mind to bear upon our dreams, we are re-creating and creating a story. Thus, in any retold dream our imagination comes into play—twice: first in our dream consciousness, where we create the dream itself, and second, when we create its story.

When we look at our dreams, what we choose to remember is important, as is what we choose to forget. In this exploration, we transform a memory into a dream.

1. Choose a memory.

It can be from as far back in time as you wish. Or it can be from yesterday.

2. Close your eyes and let it come back.

Take a few breaths. Let the details and feelings emerge.

3. Write the memory as if it were a dream.

You may expand it, add elements. Use your imagination. And write it in the present tense.

4. Do you notice any changes in the memory?

Does it feel different after you have rendered it as a dream?

Giving Your Dream a Title

Have you ever read the title of a book that really grabbed you? A title can draw the essentials of a book or story into a few powerful words. A title is a powerful distillation. Let's try it giving one to a dream.

1. Think of some great titles that have affected you.

They can be the titles of books or stories or movies or plays. What is it about each title that hooks you?

2. Choose a dream.

It's best to choose one that has some detail.

3. Take your time reviewing the dream in your journal.

What are the essential aspects of the dream?

4. Give the dream a title.
Think of it as a book. Or a story, movie, or play.

5. Try this with a few other dreams.
Does the process of selecting a title affect the way you see the dream?

Row, Row, Row Your Boat

> *Row, row, row your boat*
> *Gently down the stream.*
> *Merrily, merrily, merrily, merrily,*
> *Life is but a dream!*

We all have to row our boats, so we might as well do it gently, when we can. And merrily. Can we see our life as a dream? Or a dream as our life?

1. Choose a recent situation from your waking life.
It can be any experience that moved you in some way—happy, sad, something else entirely.

2. Close your eyes and reconstruct it in your mind.
Don't worry about accuracy because it doesn't exist.

3. Rewrite the experience as if it were a dream.
Again, you can add things, embellish. And, of course, the feelings are very important.

4. Interpret the "dream" as you would any other.
See yourself in all parts of it. You can re-create it in any way you wish.

Down the Stream
Here we experience the dream while we are awake.

1. Start the day with the commitment to treat it as a dream.
That's right. You will experience this day as a dream.

2. Imagine that you're dreaming and are aware that you're dreaming.
Essentially, you'll be watching yourself in the dream.

3. Pay attention to what you are feeling in this waking dream.
And note when and how it changes.

4. At the end of the day, write down this day's dream.
Any insights? Any interpretations?

CONCLUSION:
INFINITE VARIETIES—SUMMER OF '98

It was the summer of 1998 at Appel Farm, an arts camp for kids in southern New Jersey. Sixteen teenagers met with me for an hour a day, five days a week, for a month. We explored our dreams together, experimented, and discovered.

It was a kaleidoscope of experiences. One student never saw faces in her dreams—they were always black or darkened. We all discussed it and, for the first time in her life, she began to see faces.

Another student never heard voices in his dreams—that is, he never heard voices from outside of himself. All the voices in his dreams came from within him. After a week or two in our group, he heard a voice outside of himself for the first time. It was the voice of his grandfather.

There was a student who never saw the eyes of people in her dreams—her dream eyes were always black holes or black-painted circles—and another who always dreamed of riding in or driving a car.

There were only sixteen of us, and yet the variety of dream experiences seemed infinite.

There are not thousands of realities—there are infinite realities. But who can grasp the concept of infinity? Only the world of dreams allows us to explore them and our own infinite potential and endless possibility.

Throughout the world, across cultures and through time, humans have explored their surroundings near and far. But long before they explored the seven seas, they explored their own inner landscape—their dream consciousness. Unlike the lands on earth, the land of dreams has no boundaries. We can explore it forever to find ever richer levels of understanding.

We humans have long relied on our tribes. Ethnic, social, religious, or national—we have defined ourselves by and identified with the group to which we belong. Our tribes have nurtured us and protected us. They have provided us with a way to look at the world and ourselves. They have given us symbols and the ability to see our dream consciousness in certain ways.

Now, perhaps for the first time in the history of our species, we are able to reach beyond the tribe to use the wisdom of cultures others than ours in order to transcend all culture and tribe. Now, for the first time, we are truly able to think for ourselves, and now, each of us may realize the inner wisdom and understanding revealed in our dreams.

What an exciting time to be alive!

Notes

1. Fray Diego Durán, *Book of the Gods and Rites and the Ancient Calendar,* translated and edited by Fernanda Horcasistas and Doris Heyden (Norman: University of Oklahoma Press, 1971).

2. William Howell, "The Sea Dyak," *Sarawak Gazette* (December 16, 1908).

3. Sigmund Freud, *The Interpretation of Dreams* (New York: Avon Books, 1965.)

4. Siegfried Frederick Nadel, *Nupe Religion* (London: Routledge and Paul, 1954).

5. A well-known Sufi tale from a discourse of Osho. Retold by Sarvananda Bluestone.

BIBLIOGRAPHY

I was trained as a historian and we historians are taught to document and footnote every statement that is not common knowledge. So, by the time I finished writing this, there were close to one thousand footnotes. I included them in the original manuscript, but my editor felt that forty pages of notes was a bit excessive, and I had to agree. Our solution was to gather most of the notes into a bibliography. My inner graduate student is slightly disappointed, but my inner editor is satisfied that the curiosity of the reader will be served by this.

Alkema, B., and T. J. Bezemer. *Beknopt Handboek der Volkenjunde van Nederlandsch-Indië* [Concise Handbook of the Ethnology of the Netherlands East Indies]. Haarlem: H. D. Tjeenk Willink and Zoon, 1927.

Ammar, Hamed. *Growing Up in an Egyptian Village: Silwa, Province of Aswan.* London: Routledge and Kegan Paul, 1954.

Aserinsky, Eugene, and Nathaniel Kleitman. "Regularly Occuring Periods of Eye Motility and Concomitant Phenomena During Sleep." *Science* 118 (1953).

Barber, Elizabeth Wayland. *Women's Work: The First 20,000 Years.* New York: W. W. Norton, 1995.

Beaglehole, Ernest, and Pearl Beaglehole, "Ethnology of Pukapuka." In *Bernice P. Bishop Museum Bulletin* 150 (1938). Bernice P. Bishop Museum, Honolulu.

Beckwith, Martha Warren. *Black Roadways: A Study of Jamaican Folk Life.* Chapel Hill: University of North Carolina Press, 1929.

Bell, Charles Alfred. *The Religion of Tibet.* Oxford: Clarendon Press, 1931.

Bellman, Beryl Larry. *The Language of Secrecy: Symbols and Metaphors in Poro Ritual.* New Brunswick, N. J.: Rutgers University Press, 1984.

———. *Village of Curers and Assassins: On the Production of Fala Kpelle Cosmological Categories.* The Hague: Mouton, 1975.

Bennett, Albert L. "Ethnographic Notes on the Fang." *Journal of the Anthropological Institute of Great Britain and Ireland* 29 (1899).

Bennett, Wendell C., and Robert M. Zingg. *The Tarahumara: An Indian Tribe of Northern Mexico.* Chicago: University of Chicago Press, 1935.

Berglund, Axel-Ivar. "Zulu Thought Patterns and Symbolism." In *Studia Missionalia Upsaliensia* 22, (1976). Swedish Institute of Missionary Research, Uppsala, Sweden, and Cape Town, South Africa.

Bernatzik, Hugo Adolf. *Akha und Meau, Probleme der Angewandten Volkerkunde in Hinterindien* [Akha and Miao: Problems of Applied Ethnography in Farther India]. Innsbruck: Kommisionverlag Wagner'sche Universitats, 1947.

Biddulph, J. *Tribes of the Hindoo Koosh.* Calcutta: Office of the Superintendent of Government Printing, 1880.

Biedermann, Hans. *Dictionary of Symbolism: Cultural Icons and the Meanings Behind Them.* New York: Meridian, 1994.

Blacker, Carmen. "Japan." In Michael Loewe and Carmen Blacker, eds., *Oracles and Divination.* Boulder, Colo.: Shambala, 1981.

Bland, N. "On the Muhammedan Science of Tabír, or Interpretation of Dreams." In *Journal of the Royal Asiatic Society of Great Britain and Ireland* 16 (1856).

Blank, H. Robert. "Dreams of the Blind." *Psychoanalytic Quarterly* 27 (April 1958).

Bluestone, Sarvananda. *How to Read Signs and Omens in Everyday Life.* Rochester, Vt.: Destiny Books, 2001.

Bogaraz-Tah, Vladimir Germanovich. "The Chukchee: Material Culture—Part 1: Religion." In *Memoirs of the American Museum of Natural History* (1904).

Bohannan, Laura, and Paul Bohannan. *The Tiv of Central Nigeria.* London: International African Institute, 1953.

————. *A Source Notebook on Tiv Religion,* vol. 1. New Haven: Human Relations Area Files, 1969.

Bollig, Laurentius. "Die Bewohner der Truk-Inseln: Religion, Leben und kurze Grammatik sines Mikronesiervolkes" [The Inhabitants of the Truk Islands: Religion, Life, and a Short Grammar of a Micronesian People]. *Anthropos Ethnologische Bibliothek* 3, no. 1. Munster: Aschendorffsche Verglags, 1927.

Bourdillon, Michael F. C. *The Shona Peoples: An Ethnography of the Contemporary Shona, with Special Reference to Their Religion.* Shona Heritage Series, vol. 1. Gwelo: Mambo Press, 1976.

Bourke, John Gregory. "The Medicine-Men of the Apache." *United States Bureau of Ethnology's Annual Report to the Secretary of the Smithsonian Institution* 9 (1887–1888).

Bowers, Alfred W. *Mandan Social and Ceremonial Organization.* Chicago: University of Chicago Press, 1950.

Boyer, L. Bryce. "Folk Psychiatry of the Apaches of the Mescalero Indian Reservation." In Ari Kiev, ed., *Magic, Faith, and Healing.* New York: Free Press, 1964.

Breton, André. "What Is Surrealism?" Public lecture sponsored by the Belgian Surrealists, Brussels, June 1, 1934. Posted at www.wlv.ac.uk/~fa1871/what-surr.html.

Briggs, George W. *The Chamars: The Religious Life of India.* Calcutta: Association Press, 1920.

Browne, Charles R. "The Ethnography of the Mullet, Inishkea Islands, and Portacloy, County Mayo." *Proceedings of the Royal Irish Academy* 3, series 3 (1895).

Butt, P. T. W., and Audrey Butt. "The Azande and Related Peoples of the Anglo-Egyptian Sudan and Belgian Congo." In Daryll Forde, ed., *Ethnographic Survey of Africa, East Central Africa,* part 9. London: International African Institute, 1953.

Calame-Griaule, Genevieve. *Words and the Dogon World.* Deirdre La Pin, trans. Philadelphia: Institute for the Study of Human Issues, 1986.

Callaway, Henry. *The Religious System of the Amazulu Izinyanga Zokubula. Folk-Lore Society Publications* 15. London: Trubner, 1870.

Campbell, J. E. *Honour, Family and Patronage: A Study of Institutions and Moral Values in a Greek Mountain Community.* Oxford: Clarendon Press, 1964.

Cappelletty II, Gordon Guy. "Factors Affecting Psychological Distress within the Hmong Refugeee Community." Ph.D. dissertation, California School of Professional Psychology, 1986.

Caudill, Harry M. *Night Comes to the Cumberlands: A Biography of a Depressed Area.* Boston: Little, Brown and Company, 1963.

Chevalier, Jean, and Alain Gheerbrant. *A Dictionary of Symbols.* New York: Penguin, 1994.

Cirlot, J. E. *A Dictionary of Symbols.* New York: Philosophical Library, 1962.

Clemmer, Richard Ora. "Directed Resistance to Acculturation: A Comparative Study of the Effects of Non-Indian Jurisdiction on Hopi and Western Shoshone Communities." Ph.D. dissertation, University of Illinois, 1972.

Cline, Walter. "Notes on the People of Siwah and El Garah in the Libyan Desert." General Series in Anthropology 4. Menasha, Wis.: George Banta, 1936.

Cline, Walter, et al. "The Sinkaietk or Southern Okanagon of Washington." *Contributions from the Laboratory of Anthropology* 2, General Series in Anthropology 6. Menasha, Wis.: George Banta.

Connelly, Dianne M. *All Sickness Is Homesickness.* Columbia, Md., 1993.

Coon, Carleton Stevens. *Tribes of the Rif. Harvard African Studies,* vol. 9. Cambridge: Peabody Museum, 1931.

Cooper, John M. "The Gros Ventres of Montana: Religion and Ritual." *Catholic University Anthropological Series,* part 2, no. 16 (1956).

Covarrubias, Miguel. *Island of Bali.* New York: Alfred A. Knopf, 1938.

Crooke, W. *The Popular Religion and Folklore of Northern India,* vol. 1. Westminster: Archibald Constable, 1896.

Culshaw, W. J. *Tribal Heritage: A Study of the Santals.* London: Lutterworth Press, 1949.

de Laguna, Frederica. *Under Mount Saint Elias: The History and Culture of the Yakutat Tlingit. Smithsonian Contributions to Anthropology,* vol. 7. Washington: Smithsonian Institution, 1972.

de Ondegardo, Juan Polo. "Informaciones acerca de la Religión y Gobierno de los Incas" [Information Concerning the Religion and Government of the Incas]. *Colección de Libros y Documentos Referentes a la Historia del Peru* 3 (1916).

Delobsom, Dim. *L'Empire du Mogho-naba: Coutumes des Mossi de La Haute-Volta* [The Empire of the Mogho naba: Customs of the Mossi of Upper Volta]. Paris: Domat-Montchrestien, 1932.

Densmore, Frances "Chippewa Customs." *Bureau of American Ethnology Bulletin* 86 (1929).

———. "Northern Ute Music." *United States Bureau of American Ethnology Bulletin* 75 (1922).

———. "Yuman and Yaqui Music." *United States Bureau of American Ethnology Bulletin* 110 (1932).

Dentan, Robert Knox. "Senoi." In Frank M. Lebar, Gerald C. Hickey, and John K. Musgrave. *Ethnic Groups of Mainland Southeast Asia.* New Haven: Human Relations Area Files Press, 1964.

———. "Some Senoi Semai Dietary Restrictions: A Study of Food Behavior in a Malayan Hill Tribe." Ph.D. dissertation, Yale University, 1965.

Devereux, George. "Mohave Ethnopsychiatry and Suicide: The Psychiatric Knoweldge and the Psychic Disturbances of an Indian Tribe." *United States Bureau of American Ethnology Bulletin* 175 (1961).

Devisch, Rene. "Mediumistic Divination Among the Northern Yaka of Zaire: Etiology and Ways of Knowing." In Philip M. Peek, *African Divination Systems: Ways of Knowing.* Bloomington: Indiana University Press, 1991.

Dickson, H. R. P. *The Arab of the Desert: A Glimpse into Badawin Life in Kuwait and Sau'di Arabia.* London: George Allen and Unwin, 1951.

Dictionary of Mythology. www.geocities.com/~stilicho/mythology/oniroi.html.

Dieterlen, Germaine. *Essai sur la Religion Bambara* [An Essay on the Religion of the Bambara]. Paris: Presses Universitaires de France, 1951.

Diringer, David. *The Alphabet: A Key to the History of Mankind,* vol. 1. New York: Funk and Wagnalls, 1968.

Djurfeldt, Goran, and Staffan Lindberg, *Pills Against Poverty: A Study of the Introduction of Western Medicine in a Tamil Village.* Scandinavian Institute of Asian Studies, Monograph Series 23. London: Curzon, 1975.

Domhoff, G. William. *The Mystique of Dreams: A Search for Utopia through Senoi Dream Theory.* Berkeley: University of California Press, 1985.

Donaldson, Bess Allen. *The Wild Rue: A Study of Muhammadan Magic and Folklore in Iran.* London: Luzac and Company, 1938.

Doniger, Wendy. "Western Dreams about Eastern Dreams." In Kathy Bulkeley, ed. *Among All These Dreamers: Essays on Dreaming and Modern Society.* Albany: State University of New York Press, 1996.

Downes, T. W. "Maori Etiquette." *The Journal of the Polynesian Society* 38 (1929). The Polynesian Society, New Plymouth, New Zealand.

Downs, Richard Erskine. *The Religion of the Bare'e-Speaking Toradja of Central Celebes.* Gravenhage: Uitgeverij Excelsior, 1956.

Duchesne-Guillemin, Jacques. "La Divination dans l'Iran Ancien." In Andre Caquot and Marcel Leibovici, *La Divination*, vol. 1. Paris: Presses Universitaires de France, 1968.

Dundas, Charles. *Kilimanjaro and Its People.* London: H. F. and G. Witherby, 1924.

Durán, Fra Diego. *Book of the Gods and Rites and the Ancient Calendar.* Fernanda Horcasistas and Doris Heyden, trans. and ed. Norman: University of Oklahoma Press, 1971.

Ehrenreich, Barbara, and Deirdre English, *Witches, Midwives and Healers.* Old Westbury, N.Y.: Feminist Press, 1973.

Ehrenreich, Paul. "Beitrage zur Volkerkunde Brasiliens" [Contributions to the Ethnography of Brazil]. *Veroffentlichungen aus dem Koniglichen Museum fur Volkerkunde* 2 (1891).

Elwin, Verrier. *Muria Murder and Suicide.* Bombay: Oxford University Press, 1943.

———. *The Muria and Their Ghotu.* Bombay: Oxford University Press, 1947.

Encyclopedia Mythica. www.pantheon.org/mythica/search.html.

Evans, Emyr Estyn. *Irish Folk Ways.* London: Routledge and Kegan Paul, 1957.

Evans-Pritchard, Edward Evan. *Witchcraft, Oracles and Magic Among the Azande.* Oxford: Clarendon Press, 1937.

Elves, John C. *The Blackfeet: Raiders of the Northwestern Plains.* Norman: University of Oklahoma Press, 1971.

———. "A Unique Pictorial Interpretation of Blackfoot Indian Religion in 1846–1847." *Ethnohistory* 18 (Summer 1971).

Ewers, John C. ed., William Wildschut, "Crow Indian Medicine Bundles." *Contributions from the Museum of the American Indian* 17 (1960).

Fenton, William N. *The False Faces of the Iroquois.* Norman: University of Oklahoma Press, 1987.

Firth, Raymond. *Tikopia Ritual and Belief.* London: George Allen and Unwin, 1967.

———. "The Meaning of Dreams in Tikopia." In Evans-Pritchard, Firth, Malinowski, and Schapera, eds., *Essays Presented to C. G. Seligman.* London: Kegan Paul, Trench, Trubner and Co., 1934.

Flannery, Regina. "The Gros Ventres of Montana," part 1, no. 15: Social Life. *Catholic University Anthropological Series* (1953).

Forsyth, Thomas. "An Account of the Manners and Customs of the Sauk and Fox Nations of Indiana Tradition." In Emma Helen Blair, ed., *The Indian Tribes of the Upper Mississippi Valley and Region of the Great Lakes,* vol. 2. Cleveland: Arthur H. Clark Company, 1912.

Frederick, Jack, and Anna Gritts Kilpatrick. *Run toward the Nightland: Magic of the Oklahoma Cherokee.* Dallas: Southern Methodist University Press, 1967.

Freud, Sigmund. *The Interpretation of Dreams.* New York: Avon Books, 1965.

Fried, Jacob. "Ideal Norms and Social Control in Tarahumara Society." Ph.D. dissertation, Yale University, 1951.

Garnett, Lucy M. J. "Albanian Women." In *The Women of Turkey and Their Folk-Lore,* vol. 2. London: David Nutt, 1891.

Gay, John, and Michael Cole, *The New Mathematics and an Old Culture: A Study of Learning Among the Kpelle of Liberia.* New York: Holt Rinehart and Winston, 1967.

Gayton, Anna H. *Yokuts-Mono Chiefs and Shamans.* Berkeley: University of California, 1930.

———. "Culture-Environment Integration." *Southwestern Journal of Anthropology* 2 (1946).

———. "Northern Foothill Yokuts and Western Mono." In *Yokuts and Western Mono Ethnography,* vol. 2. Berkeley: University of California Press, 1948.

Gelfand, Michael. *Witch Doctor: Traditional Medicine Man of Rhodesia.* London: Harvill Press, 1964.

Gomes, Edwin. S*eventeen Years Among the Sea Dyaks of Borneo: A Record of Intimate Association with the Natives of the Bornean Jungles.* London: Seeley and Company, 1911.

Gonzales, Nancie L. Solien. *Sojourners of the Caribbean: Ethnogenesis and Ethnohistory of the Garifuna.* Urbana: University of Illinois Press, 1988.

Gorer, Geoffrey. *Himalayan Village: An Account of the Lepchas of Sikkim.* London: M. Joseph, 1938.

Graham, David Crockett. "The Customs of the Ch'uan Miao." In *West China Border Research Society Journal* 9 (1937).

Graham, Penelope. *Iban Shamanism: An Analysis of the Ethnographic Literature.* Canberra: Australian National University Press, 1987.

Grey, Herman. *Tales from the Mohaves.* Norman: University of Oklahoma Press, 1970.

Griffiths, Walter G. "The Kol Tribe of Central India." In *Royal Asiatic Society of Bengal Monograph Series* 2 (1946).

Grinnell, George Bird. *Blackfoot Lodge Tales: The Story of a Prairie People.* Lincoln: University of Nebraska Press, 1962.

Gusinde, Martin. *Die Selk'nam: vom Leben und Denken eines Jagervolkes auf der grossen Feurlandinsel* [The Selk'nam: On the Life and Thought of a Hunting People of the Great Island of Tierra del Fuego]. Modling bei Vien, Verlag der Internationalen Zeitschrift, 1931.

——. *Die Yamana: vom Leben und Denken der Wassemomaden am Kap Hoorn* [The Yahgan: The Life and Thought of the Water Nomads of Cape Horn]. Vienna: Anthropos-Bibliothek, 1937.

Hadley, J. Nixon. "Notes on the Socio-Economic Status of the Oklahoma Seminoles." In Wilton Marlon Krogman, *The Physical Anthropology of the Seminole Indians of Oklahoma*. Rome: Comitato Italiano per lo Studio del Problemi della Populazione, 1935.

Hake, Andrew. *African Metropolis: Nairobi's Self-Help City*. London: Sussex University Press, 1977.

Hara, Hiroko Sue. "Hare Indians and Their World." Ph.D. dissertation, Bryn Mawr College, 1964.

Harner, Michael J. *The Jivaro: People of the Sacred Waterfalls*. Garden City: Anchor/Doubleday, 1973.

Harrington, Mark Raymond. "Sacred Bundles of the Sac and Fox Indians." *University of Pennsylvania Museum Anthropological Publications* 4, no. 2 (1914).

Harwood, Alan. *Rx-Spiritist as Needed: A Study of a Puerto Rican Community Mental Health Resource*. The Anthropology of Contemporary Issues Series. Ithaca: Cornell University Press, 1987.

Hawkins, Ben. "A Sketch of the Creek Country in 1798 and 1799." In John R. Swanton, *Religious Beliefs and Medical Practices of the Creek Indians. Forty-Second Annual Report of the Bureau of American Ethnology* (1928).

Heckewelder, John. "An Account of the History, Manners, and Customs of the Indian Nations Who Once Inhabited Pennsylvania and the Neighboring States." In *Transactions of the Historical and Literary Committee of the American Philosophical Society*. Philadelphia: Abraham Small, 1819.

Henry, Joseph. *L'ame d'un peuple Africain. Les Bambara: Leur vie psychique, ethique, sociale, religeuse* [The Soul of an African People. The Bambara: Their Psychic, Ethical, Religious and Social Life]. Munster: Bibliotheque-Anthropos, Druck und Verlag der Aschendorffschen Buchhandlung, 1910.

Hermanns, Matthias. *The Indo-Tibetans: The Indo-Tibetans and Mongoloid Problem in the Southern Himalayas and North-Northeast India*. Bombay: K. L. Fernandes, 1954.

Hewitt, F. N. B. "The Iroquoian Concept of the Soul." *Journal of American Folklore* 8, no. 28 (1895).

Hilger, M. Inez. "Arapaho Child Life and Its Cultural Background." *U.S. Bureau of American Ethnology Bulletin* 148 (1952).

——. "Chippewa Child Life and Its Cultural Background." *Bureau of American Ethnology Bulletin* 146 (1951).

Hill, Brian, compiler. *Gates of Horn and Ivory*. New York: Taplinger, 1968.

Hockings, Paul. *Sex and Disease in a Mountain Community*. New Delhi: Vikas Publishing House, 1980.

Holas, Bohumil. "Quelques Recettes employées au Senegal pour provoquer les rêves" [Some Methods Used in Senegal to Evoke Dreams]. *Notes Africaines* 32 (1946).

Hollis, Alfred Claud. *The Masai: Their Language and Folklore*. Oxford: Clarendon Press, 1905.

Holmberg, Allan R. "Nomads of the Long Bow: The Siriono of Eastern Bolivia." *Institute of Social Anthropology Publication* 10 (1950).

Honigmann, John J. "Culture and Ethos of Kaska Society." *Yale University Publications in Anthropology* 40 (1949).

Howell, Signe. *Society and Cosmos: Chewong of Peninsular Malaya*. Singapore: Oxford University Press, 1984.

Howell, William. "The Sea Dyak." *Sarawak Gazette* (December 16, 1908).

http://library.thinkquest.org/C005545/english/sleep/REM.htm.

Hulbert, Archer Butler, and William Nathaniel Schwarze. "David Zeisberger's History of the Northern American Indians." *Ohio Archaeological and Historical Publications* 19 (1910).

Hultkrantz, Ake. *Native Religions of North America*. San Francisco: HarperSanFrancisco, 1987.

Hungry Wolf, Adolf. *The Blood People: A Division of the Blackfoot Confederacy*. New York: Harper and Row, 1977.

Hunt, Muriel Eva Verbitsky. "The Dynamics of the Domestic Group in Two Tzeltal Villages: A Contrastive Comparison." Ph.D. dissertation, University of Chicago, 1962.

Itkonen, Toivo Immanuel. *The Lapps in Finland up to 1945,* vol. 2. Porvoo, Helsinki: Werner S(char)derstr(char)m Osakeyhti(char).

Jefferson, James. *The Southern Utes: A Tribal History.* Colorado: Southern Ute Tribe, 1972.

Jenness, Diamond. "The Ojibwa Indians of Parry Island: Their Social and Religious Life." In *Bulletin of the Canada Department of Mines* 78 (1935). National Museum of Canada, Ottawa.

Jones, John Alan. "The Sun Dance of the Northern Ute." *United States Bureau of American Ethnology Anthropological Papers* 47 (1955).

Jones, William. "Mortuary Observances and the Adoption Rites of the Algonkin Foxes of Iowa." *International Congress of Americanists 15th Proceedings* 2 (1906).

Jorgensen, Joseph Gilbert. *The Sun Dance Religion: Power for the Powerless.* Chicago: University of Chicago Press, 1974.

Journal of Neuroscience (September, 1994). Posted at: www.sfn.org/content/Publications/BrainBriefings/rem_sleep.html.

Jung, Carl. "The Aims of Psychotherapy." In *Collected Works* vols. 9 and 16 (1931).

Karsten, Rafael. *The Religion of the Samek: Ancient Beliefs and Cults of the Scandinavian and Finnish Lapps.* Leiden: E. J. Brill, 1955.

———. "The Head-Hunters of Western Amazonas: The Life and Culture of the Jibaro Indians of Eastern Ecuador and Peru." *Societas Scieniarum Fennica: Commentationes Humanarum Litterarum* 7, no. 1 (1935).

Kelley, Isabel T. "Chemehuevi Shamanism." In Robert H. Lowie, ed. *Essays in Anthroplogy Presented to A. L. Kroeber in Celebration of His Sixtieth Birthday, June 11, 1936.* Berkeley: University of California Press, 1936.

———. "Ethnography of the Surprise Valley Paiute." *University of California Publications in American Archaeology and Ethnology* 31 (1932).

———. "Southern Paiute Shamanism." *University of California Anthropological Records* 2 (1939).

Kemp, P. *Healing Ritual: Studies in the Technique and Tradition of the Southern Slavs.* London: Faber and Faber, 1935.

Kephart, Horace. *Our Southern Highlanders: A Narrative of Adventure in the Southern Appalachians and a Study of Life Among the Mountaineers.* New York: Macmillan, 1929.

Kerewskiy-Halpern, Barbara. "Watch Out for Snakes!: Ethnosemantic Misinterpretation and Interpretation of a Serbian Healing Charm." *Anthropological Linguistics* 25 (Fall 1983).

Kinietz, Vernon. "Delaware Culture Chronology." *Indiana Historical Society Prehistory Research Series* 3, no. 1 (1946).

Kinietz, W. Vernon. "Chippewa Village: The Story of Katikitegon." *Cranbrook Institute of Science Bulletin* 25 (1947).

Klapka, Jerome. "Dreams" at ftp://uiarchive.cso.uiuc.edu/pub/etext/guten-berg/etext97/jjdrm10.txt

Koentjaraningrat, R. M. *A Preliminary Description of the Javanese Kinship System.* Southeast Asia Studies Cultural Report Series, vol. 4. New Haven: Yale University Press, 1957.

Kohl, G. *Kitchi-Gami.* London: Chapman and Hall, 1860.

Krasheninnikov, Stepan. *The History of Kamtschatka, and the Kurilski Islands with the Countries Adjacent.* Richmond: Richmond Publishing Co., 1973.

Krige, Eileen Jensen. *The Social System of the Zulus.* Pietermaritzburg: Shuter and Shooter, 1965.

Kroeber, Alfred Louis. "The Arapaho." *American Museum of Natural History Bulletin* 18 (1902–1907).

———. "The Mohave: Concrete Life." *Handbook of the Indians of California. U.S. Bureau of American Ethnology Bulletin* 78 (1953).

———. "The Mohave: Dream Life." *Handbook of the Indians of California. U.S. Bureau of American Ethnology Bulletin* 78 (1953).

Kronenberg, Andreas. *"Die Teda von Tibesti"* [The Teda of Tibesti]. *Beiträge sur Kulturgeschichte und Linguistik* 12 (1958).

Kuei Li, Fang, and Ronald Scollon. *Chipewyan Texts.* Taipei, Taiwan: Academica Sinica, Institute of History and Philology, 1976.

Laberge, Stephen, and Howard Rheingold. *Exploring the World of Lucid Dreaming.* New York: Ballantine, 1990.

Lambrecht, Francis. "The Mayawyaw Ritual: Illness and Its Ritual." *Journal of East Asiatic Studies* 4 (1955).

―――. "The Mayawyaw Ritual," parts 1 and 2. *Catholic Anthropological Conference Publications* 4, no. 2 (1935).

Landes, A. "Notes sur les Moeurs et superstitions populaires des Annamites" [Notes on the Customs and Popular Superstitions of the Annamese]. *Excursions et Reconaissances* 4 (1881).

Landes, Ruth. *Ojibwa Sociology. Columbia University Contributions to Anthropology,* vol. 24. New York: Columbia University Press, 1937.

Landor, Arnold Henry Savage. *Korea or Cho-sen: The Land of the Morning Calm.* London: W. Heinemann, 1895.

Lantis, Margaret. "Fanti Omens." *Africa* 13 (1940).

"The Lapps." *Indiana University Subcontractor's Monography.*

Latcham, Richard E. "Ethnology of the Araucanos." *Journal of the Royal Anthropological Institute of Great Britain and Ireland* 39 (1909).

Laufer, Berthold. "Inspirational Dreams in Eastern Asia." In *Journal of American Folk-Lore* 44 (April/June 1931).

Lawlor, Robert. *Voices of the First Day: Awakening the Aboriginal Dreamtime.* Rochester, Vt.: Inner Traditions, 1991.

Leach, Edmund Ronald. *Pul Eliya, a Village in Ceylon: A Study of Land Tenure and Kinship.* Cambridge: Cambridge University Press, 1961.

Lesser, Alexander. "The Pawnee Ghost Dance Hand Game." *Columbia University Contributions to Anthropology,* vol. 16. New York: Columbia University Press, 1933.

Lincoln, Jackson Steward. *The Dream in Primitive Cultures.* New York: Johnson Reprint Company, 1970. Originally published by Cressett Press in 1935.

Lot-Falck, Eveline. "La Divination dans l'Arctique et l'Asie septentrionale." In Andre Caquot and Marcel Leibovici, eds., *La Divination,* vol. 2. Paris: Presses Universitaires de France, 1968.

Lowie, Robert H. *The Crow Indians.* New York: Farrar and Rinehart, 1935.

―――. *Ethnographic Notes on the Washo.* Berkeley: University of California Press, 1939.

―――. "The Sun Dance of the Crow." *Anthropological Papers of the American Museum of Natural History* 16 (1915).

―――. "The Tobacco Society of the Crow Indians." *Anthropological Papers of the American Museum of Natural History* 21, part 2 (1919).

————. "The Religion of the Crow Indians." *Anthropological Papers of the American Museum of Natural History* 25 (1922).

MacInnes, John. "The Seer in Gaelic Tradition." In Hilda Ellis Davidson, ed., *The Seer in Celtic and Other Traditions*. Edinburgh: John Donald Publishers, 1989.

Mackenzie, D. R. *The Spirit-Ridden Konde*. London: Seekyl Service, 1925.

Madsen, William. *Mexican-Americans of South Texas*. New York: Holt, Rinehart, and Winston, 1973.

Malinowski, Bronislaw. *The Sexual Life of Savages in Northwestern Melanesia*, vols. 1 and 2. New York: Horace Liveright, 1929.

Mangin, Eugene. *Les Mossi, essai sur les us et coutumes du people mossi au Soudan Occidental* [Essay on the Manners and Customs of the Mossi People in the Western Sudan]. Paris: Augustin Challamel, 1921.

The Maori, vol 1. Wellington, New Zealand: Board of Maori Ethnological Research, 1924.

Marshall, Lorna. "!Kung Bushmen Religious Beliefs." In *Africa* 32 (1962).

Masse, Henri. *Croyances et coutumes Persanes* [Persian Beliefs and Customs]. Paris: Librairie Orientale et Americaine, 1938.

Matthews, Caitlín, and John Matthews. *Encyclopedia of Celtic Wisdom: A Celtic Shaman's Sourcebook*. Rockport, Mass.: Element, 1994.

Matthews, John. "By Stick and Stone: Celtic Methods of Divination." In John Matthews, ed., *The World Atlas of Divination: The Systems, Where They Originated, How They Work*. Boston: Little, Brown, 1992.

McClintock, Walter. *The Old North Trail, or Life, Legends and Religion of the Blackfoot Indians*. Lincoln: University of Nebraska Press, 1968.

McIlwraith, Thomas F. *The Bella Coola Indian*, vol. 1. Toronto: University of Toronto Press, 1948.

Metraux, Alfred. "Myths and Tales of the Matako Indians (The Gran Chaco Argentina)." *Ethnological Studies* 9 (1939).

Monteil, Charles. *Les Bambara du Segou et du Kaarta: Étude historique, ethnographique et litteraire d'une peuple du Soudan Française* [The Bambara of Segou and Kaarta: A Historical, Ethnographical and Literary Study of a People of the French Sudan]. Paris: Emile Larose, 1924.

Morgan, Lewis Henry. *League of the Ho-D-No-Sau-Nee or Iroquois*, vol. 1. New York: Dodd, Mead, and Company, 1901.

Morgan, William. "Navajo Dreams." *American Anthropologist* 34 (1932).

Morse, Edward S. "Korean Interviews." *Popular Science Monthly* 51 (1897).

Munro, Neil Gordon. *Ainu Creed and Cult*. New York: Columbia University Press, 1963.

Murphy, Robert F. "Mundurucu Religion." *University of California Publications in American Archaeology and Ethnology* 49 (1958).

Murphy, Robert F., and Buell Quain. *The Trumai Indians of Central Brazil.* Locust Valley, N.Y.: J. J. Augustin, 1955.

Musil, Alois. "The Manners and Customs of the Rwala Bedouins." *American Geographical Society Oriental Explorations and Studies* 6 (1928).

Nadel, Siegfried Frederick. *Nupe Religion.* London: Routledge and Paul, 1954.

Naik, T. B. *The Bhils: A Study.* Delhi: Bharatiya Adimjati Sevak Sangh, 1956.

Nelson, Lowry. *The Mormon Village: A Pattern and Technique of Land Settlement.* Salt Lake City: University of Utah Press, 1952.

Nimuendaju, Curt. "The Tucuna: Habitat, History, and Language." *Bureau of American Ethnology Bulletin* 143 (1948).

Noone, Richard, with Dennis Holman. *In Search of the Dream People.* New York: William Morrow, 1972.

Nordenskiold, Erland. "An Historical and Ethnological Survey of the Cuna Indians." In *Comparative Ethnological Studies* 10. Göteborg, Sweden: Göteborg Museum (1938).

Obermeyer, Gerald Joseph. "Structure and Authority in a Bedouin Tribe: The Aishaibat of the Western Desert of Egypt." Ph.D. dissertation, Indiana University, 1968, 1973.

Opler, Marvin Kaufman. "The Southern Ute of Colorado." In Ralph Linton, ed., *Acculturation in Seven American Indian Tribes.* Gloucester, Mass.: Peter Smith, 1963.

Opler, Morris Edward. *An Apache Life-Way: The Economic, Social, and Religious Institutions of the Chiricahua Indians.* Chicago: University of Chicago Press, 1941.

———. "The Creative Role of Shamanism in Mescalero Apache Mythology." *Journal of American Folkore* 59 (1946).

———. "A Summary of Jicarilla Apache Culture." *American Anthropologist New Series* 38 (1936).

Park, Willard Z. *Shamanism in Western North America: A Study in Cultural Relationships.* Evanston: Northwestern University Press, 1938.

———. "Paviotso Shamanism." *American Anthropologist* 36 (1934).

Parker, Arthur C. *Seneca Myths and Folk Tales.* Buffalo: Buffalo Historical Society, 1923.

Parman, Susan. *Dream and Culture: An Anthropological Study of the Western Intellectual Tradition.* New York: Praeger, 1991.

Parsons, Elsie Worthington Clews. *Mitla, Town of the Souls, and Other Zapoteco-Speaking Pueblos of Oaxaca, Mexico.* Chicago: University of Chicago Press, 1970.

Pavlovic, Jeremija M. "Folk Life and Customs in the Kragujevac Region of the Jasenica in Sumdaija." New Haven: Unpublished Manuscript in Human Relations Area Files, 1973.

Playfair, Alan. *The Garos.* London: David Nutt, 1909.

Porter, J. R. "Ancient Israel." In Michael Loewe and Carmen Blacker, eds., *Oracles and Divination.* Boulder, Colo.: Shambala, 1981.

Porter III, Robert William. "History and Social Life of the Garifuna in the Lesser Antilles and Central America." Ph.D. dissertation, Princeton University, 1984.

Radcliffe-Brown, A. R. *The Andaman Islanders: A Study in Social Anthropology.* Cambridge: Cambridge University Press, 1922.

Radha, Swami Sivananda. *Realities of the Dreaming Mind.* Boston: Shambala, 1996.

Rattray, R. S. *Religion and Art in Ashanti.* Oxford: Clarendon Press, 1927.

Ray, Verne F. *Cultural Relations in the Plateau of North America.* Los Angeles: Southwest Museum, 1939.

————. "The Sanpoil and Nespelem: Salishan Peoples of Northeastern Washington." *University of Washington Publications in Anthropology* 5 (December 1932).

Redfield, Robert, and Alfonso Villa Rojas. *Chan Kom: A Maya Village.* Chicago: University of Chicago Press, 1934.

Roberts, H. H., and Morris Swadesh. "Songs of the Nootka Indians of Western Vancouver." *Transactions of the American Philosophical Society* 45, part 3 (1955).

Rockhill, W. Woodville. "Notes on Some of the Laws, Customs and Superstitions of Korea." *American Anthropologist* 4 (1891).

Roseman, Marina Louise. "Sound in Ceremony: Power and Performance in Temiar Curing Rituals." Ph.D. dissertation, Cornell University, 1986.

Roux, J. P. and P. N. Boratav. "La Divination chez les Turcs." In André Caquot and Marcel Leibovici, eds. *La Divination*, vol. 2. Paris: Presses Universitaires de France, 1968.

Sanders, Irwin T. *Balkan Village.* Lexington: University of Kentucky Press, 1949.

Sandin, Benedict. *Iban Adat and Augury.* Penang: Penerbit Universiti Sains Malaysia for School of Comparative Social Sciences, 1980.

Scheffer, John. "The History of Lapland." In Rafael Karsten, *The Religion of the Samek: Ancient Beliefs and Cults of the Scandinavian and Finnish Lapps.* Leiden: E. J. Brill, 1955.

Seligman, G. C. Introduction in Jackson Steward Lincoln, *The Dream in Primitive Cultures.* New York: Johnson Reprint Company, 1970. Originally published by Cressett Press in 1935.

Serjeant, R. B. "Islam." In Michael Loewe and Carmen Blacker, eds., *Oracles and Divination.* Boulder, Colo.: Shambala, 1981.

Simpson, G. E. *The Heart of Libya: The Siwa Oasis, Its People, Customs and Sport.* London: H. F. and G. Witherby, 1929.

Smith, Huron H. "Ethnobotany of the Meskwaki Indians." *Public Museum of the City of Milwaukee Bulletin 4*, no. 2 (1928).

Smith, James G. E. "Chipewyan." In June Helm, ed., *Handbook of North American Indians* 6 (1981).

Smith, Richard J. *Fortune-Tellers and Philosophers: Divination in Traditional Chinese Society*. Boulder, Colo.: Westview Press.

Smithson, Carla Lee, and Robert C. Euler. "Havasupai Religion and Mythology." *University of Utah Anthropological Papers* 68 (Salt Lake City, 1964).

Sobotka, Primus. *Feste und Brauche der Slaven* [Festivals and Customs of the Slavs], vol. 1. Vienna: Kaiserlich-koniglichen Hof-und Staatsdruckerei, 1894.

Speck, Frank Gouldsmith. *Naskapi: The Savage Hunters of the Labrador Peninsula*. Norman: University of Oklahoma Press, 1935.

Spier, Leslie. "Havasupai Ethnography." *Anthropological Papers of the American Museum of Natural History* 24 (1928).

———. "Klamath Ethnography." *University of California Publications in American Archaeology and Ethnology* 30 (1930).

———. "Yuman Tribes of the Gila River." *University of Chicago Publications in Anthropology Ethnological Series*. Chicago: University of Chicago, 1933.

Spoehr, Alexander. "Kinship System of the Seminole." *Field Museum of Natural History Anthropological Series* 23, no. 2. Field Museum of Natural History, Chicago.

Staiano, Kathryn Vance. "Interpreting Signs of Illness: A Case Study in Medical Semiotics." In *Approaches to Semiotics* 72 (1986).

States, Bert O. *Dreaming and Storytelling*. Ithaca: Cornell University Press, 1993.

Steggerda, Morris. "Maya Indians of Yucatán." *Carnegie Institution of Washington Publication* 531 (1941).

Stevenson, Matilda Coxe. "The Zuni Indians: Their Mythology, Esoteric Fraternities, and Ceremonies," *Twenty-Third Annual Report of the Bureau of American Ethnology to the Secretary of the Smithsonian Institution, 1901–1902* (1904).

Steward, Julian Haynes. "Culture Element Distributions 13, Nevada Shoshoni." *University of California Publications Anthropological Records* 4, no. 2 (1941).

Stewart, Kenneth M. "Chemehuevi Culture Changes. In *Plateau* 40 (1967).

———. "Mohave." In Alfonso Ortiz, ed., *Handbook of North American Indians*, vol. 10 (1983).

Stewart, Kilton. "Dream Theory in Malaya." In Charles T. Tart, ed., *Altered States of Consciousness: A Book of Readings*. New York: John Wiley and Sons, 1969.

Stross, Brian. "Aspects of Language Acquisition by Tzeltal Children." Ph.D. dissertation, University of California, Berkeley, 1969.

Sverdrup, Harald Ulrich. *Hos Tundrafolket* [With the People of the Tundra]. Oslo: Gyldendal Norsk Forlag, 1938.

Swanton, John R. "Religious Beliefs and Medical Practices of the Creek Indians." *Forty-Second Annual Report of the Bureau of American Ethnology* (1928).

Talmage, James E. *A Study of the Articles of Faith, Being a Consideration of the Principal Doctrines of the Church of Jesus Christ of Latter-day Saints.* Salt Lake City: The Church of Jesus Christ of Latter-day Saints, 1976.

Tantaquidgeon, Gladys. *A Study of Delaware Indian Medicine Practice and Folk Beliefs.* Harrisburg: Pennsylvania Historical Commission, 1942.

Terwiel, B. J. *Monks and Magic: An Analysis of Religious Ceremonies in Central Thailand.* New Haven, Conn.: Human Relations Area Files, 2000.

Textor, Robert Bayard. *Roster of the Gods: An Ethnography of the Supernatural in a Thai Village.* New Haven, Conn.: Human Relations Area Files, 1973.

Tick, Edward. *The Practice of Dream Healing: Bringing Ancient Greek Mysteries into Modern Medicine.* Wheaton: Quest Books, 2001.

Tomasic, Dinko. *Personality and Culture in Eastern European Politics.* New York: George W. Stewart, 1948.

Tschopik Jr., Harry. "The Aymara." *Bureau of American Ethnology Bulletin* 143, no. 2 (1946).

———. "The Aymara of Chucuito, Peru: Magic." *Anthropological Papers of the American Museum of Natural History* 44.

Turnbull, Colin M. "The Mbuti Pygmies: An Ethnographic Survey." *American Museum of Natural History Anthropological Papers* 50. New York: American Museum of Natural History, 1965.

Underhill, Ruth Murray. *Papago Indian Religion. Columbia University Contributions to Anthropology,* vol. 33. New York: Columbia University Press, 1946.

———. *Social Organization of the Papago Indians. Columbia University Contributions to Anthropology,* vol. 30. New York: Columbia University Press, 1939.

Van de Castle, Robert. *Our Dreaming Mind.* New York: Ballantine, 1994.

Variakojis, Danguole Jurate. "Concepts of Secular and Sacred Among the White Mountain Apache as Illustrated by Musical Practice." Ph.D. dissertation, Indiana University, Bloomington, 1969.

Viski, Karoly. *Hungarian Peasant Customs.* Budapest: Dr. George Vajna and Co., 1932.

Vogel, Gerald, David Foulkes, and Harry Trosman. "Ego Functions and Dreaming During Sleep Onset." In Charles T. Tart, ed., *Altered States of Consciousness: A Book of Readings.* New York: John Wiley and Sons, 1969.

von den Steinen, Karl. *Unter den Naturvolkern Zentral-Brasiliens. Reiseschilderung und Ergebnisse der Zweiten Schingu Expedition, 1887–1888* [Among the Primitive Peoples of Central Brazil: A Travel Account and the Results of the Second Xingu Expedition 1887–1888]. Berlin: Dietrich Reimer, 1894.

Wagley, Charles. "Tapirape Shamanism." *Boletim do Museu Nacional New Series Antropologia* 3 (1943). Ministry of Education and Health, Rio de Janeiro, 1943.

Wallace, Ernest W., and E. Adamson Hoebel. *The Comanches: Lords of the South Plains.* Norman: University of Oklahoma Press, 1952.

Wallis, Wilson D., and Ruth Sawtell Wallis. *The Micmac Indians of Eastern Canada.* Minneapolis: University of Minnesota Press, 1955.

Warner, W. Lloyd. *A Black Civilization: A Social Study of an Australian Tribe.* New York: Harper and Brothers, 1937.

Waugh, F. W. "Iroquois Foods and Food Preparation." *Canada Department of Mines Geological Survey, Memoir* 86, no. 12 (1916).

Weiss, Jerome. "Folk Psychology of the Javanese of Ponorogo." Ph.D. dissertation, Yale University, 1977.

Whiting, Beatrice Blyth. "Paiute Sorcery." *Viking Fund Publications in Anthropology* 15 (1950). Viking Fund, New York.

Wilson, Monica Hunter. *Good Company: A Study of Nyakyusa Age-Villages.* London: Oxford University Press, 1951.

———. *Rituals of Kinship Among the Nyakyusa.* London: Oxford University Press, 1957.

Winstedt, Richard Olof. *The Malays: A Cultural History.* New York: Philosophical Library, 1950.

———. "Karamat: Sacred Places and Persons in Malaya." In *Journal of the Royal Asiatic Society* 2 (1924).

Wissler, Clark. "Ceremonial Bundles of the Blackfoot Indians." In *American Museum of Natural History Anthropological Papers* 7, part 2 (1912).

www-groups.dcs.st-and.ac.uk/~history/Mathematicians/Wren.html

www.britannia.com/history/monarchs/mon23.html

www.totse.com/en/fringe/fringe_science/chladni1.html.